THE LONG TRUCE

THE LONG TRUCE

*How Toleration Made the World Safe
for Power and Profit*

A. J. CONYERS

SPENCE PUBLISHING COMPANY • DALLAS
2001

Published in the United States by
Spence Publishing Company
111 Cole Street
Dallas, Texas 75207

Library of Congress Cataloging-in-Publication Data

Conyers, A. J., 1944-
    The long truce : how toleration made the world safe for power and profit /
A.J. Conyers.
        p. cm.
    Includes bibliographical references and index.
    ISBN 1-890626-36-8 (alk. paper)
        1. Toleration—History.   2. Religious tolerance—Christianity—History.
    3. Power (Social sciences)—History.   4. Secularization—History.   I. Title.

HM1271.C665 2001
179'.9—dc21   2001017021

Printed in the United States of America

To my father,

Ab Conyers

As from one man's face many likenesses are reflected in a mirror, so many truths are reflected from one divine truth.

Peter Lombard

Modern nationalism, as a state of mind and cultural reality, cannot be understood except in terms of the weakening and destruction of earlier bonds, and of the attachment to the political state of new emotional loyalties and identifications.

Robert A. Nisbet

And the only sure and certain result which accrues from contemplating this spectre [of an empty transcendence] seems to be the rather barren law of toleration, i.e., of refraining from absolutising, and therefore in fact of avoiding all positive statements concerning its binding content and direction. . . . We must certainly insist, however, that [by the term 'God'] we necessarily have something very different in view.

Karl Barth

Whenever the state becomes the executor of all the vital and cultural activities of man, it forfeits its own proper dignity, its specific authority as government.

Dietrich Bonhoeffer

It would be a gain to the country were it vastly more superstitious, more bigoted, more gloomy, more fierce in its religion than at present it shows itself to be.

John Henry Newman

The opposite of love is not hate, but power.

Marion Montgomery

Contents

Preface

T HIS BOOK BEGAN WITH AN INTUITION concerning a remarkable coincidence in modern history. It was apparent to me that the idea of toleration as we have received it in the tradition of John Locke and John Stuart Mill first came into prominence *along with* the rise of the modern nation-states. My intuition was that there might be some connection. Yet it would be strange and ironic, from one point of view, if an interest in a stronger, more centralized and authoritarian government were to be accompanied by an emphasis upon very non-authoritarian ideas about religion. Was there a connection? Or was it *merely* a coincidence, an historical accident with no meaning at all?

Further investigation proved that my intuition has considerable historical support. Each of the early theorists of toleration—without exception among the major figures—also had a significant bent at some point in his career toward securing the sovereign authority of the state. This was clearly true of Jean Bodin and Pierre Bayle, who were absolutists, but it was also true in a more complicated sense of John Locke. Even a number of minor figures—often making a virtue of necessity—calling for toleration, usually for their own religious community, did so by appealing to the growing sovereign power of the state against the petty oppressions of local, regional, and church officials. Unintentionally, and with less theoretical purpose, they were strengthening the centralizing trend of the modern state.

The historical coincidence is seen not simply in the genesis of these two trends. The movement toward strong centralized governments was accompanied by a sustained secularization of public life and a trend toward relaxing the moral discipline of society. Furthermore, where one is found—primarily in large Western or westernized nation-states—it is likely that the other is found as well. In Western Europe, Great Britain, and North America one finds both the large states, supported by extensive economic development, and a highly articulate public philosophy of tolerance in its religious, moral, and social dimensions.

Why such a coincidence is, in fact, more than a coincidence is the subject of this book. The recognition of how these trends have developed together throws light upon a number of related questions. Why is there often found, in those of the ideological left, a tendency to support movements that disparage or undermine the privileged position of the family? Why should those who favor strong government intervention in almost every area of life also ally themselves with movements such as "gay rights" and abortion on demand? Why is it so often true that those who defend the individual against all sorts of infringements—by the family, the church, the local community— seem to have little passion for securing them against an imposing government bureaucracy?

There are, of course, pure libertarians such as Governor Jesse Ventura who profess to be against any kind of restraint on an individual who is not harming someone else. But these are more specimens for our curiosity than examples of a movement. In our era, for some time now, liberal democracy has proved to be a movement of considerable staying power. And in this very modern movement we find the irony of individuals set free from every association to which they are naturally attached—and at the same time bound with bands of iron to the strongest and most comprehensive regimes in history, not coincidentally regimes involved almost continually in wars and the preparation for war on a scale never before seen. The very preoccupation with "freedom" in modern democratic countries bears some irony, as Hannah Arendt recognized. She agreed with the prophetic insight of Vilfredo Pareto at the turn of the century, who observed that "freedom . . . by which I mean the power to act shrinks every day, save for criminals, in the so-called free and democratic countries."[1] The problem is that we have become so accustomed to the modern world that we no longer really notice such things.

Part of the motivation for this project comes from my conviction that even destructive ideas are often founded on practices that are both good and true. Such is the case with toleration. As a virtue of instrumental value to the modern state, it is ill used. But as a practice among peoples so diverse in culture and religion that they can barely understand one another, it is an indispensable point of departure from which to discover a common humanity and a common destiny. Not that one book will accomplish such a thing, but there is good work to be done in rescuing an idea from long abuse and restoring it as something both useful and timely.

I HAVE HAD MUCH HELP ALONG THE WAY. I am grateful for the confidence of my publisher Tom Spence and for the helpful guidance of Mitch Muncy, Spence Publishing Company's editor in chief. My graduate assistants at Baylor University's George W. Truett Theological Seminary—Melanie Moore, Ann Bell, Joe Shilo, Rachel Stephen, Jay Smith, Eric Herrstrom, and Matt Sciba—were of immense help. My family was a constant source of inspiration and courage during the long haul of research and writing. My wife, Deborah, as always, is my companion in thinking through the really important matters of life and is often the wisest person I know. This book is dedicated to my father, now in his eighty-eighth year, who has always had a devotion to the life of the mind, and to our family, through many trials and joys. I also must thank colleagues at several institutions who helped by sending me in the right direction at a number of critical points. These include Donald Livingston at Emory University, Susan Mendus at the University of York, Peter Jones at the University of Edinburgh, Father Timothy Vaverek of St. Joseph Parish, as well as Millard Erickson and Bill Hair of Baylor University. It is also with much gratitude that I remember the many interested inquiries and words of encouragement from my students and colleagues.

THE LONG TRUCE

The Cunning of History

Therefore let us unite with those who devoutly practice peace, and not those who hypocritically wish for peace.

First Clement

THINK OF THIS BOOK as an extended essay on the definition of a term according to its modern usage. Behind all of the philosophical streams that feed into our use of "tolerance" or "toleration" is the simple fact that for our century, and increasingly since the seventeenth century, it has taken its place in what many would describe as a list of virtues. But if it is a virtue, then it operates in a very peculiar way. Compare "tolerance," if you will, with the virtue "love." Among the classic virtues, no one seems prepared to exclude love, no matter how ancient and traditional it has become. If you were to ask if there is enough love in the world (or, for that matter, in the country, in the church, in Oshkosh, or in a particular family), the answer would almost invariably be "No." There seems never to be too much love; and almost always there is not enough. So inconceivable is the notion of a superabundance of love that we would each demand at once how there could be too much love.

One might say the same thing about other of what we call virtues. How could there be too much hope? Too much faith? Too much humility or prudence? Now when we install toleration as a virtue, something very different seems to be the case. Suppose we apply toleration to the area of speech. We stand in principle for toleration toward any expression whatsoever, no matter how much that expression might differ from our own opinion or sentiment. Can this "virtue" ever in principle be applied in an unlimited way? While we might, in our age, tolerate blasphemy or obscenity, we would likely still draw the line at libel, slander, fraud, inciting to riot, and "crying 'Fire!' in a crowded theatre." Add to that the contemporary sensitivity to "hate speech," highly charged expressions of disdain for particular groups, language motivated by racial antipathy or what is commonly called "sexism." Many today draw the line at "homophobic" expression—however and for whatever reason that might be defined and circumscribed.

So, from the very beginning, writers such as John Locke have suggested that there are limits of toleration that must be observed. Locke drew the line when it came to Catholics and atheists, which seem rather strange restrictions today. But most of us, while not agreeing to Locke's demarcation, would probably draw the line somewhere. And the discussion of these limits has gone on ever since. Yet this is not normally the way with virtues.

But if toleration is something other than a virtue, then what is it? What part does it play in the ethical vocabulary of our times? To answer that question, I would like briefly to give an account of the rise and prominence in our time of the idea of toleration.

A Brief History of Toleration

The idea of toleration as an explicit public virtue was born in the midst of the trials of the seventeenth century. The Reformation, which had divided the Western church, was a century in the past. On the continent, religious wars had devastated communities and exacted a toll in some regions of up to a third of the population. While religious differences were clearly not the only reason for conflict, and sometimes served as a mere ideological rationalization for the seizure of land and power, they were also the occasion for the protraction and exacerbation of conflicts. These wars came to a head in what we know as the Thirty Years War, a series of conflicts so devastating that they appeared to some positive proof that the end of time was upon them. To others they proved the vacuity and madness of religion, which had come to be not the consolation for human suffering but its principle cause. The time was indeed ripe for taking a new look at religious conflict.

A parallel development was both more political and more secular in nature. Europe had seen for the past two hundred years the rise, by fits and starts, of nation-states, political entities taking in large territories and uniting peoples heretofore politically unrelated. War was both the emergency that created the demand for and the opportunity to effect the large-scale concentration of power. Over the next three centuries the world saw a continuation of the trend toward larger and more comprehensive governments and of the tendency to identify peoples with large, powerful ruling centers, rather than with the variety of associations that had always made up complex human society. Even though in our time we have become accustomed to thinking almost exclusively in terms of nation-states with broad powers exercised over vast territories and diverse peoples, the rise of the nation-state brought about an astounding change in social arrangements.

This change, furthermore, occasioned the isolation of the individual. People began to think of themselves not so much in terms of their social setting, or their families, or their churches, but as autonomous free agents. They viewed their associations with others as accidental and volitional, not necessary and obligatory. Therefore, the identity of the individual was less and less to be found in his primary relationships in the community. It appeared theoretically possible—though it was still not practically so—that the individual could choose his group identity. It seemed, therefore, (again, more on the level of theory than practice) that the individual gave rise to the group rather than the group making the life of the individual possible. At the same time, as his primary associations faded, his identity with a "nation" became more pronounced: more and more, he became American, or German, or Italian, or French. The result was a powerful state and a lonely individual, two distinctive features of the modern period. I agree with Robert Nisbet that "the single most decisive influence upon Western social organization has been the rise and development of the centralized territorial state . . . . The conflict between the central power of the political state and the whole set of functions and authorities contained in church, family, guild, and local community has been, I believe, the main source of those dislocations of social structure and uprootings of status which lie behind the problem of community in our age."

What part does toleration play in these twin developments of large centralized states and the isolation of the individual? Is it merely coincidental that wherever highly organized industrial powers with a central bureaucratic government is found anywhere in the world, one also finds the presence of a strong "ethos of tolerance?"

To understand quite how modern and how Western this doctrine of toleration is, we must first distinguish it from the ancient and universal *practice* of toleration. We will see that what would later be called toleration certainly had its place in the history and culture of Hebrew and Christian peoples, and in many other cultures as well. But the practice was always subordinated to some higher goal and was hardly ever thought of as a kind of isolated item in moral philosophy as it is today. Close to the beginning of the modern era, Johannes Althusius would speak of it as "moderation."[1] But the doctrine that developed, often with the most tenuous relationship to that earlier practice, was not simply moderation. It was a statement about the needs of the times: the need for broader authority than the splintered church could provide, the need to take advantage of secular opportunities emerging with the discoveries, the conquests, and the crises that suddenly erupted throughout modern Europe.

It is no coincidence, I contend, that the idea of toleration became so prominent at the same time that these large nation-states were coming into their own. And it is no coincidence, furthermore, as the world continues to appear a dangerous place in which to live, and as we rely on political power (that is, violent force) to meet crises, that there is a continued emphasis upon what we have learned to call toleration. When the nation must be mobilized to meet a crisis, or when the state has assumed both the right and the duty to see that national life functions well, the kinds of distinctions that make up the fabric of a society tend to obstruct the efficiency needed for effective action. The doctrine of toleration, while preached sincerely and not at all for purposes of state, neutralizes those inconvenient distinctions, eroding their capacity to draw groups together for purposes other than those of the central government.

The Strategy of Toleration

Let me return to my original question. Is toleration a virtue, as modern usage tends to suggest, or is it something else? The best answer to that question, I contend, is that toleration is not, strictly speaking, a virtue—at least it does not function as a virtue in the classical sense, even if it can properly be called a secular virtue. It is, instead, a *strategy*. It calls upon virtues, such as patience, humility, moderation, and prudence; but toleration itself relates to these qualities not as another quality of the same sort but as a policy intended to achieve some other end. A virtue strengthens our relationships. From a Christian perspective, all virtues serve the interests of love, love being the chief virtue and the goal of life. Humility, patience, and prudence make it possible to love God, the world, and human

beings, all in their proper order and proportion. Virtues are inter-
connected and, in a sense, are all one. They are themselves the goal
of human life. We are created for this: to be capable of loving.

   Toleration, on the other hand, eases the tension created by the fact
that we are different, that we understand things differently, that we have
experienced life in different ways, that we reason imperfectly, and so
on. It is not an end in itself but finds a goal in something else: it seeks
harmony, the capacity to live together in spite of our differences. But
toleration is not in itself harmony or peace; rather it is a strategy, a
modus vivendi that seeks to achieve harmony or peace within community life. Since a virtue is a good thing in itself, we are not concerned about the purpose it serves even though we are not prevented
from thinking about that. We can very well want to promote love,
even though we may not bother to think what are the further results
of love. In the case of a strategy, everything depends upon what
purpose that strategy serves. The goodness of the strategy (as opposed to its effectiveness) depends entirely on whether it serves a
good purpose. Thus, the way we feel about a community that "tolerates" child abuse will usually be quite different from the way we feel
about a community that "tolerates" the Jewish faith. One can easily see
why this strategy is important in the effort to form large, centralized
nation-states. The greater the population, and the more diverse, the
greater is the threat to a nation's unity. For the more diverse the
peoples, the more they are bedeviled by their different ways of seeing, understanding, and desiring. The rise of the nation-state in
modern times, with its central authority and its political ambitions
to maintain and even extend rule, made the governance of diverse
populations a critical necessity. How could that be achieved when the
basis of power was narrow and the scope of the governed population
and territory was broad? Michael Walzer has pointed out that the nation-state is not so called because it has ethnically homogeneous
populations. "It means only," he says, "that a single dominant group
organizes the common life in a way that reflects its own history and

culture and, if things go as intended, carries the history forward and sustains that culture."[2]

This means that minority groups within the nation-state must be brought under the central power and must not pose a danger to the overall political design. Differences in the culture, especially those differences, such as religion, that claim universal validity, must somehow be neutralized if the central power is to prevail in extending its authority over the entire populace. To the extent that minorities maintain their claim to some kind of independent authority (such as happens in the church), measures must be taken to assure that it does not interfere with the machinery of government. This can be done by insisting on agreement among all citizens with regard, let us say, to religion. That was the solution in Louis xiv's France of the Revocation of the Edict of Nantes, which withdrew the freedoms given formerly to Protestants. Or it might be done by insisting that the state will take no part in religious disputes, suggesting that religion be restricted to the sphere of private choice. This has been the route more commonly taken by Western states since the middle of the nineteenth century. One of these choices we would call the establishment of religion by the state, and the other we would call "religious toleration." Yet it is important to point out that in *both* cases the authority of the religious group is diminished; and in both cases, the power of the state is assumed to be of paramount importance.

That is why, as Michael Walzer pointed out, "toleration in nation-states is commonly focused not on groups but on their individual participants."[3] In liberal democracies especially, the efforts at centralizing power can appear to have an enormously liberating effect. The latitude given to individuals is increased with respect to the social connections that once demanded a certain loyalty and discipline of them, but whose authority is now diminished. All belong to the state, and to that extent they belong less to the church, the guild, the regional culture, and the family. As Tocqueville demonstrated for his own time, the so-called French Revolution was anything but a revolution. It continued and exaggerated the trend toward centralizing all authority that had begun two centuries earlier. The true issue of the French Revolution was not *liberté, egalité, fraternité*, but Napoleon, War, Empire.

Toleration as a modern doctrine (as opposed to an ancient practice which I will distinguish later) has little to do with the survival of minority groups and everything to do with the centralizing of power. It is not for the sake of the authority that naturally subsists within the group that toleration is offered, but it is for the sake of drawing the group more securely within the new authority, an authority that is essentially alien from the group itself. And if we consider that groups exist with their own peculiar sense of social ends and their own system of authority, then we find that the central power makes peace with groups by detaching them from their spiritual essence and then testifying to its respect for the dispirited remains of what was once both the body and soul of a culture.

Take the family in contemporary America as an example. In Mrs. Clinton's American "village," concern for the family would be of paramount importance, especially concern for the children. Yet it is precisely the authority of the family that must be taken over by the larger state, which is assumed to be more competent and caring in its provision of services for the individual members of the family. Wives need more protection from their husbands, husbands need intervention with their bosses, and children need intercession with everyone. Thus, for the sake of the group (and we need not doubt the sincerity of the effort), the individuals are plucked one by one from their vital dependence upon the group, leaving the group to exist in name only.

Before leaving this point, I want to clarify what I do *not* mean by "strategy" when I say that toleration is a strategy. I am, of course, not making the point that some sort of political cabal intends to sell everyone on this notion of toleration for the sake of amassing more power. Nor would I say that the principal writers and speakers on behalf of toleration always have an interest in promoting a centralizing state or of breaking down the old feudal arrangements. Rather, it works in something of the way Hegel had in mind when he wrote of the "cunning of history." There is a bit of mystery in the way these two public goals—sovereignty and toleration—work together, but it is not entirely a mystery.

Betrand de Jouvenel's insights into the authority of groups helps us to understand how the two ideas of sovereignty and toleration might work in tandem. Within every group that has any lasting life there emerges a system of authority for that group. That system of authority may be very subtle and difficult to detect, but the group operates as a group because it has discovered some internal discipline that keeps it intact. This is true whether we are speaking of a family, a regular gathering of friends at the local café, a professional guild, a religious order, or members of a large population who somehow think of themselves as belonging to each other more than to people of other regions. The individuals, consciously or not, take upon themselves the characteristics and disciplines of that group so that they can be identified as belonging to that group. Of course, we might think of the church as being an especially serious endeavor to create a community and to communicate the disciplines that belong to that group, with eschatological aims in mind.

It is not difficult to understand the conflict implied when one power seeks to make itself sovereign. No one has to design the overthrow of church authority to know instinctively that here is one serious barrier to the rise of an organized regional authority. The clash might come, as in the reign of Henry VIII, with a brazen grab for power (and as Eric Voegelin phrased it, "for scandalous reasons"). Or it might be an open policy of the state, as in the case of the former Soviet Union or the present People's Republic of China. Most often, however, the conflict is subterranean in its effect, and the tension expressed among these rival powers is always a factor in the priori-

ties shown both by the political leaders and the advocates of toleration as a public doctrine.

Dietrich Bonhoeffer saw this as a conflict between the "natural"
and the "organized" in which the "organized" is by definition "unnatural." The "unnatural consists essentially in organization, and the natural cannot be organized but is simply there." He undoubtedly had in
mind the highly organized regime of Hitler's state in this wartime
writing. No doubt it was with great hopes for the outcome of
Germany's crisis that he concluded that, "in the long run every organization collapses, and the natural endures and prevails by its own
inherent strength; for life itself is on the side of the natural."[4] We can
be sure, however, that the efforts to organize larger concentrations of
power will continue to be a part of modern political life. It helps to
clarify our life together if we realize that the two will always live in
some kind of tension with each other—the organized and the spontaneous authorities, the sacred and the secular authorities, the comprehensive power that instinctively wants no competitor and the
authority that grows from neighborhoods and families and congregations. Toleration plays a part in this tension. As an ancient practice it makes possible the catholic vision of life together, so that the
different associations both reinforce and give balance to one another,
and so that there is on the horizon a view of the whole world and all
of humanity as an interlinking community. As a modern doctrine,
however, toleration becomes the solvent that dissolves the lesser powers, making way for the highly organized state. I believe the issue is
partly expressed in the unscientific maxim that groups arise from the
power of love and the organization of the state arises from the love
of power. However we might want to qualify this "proverb," we have
the beginnings of a depiction of the modern crisis, which is, in a real
sense, the struggle between the love of power and the power of love.

Is Centralizing Power Inevitable?

In *Sovereignty*, F. H. Hinsley makes the case that the evolution toward larger states with a central bureaucratic authority was inevitable. The complexity of relationships and tasks in many areas of life, including the economic and the military, made necessary the social organization that could meet the challenge of new complexities. It is, of course, often comforting to think that the way things have happened was inevitable and unavoidable and that matters will never change. We can console ourselves with the thought that the extremities of this movement toward a strong state in Nazi Germany or Stalinist Russia is simply the extreme edge of a basically unavoidable trend in the world toward high concentrations of power and the intimate intrusion of politics into every facet of life.

Yet we do well, I think, to at least nurture a suspicion that the inescapable nature of this tyranny of bureaucrats and this authority vested in distant officers of the state is a modern superstition. Even if there is going to be, for a long time yet, more or less centralized powers vested with certain tasks (such as defense), must we conclude that these same powers necessarily take responsibilities that might more naturally belong to other elements of society?

In fact, a tradition exists in the West that has had some influence on our institutions but which varies considerably from this majority view of the state as the comprehensive expression of society. One of the chief exponents of this alternative view—a view that stands in marked contrast to that of Thomas Hobbes—was Johannes Althusius. Otto Gierke, writing in the latter part of the nineteenth century, considered Althusius the "most profound political thinker between Bodin and Hobbes."[5] Althusius was of the Reformed (Calvinist) faith. A German scholar trained at Basel, he was born in Diedenshausen, Westphalia, around 1557. His greatest work, *Politica*, which sets forth a theory of political life, was published in 1603. This work appeared just before he was named Syndic (city attorney) for Emden in East Friesland, one of the early German cities to turn toward the Reformed expression of Protestant Christianity, which was accorded the name "Geneva of the North."

Althusius began with the assumption that the political life was the life of the community, not simply those things related to government and the state. In addition to the state, which is a kind of community, there are also other kinds of human associations. Politics really regards how we live in community with one another; and often the most important group, the group that exerts the most influence on us, is *not* the state. It is likely to be the family, the church, the collegium (those associated by virtue of their common work), the guild, or the regional community. These groups each have their own end or goal. In fact, Althusius contended that just as the individual has a vocation (an important feature of Protestant theology) so has the group—in its own way and for a given purpose.

A full discussion of the life of a commonwealth, therefore, required an assessment of the different kinds of associations that make up the body politic (*consociatio*). He begins by saying that "Politics is the art of associating (*consociandi*) men for the purpose of establishing, cultivating, and conserving social life among them."[6] The subject matter is more comprehensive than, say, a discussion of the "governing of the political state" or the "power relationships of interest groups within a democracy." Instead it includes the consideration of how and why people live together, a matter prerequisite to any understanding of how they are governed or how power operates in the national life. For Althusius, the proper beginning of political thought is the recognition that human beings live in natural communities that occur spontaneously and that nowhere do they live alone— or, if they do, they live in an unnatural state. Political life is about living together: "Whence it is called 'symbiotics'."[7]

At the threshold of the modern age (and Althusius is indeed a modern man in important respects), he rejects the growing tendency to think of persons in isolation, as individuals first and as members of a group only secondarily. As Althusius reckons,

> The end of Political "symbiotic" man is holy, just, comfortable, and happy symbiosis, a life lacking nothing either necessary or useful. Truly, in living this life no man is self-sufficient (*autarkas*), or adequately endowed by nature. For when he is born, destitute of all help, naked and defenseless, as if having lost all his goods in a shipwreck, he is cast forth into the hardships of this life, not able by his own efforts to reach a maternal breast, nor to endure the harshness of his condition, nor to move himself from the place where he was cast forth. By his weeping and tears, he can initiate nothing except the most miserable life, a very certain sign of pressing and immediate misfortune. Bereft of all counsel and aid, for which nevertheless he is then in greatest need, he is unable to help himself without the intervention and assistance of another.[8]

As a result of certain trends in modern thought it became more customary to think in terms of individuals governed by a central administration. Leave aside for the moment whether that governance was a royal authoritarian one based on compact, authoritarian based on divine right, or more or less democratic. It was consequently common to see a consideration of social groups with their own identity and system of governance fade from conscious consideration. Resorting to the greatest public power available, of course, diminishes the role played by authorities closer to home, authorities of a different order. It is significant, therefore, that Althusius considered it indispensable to first attend to the function of five "associations" whose work is different from, and whose goals are distinct from, the state's: the family, the collegium, the city, the province, and the church.

The significance of this intentional regard for non-governmental associations cannot be overestimated. The modern reader is at first struck by the realism of such an approach. There is a shock of sudden recognition. For all these years the tendency has been to think of political life as business transacted between the citizen, defined as a member of the state, and the government. Family and religion, as well as friendships, have been relegated to the private sphere and come into view only as incidentals in public life: the essentials of public life take place within the two great brackets of the governing apparatus and the individual citizen. Trade, manufacture, banking, monetary policy, education of the young, provision for the destitute, the ill, and the aged, all relate more or less directly to the demands of individuals and the policy of government. These two poles become luminous in the modern mind, while associations once regarded as having little or nothing to do with the state, and yet which held their own separate authority for the individual, fade from sight. They serve the individual, or are beneficiaries of state operations, but have lost the dignity, independence, and authority they once had. Only the state and the individual are privileged with that status.

I use the term "bipolar vision of society" to describe this bracketing of all of life, in the modern mind, between the individual and the state. It is mostly accidental that I happen to use a term that mimics the psychologist's description of the personality under the spell of periodic swings from depression to mania. But it seems to me a fitting coincidence: for the condition of the modern psyche moves from the depressed realization of the private person in isolation, to the maniacal illusion of god-like omnipotence through the collective powers of the state. The modern self-image seems suspended between the twin obsessions with its lonely despair and its immoderate ambitions.

Althusius's recognition of the associations and their importance to political life (that is, to symbiotic existence) comes, as I say, with a shock of awareness. These associations still do have—as they always have had—a profound effect on our lives. As Bonhoeffer said, when he touched on this very topic, the natural will always outlive the organized, even though the organized will seem momentarily to obliterate the natural. We become conscious of this effect, perhaps, when the natural has been for some time in eclipse. A society that becomes aware that it is bereft of families that function as families becomes acutely aware of why families and family life must be protected.

I live in a city bisected by a major north-south interstate highway. Consequently the homeless, dispossessed, and destitute traveling this artery spill over into our community; many who subsist on the streets are from this very locale. The scene, of course, is not confined to Waco, Texas. A little travel is enough to acquaint us with the fact that similar conditions, with the increase of homelessness and the prevalence of begging, exist throughout North America and in parts of Western Europe, the most prosperous regions ever to exist over a long period of time in the entire course of history. The reasons for these conditions are varied. But undoubtedly, beyond any other explanation, these are the children of people who learned decades ago that individual fulfillment and happiness was far more important than the maintenance of the family. Ask them why they are there—as I have done again and again—and they will answer (it is most of the time a true answer), "I have nowhere to go." Extended families have dispersed; homes, so ubiquitous years ago, have disappeared.

The logic was compelling, in fact invincible, in light of the modern conviction that the individual is the only unit of society worthy of making serious demands. The sad result, however, is that where once there were families who were honor-bound to care for those of its members that fell by the wayside, now often no one in particular is left to take that responsibility. It was assumed that the state would take up that function and handle it more professionally and competently than the traditional (and therefore benighted) family ever could. And in many ways the state tried, especially in Western Europe, but even to a large degree in North America. But where everyone is responsible, no one in particular takes responsibility, and the state—as opposed to the family, even with all its problems—provides a cold and antiseptic home, as experience has proved.

A Substitute for Love

Just how far have we come from a society that is conceptually one made up of multiple associations with overlapping authorities and with somewhat independent roles to play? How far have we moved from awareness of the "associations" with their own integrity, to this modern "bipolar" concept of social life?

Three questions will suggest the profound shift that has taken place from the authority of private and public associations to that of the state:

1. To what degree do parents have authority regarding medical procedures, including abortion, for their minor children?

2. To what extent are members of a religious group free to offer prayers in public if the public event, such as a public school graduation or a football game, is *nominally* associated with the state? And does it matter that the people attending the event are members of a family, members of a religious community, members of a local community with a character very different from the larger nation? Does anything matter except that these people are citizens of the state? Should that be the only thing that matters?

3. How often is it assumed, by public officials and the media, that where families have failed to live up to their responsibilities, it is the duty of the state to fill in the gap? Should it be assumed that competencies that naturally belong to the family can satisfactorily be excercised by the state? Does it matter that the nature of "family" and the nature of "state" are quite different?

One could almost say that Althusius represents a path not taken by modernity. But that would not be entirely correct. The idea of covenant relationships among distinct associations has always had some effect upon modern life. The Constitution of the United States, and the actual political life of America through most of the nineteenth century grows from a federal or covenantal understanding of political relationships among distinct communities. So insistent were the American Founders upon *not* formulating a centralized empire that what Althusius would have called provinces, they tended to call "commonwealths" or "states." Also, the covenant concept of society has influenced modern theological thinkers from John Calvin to Martin Buber to Jürgen Moltmann. Their concern usually was to see social reality in a light other than the highly centralized and highly organized vision of the state that was its alternative. The same insight in various forms has shown up among political and legal thinkers as diverse as John Calhoun and Lani Guinier.

But the important point to see is that the struggle between these views was not an even one. As Daniel Elazar wrote, in "the struggle over European state-building in the seventeenth century, the Althusian view, which called for the building of states on federal principles—as compound political associations—lost out to the view of Jean Bodin and the statists who called for the establishment of reified centralized states where all powers were lodged in a divinely ordained king at the top of the power pyramid or in a sovereign center."[9] In the twentieth century the movement toward the centralized large states and its bipolar vision of society has continued. The crisis attendant on this development also surfaced in the course of our era. The religious wars that had occasioned this movement three hundred years earlier have been vastly overshadowed by the clash of titans in Europe and Asia. The contending powers have been this time utterly secular in their aims and in their philosophies, as well as utterly ruthless in their methods. Tens of millions of casualties, cities ruined and rebuilt at great costs, the buildup of arms to undreamed of proportions, the domestic slaughter of millions accomplished with bureaucratic efficiency for reasons based on secular ideologies, and the unleashing of new torrents of religious fanaticism might now begin to awake the suspicion that the West—and with it the world at large—has taken the wrong path.

But movements three hundred years old are not easily abandoned. And the ideologies that support them have in their favor their own version of the moral order. People become used to what seems to them the received wisdom of the world in which they live; their vocabulary and sense of values are shaped by it. The new moral order naturally mimics the old one. It does not and cannot invent the moral sensibilities of people, but it can distort; it can mistake strategy for virtue.

Chapters two through seven explore the story of how the moral philosophy that supports the movement toward nation-states has taken shape. Its central tenet is the doctrine of toleration, and toleration plays a critical role in the crisis faced by the West as it entered into what we now call the modern era. The crisis seemed unresolvable on the grounds of theology or speculative philosophy, and so it was met on the basis of pragmatics. In a world vision governed by a concept of the Good, love becomes the principle virtue. But when the search for what is good is abandoned, when survival becomes the order of the day, and peace means merely the absence of danger, then the temptation is to abandon speculation for pragmatic goals. Material prosperity and safety become the measures of life's accomplishments, goals that fall well within the limits of pragmatic considerations. In such cases, toleration is the pragmatist's substitute for love.

The balance of this book is devoted, first, to exploring the full implications of the modern doctrine of toleration and the alternative views of life offered by modern and contemporary thinkers and, second, to the recovery of what is authentic in the tradition of toleration, a tradition that is fully religious and not secular, and one that is properly located in a practice of religious virtues rather than in the doctrine of a secular virtue.

2

The Ecumenical Impulse

*The truth is that people who worship health
cannot remain healthy.*

G. K. Chesterton

RELIGIONS BOTH ESTABLISH AND DENY COMMUNITY. By attempting to say something that is universally valid, they potentially
embrace the world. At the same time, the religions most conscious of their universalizing claims immediately become the rival,
even the enemy, of every contrary claim. Thus we see the irony of
religion. Without religion, no community with a catholic perspective takes shape. But with competing religions, community is imper-
iled. The world is both drawn together and split apart by the same
force.

And make no mistake, in the modern era especially it is the world
that is at stake. Our minds are inevitably fixed on the goal of truth
that is valid for the world at large, action that is universally justified,
values that pertain to all humanity. Today, for instance, we find the
goal of "human rights" compelling.[1] We sense that it is along the line
of "equal rights for all peoples" that the path of progress lies. The
impetus of community building at any stage implies a universal end

in which all are included and none excluded. Just as the church was from the beginning an Apostolic community, indicating its exclusive origin, it points toward the goal of an ecumenical community, indicating its catholic and inclusive horizon. This catholic sentiment was drummed into us by Christianity, Hebrew prophetism, Greek philosophy, and Roman law; and there is no going back, even if the fragmented pagan world still has its appeal among modern academics with their postmodern protests.

One might think of the modern era, at least since the seventeenth century, as a long crisis: it has been a crisis testing religion's, especially the Christian religion's, ecumenical claims. Early in the modern period, that ecumenical sentiment was tested by the outbreak of rival visions, each claiming universal validity. Wars in sixteenth and seventeenth century Europe, inflamed by religious conviction, gave rise to fanaticism, fanaticism gave rise to cynicism, and cynicism gave rise to secular expediency. That expediency took the form of a new kind of societal structure, the secular state, which could stand at arm's length from the passions that had produced the killing fields of seventeenth century Europe and help take advantage of less idealistic opportunities now arising in trade and commerce. As William H. McNeill wrote, "The creation of such a New Leviathan—half inadvertently perhaps—was certainly one of the major achievements of the seventeenth century, as remarkable in its way as the birth of modern science or any of the other breakthroughs of that age."[2] The refocusing of social energies on the state, rather than on religious and regional associations, continued and was even radicalized during the period of the French Revolution and its aftermath in Europe. In *The Quest for Community*, Robert A. Nisbet saw in that period a "general sterilization of associative allegiances that were not of the state, a subtle transmutation of social statuses into political status, and a general assimilation of human purposes and devotions into the single structure of the people's state."[3]

By the twentieth century that same ecumenical impulse was being tested by new secular ideologies making equally universal claims. The touchstone no longer being that of transcendent truth, the claim was made instead for class, race, "history," and autonomous individual freedom. The wars of the twentieth century were no longer religious wars, but they were wars with ecumenical claims nonetheless, wars fired by ideologies with cosmic ambitions, wars "to make the world safe for democracy." It is no accident that the Communist Internationale strikes the ear as an apocalyptic hymn:

> Arise, ye prisoner of starvation,
> Arise, ye wretched of the earth,
> For justice thunders condemnation,
> A better world's in birth

> 'Tis the final conflict
> Let each stand in his place,
> The Internationale
> Shall be the human race.

The secular ideologies of the twentieth century—so much like the movements of earlier times that were, under the pressure of civilizing forces still vigorously present in society, confined to "fringe group" phenomena—had deep roots in the symbols and expectations that were already available to Western people. Karl Löwith, for instance, has shown that it is not by chance that the proletarian movement of the Communist Party looked so much like "the world-historical mission of the chosen people," and that the "redemptive and universal function of the most degraded class is conceived on the religious pattern of Cross and Resurrection," and furthermore that "the whole process of history as outlined in the *Communist Manifesto* still corresponds to the general scheme of the Jewish-Christian interpretation of history as providential advance toward a final goal."[4]

And in the twentieth as in the seventeenth century, when the ordering principle appears discredited, "each thing meets in mere opugnancy," as Shakespeare predicted:

> Force should be right, or rather, right and wrong,
> Between whose endless jar justice resides,
> Should lose their names, and so should justice too.
> Then everything includes itself in power,
> Power into will, will into appetite;
> And appetite, an universal wolf,
> So doubly seconded with will and power,
> Must make perforce an universal prey,
> And last eat up himself.[5]

In their book on the seventeenth century, Carl Freidrich and Charles Blitzer dubbed the seventeenth century the "age of power."[6] "Power" is in fact the correct focus. There were two preoccupations of the era, both related to the religious wars breaking out during most of the century. One was sovereignty, its importance in an unstable world, its meaning, and its means. The other was "toleration."

At first it would appear that the two preoccupations are unrelated. Or if they are related, it is because they are both reactions to the threat of civil unrest and the steady drumbeat of wars fueled by religious convictions. But what is clear, upon further examination, is that the two ideas are animated by a single concern: how can people live together in peace? The answer to that question might be approached separately, either on the ground of sovereign power or on the ground of religious (and later broader moral and social) toleration. But when the two are brought together in a single focus the answer must take this form: some authorities must prevail while others are given up. Or, to state it differently: some authorities—those that make no claim but the claim to power—must prevail in the public arena, while other authorities—those that make claim to universal validity—are confined to the sphere of private convictions. The first question I will take up is whether, in examining the modern history of the idea of toleration, that idea is not best understood in its relation to the growth of a powerful state in the course of the last three centuries.

A second question is whether a condition of toleration is actually promoted by secular aims and in a secular environment. It asks whether, in fact, one must return to those theological questions that were dropped, out of expediency, and do the hard work of thinking publicly and seriously about ultimate issues of human existence. To think about toleration is necessarily to think about theology, either negatively or positively. Negatively, it is to make the judgment that thinking about God and about what are the ultimate questions of human destiny can be set aside. We surmise that they cannot be resolved, anyway. Consequently, we will "buy time" to pursue goals that are secular in nature and do not depend, we think, on the outcome of religious disagreements. Or, positively, it is to make the judgment that questions of human nature, human destiny, and whether or not we stand accountable to that which is greater than ourselves, are essential to the whole prospect of community. It means that to search for that truth, and to find a modus vivendi in which we can do so together, is an essential part of that hope for a life of peace, whether in a local community or in larger communities.

The Modern Metamorphosis of Toleration

Having once lived in Charleston, South Carolina, I return when possible and walk the narrow streets and alleys of this well-preserved old city, settled for three hundred years close by the Atlantic Ocean. I am often struck that in Charleston one can see in the very brick and mortar the results of a growing conviction, during the seventeenth century, concerning religious toleration. Here on Church Street, beside the stately St. Phillip's Episcopal Church is the ornate meeting house of the Huguenots, evidence of the early influx of persecuted French Protestants. The city streets are marked throughout by Hu-

guenot names—Ravenel, Legare, Rhette, and Inabenet. Only blocks
away from the Huguenot church stands the temple of one of America's
oldest Jewish congregations and the first Reform congregation. Then
there is the mother church of Baptists in the South, moved there at a
time when the Baptists were finding Carolina more tolerant of their
peculiar doctrine and extreme practices than much of New England.

The emphasis, in Charleston's early settlement, on religious openness had much to do with John Locke, whose teachings of religious
toleration were embedded in the constitution of Carolina, and who
served as secretary to the English colonial founders of Carolina. But
it also reflected a growing sentiment in the seventeenth century.
Europe had grown weary of religious wars and the "new world" was
their chance to begin again with a new policy: one that promised
peace, but also one that did not spoil prosperity, which was in the
minds of some what the New World was all about. These matters were
weighing heavily on ambitious European spirits as their prospects
across the Atlantic grew brighter and as it dawned upon the later set-
tlers and their financial backers in Europe just how enormous the
profits might really be.

We have good reason to wonder why the idea of toleration did
not weigh heavily in intellectual history until modern times. In the
English language the word "tolerance" or "toleration" was rarely used
in reference to public policy or a public philosophy—even in referring to religious attitudes—until well into the seventeenth century.
By the turn of the eighteenth century it had become a prominent idea,
a policy in several European states, the cry of religious dissidents, and
the doctrine which most obviously marked off modern society from
the earlier feudal society with its understanding of the compactness
of religion, laws, community, fealty, and piety.

At the same time, one can not say that medieval and ancient societies were without toleration. The ancient church, for instance,
found itself with a largely Hebrew faith that it was eager to share with
a pagan world. Yet it did so, for the most part, without arguing that

nothing in pagan culture was worth keeping. Following the example of the Jewish philosopher Philo, they found points of agreement with Plato, Heraclitus, and Aristotle.[7] The remarkable openness of the church toward other cultures and alien philosophies—especially among the Alexandrian Christians and the Cappadocian Fathers—is at least part of the reason the Christian faith so quickly and thoroughly infiltrated and then dominated the Mediterranean world.

The High Middle Ages was, by any standard, a period of remarkable creativity and energy in western Christendom. Yet the dominance of Christian life and thought in the West did not occur among people who had determined to shut out alien influence. The situation was quite the opposite. We might see instances of this cultural openness in the sciences, mathematics, and the arts. But to confine ourselves to the intellectual life of the church, we find that Christian thought would never have been the same without massive infusions of the intellectual labors of the Muslim world of Alfarabi and Avicenna, and the Jewish philosophy of Maimonides and Gersonides.

Stalin once railed in a speech against those comrades he called "troglodites." These people were what one might call fundamentalist Marxists; they wished to rip up all the capitalist railroads and replace them with socialist railroads. The church has had its share of Christian troglodites in every age; but they most typically were found on the fringes of Christian civilization. Too much of the progress of Christian thought has been associated with the dialogue initiated by Christians with non-Christian traditions for us to think that the pattern is accidental. This does not mean, of course, that Christian thinkers simply incorporated alien ideas, not even that they selected what was most congenial to Christianity. Sometimes the alien concept was thought to be antagonistic to Christianity. In its opposition, however, it contributed to the deepening of Christian thought. Thus—like the oyster developing a pearl around an irritating grain of sand—Christian thinking grows and develops in a way that would not be possible without its introduction to an offending idea.

For instance, at a time when much of the Christian world felt threatened by new infusions of Aristotelian thought from the scholars of Islam, Thomas Aquinas considered it worthwhile to subject Aristotle's thought to a critique based upon revelation and reason. When Aristotle taught that the world was eternal, such teaching appears to deny what is taught in the Bible, namely that the world is created. For Aristotle the world had no beginning. It always existed. For Christians the world had a definite beginning. There seemed an unbridgeable impasse. But Aquinas showed that even if Aristotle's "eternal world" were granted, one still found in Aristotle a world that is contingent and thus dependent upon God. This, he taught, was the heart of the doctrine of creation, because the teaching on the world's beginning was not so much about a genesis of time, which could hardly be imagined, as it was about the difference between necessary and contingent being. Thus, Aquinas corrects Aristotle and at the same time makes him useful in the explication of revealed truth.[8]

Two matters, in light of what we've just noted come into view, and they appear to be strangely out of sync with each other. One is that the practice of toleration developed—not evenly, nor thoroughly, nor self-consciously, but quite genuinely—in the context of a Christian society and in the intellectual life of the church. The other is that toleration as a public policy or as a self-conscious public virtue does not appear prominently until a time when political life was marked by increasing secularity. Why this seeming disparity? Is the tolerant practice of the ancient and medieval Christian community the same as the doctrine of toleration in a secularizing modern West? Is the new awareness of toleration as a needed public virtue simply the culmination of long development in the West, an awareness not unlike the slow recognition of the evils of slavery, the broadening of civil rights, the extension of suffrage in the U.S. to women and African-Americans? Or does the modern doctrine of toleration, while preserving much of the earlier classical and Christian ethic, in its later forms prove to be a departure from the practice of toleration as it might have existed in the West? To answer these questions one must first look at the character of what is taken to be both the earlier practice and the later doctrine.

Toleration in the Bible

One must make a distinction between the practice of toleration and the doctrine that, as we will show, developed its peculiar character in modern times, and that developed in a form that was peculiarly suited to modern conditions. The practice of toleration is much older, just as there was certainly the practice of "art" long before there was a concept of art. The West drew from a tradition of toleration much deeper and older than is apparent in its sudden appearance in the seventeenth century. We can detect the early roots of that tradition in the fundamental text of Western culture, the Bible.

The Bible is, historically speaking, the product of Hebrew prophetism. From a purely secular point of view, this movement was an unaccountable cataclysm in the realm of the moral and religious life of a nation, one that made an indelible impression upon the Hebrew people between the eighth and the fourth centuries before Christ. It left one small nation, clinging desperately to an impoverished homeland in one small corner of the Mediterranean world, infused with an unshakable conviction. Today we would call that conviction "ethical monotheism." They believed in one God, unlike their neighbors; but they also believed that the character of that God was such that he demanded justice among His people. The center of religious life had moved from the outward observance of a cultic order to the inward obedience of the morally aware human heart. Hence, in the Deuteronomic prophecies we read: "Has the Lord as great delight in burnt offering and sacrifices, as in obeying the voice of the Lord? Behold, to obey is better than sacrifice, and to hearken than the fat of rams" (1 Sam. 15:22).

Clearly, the prophetic movement in its initial effect was the op-

posite of toleration. Monotheism is by its very nature an undemo-
cratic and intolerant view of life. And if that one God has an interest
in the conduct of human life, then the effect upon human behavior
would logically be less latitude, not more. The Old Testament prophet
pronounced anathema against the gods of Israel's neighbors. He
scolded Israel for imitating the ways of the Canaanites and the Egyp-
tians. For the prophet, the worst villain of Israel was the one who
dared compromise the exclusive worship of Yahweh. And the heroes
were often those who struck down the ones who would compromise,
with swift revenge for their religious betrayal. The prophet is animated by a desire to purify Israel from the illusions and the moral
temptations of other gods. The prophet Elijah taunts the priests of
Baal, whose frantic efforts receive no answer from a god who is either hard of hearing or out of the country, or perhaps answering the
call of nature (1 Kings 18). Isaiah challenges the foreign gods to "Tell
us what is to come hereafter, that we may know you are gods," and
concludes, "Behold, you are nothing, and your work is nought; an
abomination is he who chooses you" (Isa. 41: 23, 24). In prophecies
such as Ezra and Nehemiah, there are strong injunctions against in-
termarriage with foreign women. All of this stems from Israel's devotion to the exclusive worship of the one God, with its implied moral
and cultic purity. The trend in biblical traditions, even at its earliest
stages, is contrary to tolerance. It is the opposite to openness toward
the plurality of religions and the variety of moral communities in the
ancient Mediterranean world.

At the same time we see a paradoxical trend in Hebrew exclu-
sivism, and later also in the Christian's exclusive claims. The moment
someone confesses to believe in one God, that person excludes all
other gods; but necessarily, he is saying that all people belong in some
fashion to that same God. To reject the god of the foreigner on monotheistic and exclusive grounds is to accept the foreigner himself as a
fellow human being, tied in kinship by the fact of their both being

created by the same God. In one and the same gesture, one rejects the foreign gods and embraces the foreigner.

The Old Testament is crowded with examples of this peculiar paradox. The prophet Jonah is commanded to go to the despised Ninevites to warn them of God's judgment. He hates the Ninevites and goes to great lengths to disobey the command, bringing God's judgment upon himself. Finally, after going to Ninevah and warning the Ninevites, he is dismayed to find them repenting and the judgment averted. While Jonah sulks, God says to him, "And should I not pity Nineveh, that great city, in which there are more than a hundred and twenty thousand persons?" (Jon. 4:11).

Ruth is a Moabite woman, who comes to be married to an Israelite named Boaz and becomes a mother of the line of David and the coming Messiah. Abimelech, the king of Gerar, is described as a person who fears the Lord (Gen. 20:1-18). Jethro is Moses' father-in-law and a priest of Midian, yet he too is described as one who receives and recognizes the revealed truth of Moses' God (Exod. 18:1-12). Melchizedek is descibed as "priest of God Most High," yet he precedes the covenant of Abraham. Alongside the exclusive implications of a monotheistic religion, one must also consider these and numerous other exceptions, exceptions that imply what Clark Pinnock described as a "wideness in God's mercy."[9]

In the New Testament it is difficult not to see that there is an identification of Christ, in whom all find salvation, with a Source of truth that is broader than the mere story of Jesus and certainly broader than given institutional developments. The Fourth Gospel identifies Jesus with the "logos," the "Word." For ancient people who knew of the teachings of Heraclitus this invoking of the "logos" was significant. It was that reality which gave meaning and permanence to things, and that extended through all of the changing, shifting particularities of the world drawing them together in a comprehensive wholeness. This same writer (traditionally the Apostle John, although the gospel itself is anonymous as are all the gospels) speaks of Jesus' coming in these terms: "The true light that enlightens every man was coming into the world" (John. 1:9). To the extent that any truth had come into the world, this human being was the embodiment of that truth. That is not so much a claim of exclusive truth as it is a claim identifying all wisdom with its true, incarnate reality in the historical appearance of Jesus Christ.

The Apostle Paul makes a similar point when he draws upon a Deuteronomic teaching on the essence of the law in order to explain what it means to believe in Jesus Christ. What he says in Romans is this: "But the righteousness based on faith says, Do not say in your heart, 'Who will ascend into heaven?' (that is, to bring Christ down) or 'Who will descend into the abyss?' (that is, to bring Christ up from the dead). But what does it say? The word is near you, on your lips and in your heart (that is, the word of faith which we preach); because if you confess with your lips that Jesus is Lord and believe in your heart that God raised him from the dead, you will be saved" (Rom. 10:6-9). When a reader sees what Paul is drawing from here, it becomes clear that he intends to say the same thing about Christ that the Mosaic speech in Deuteronomy says about the law: "For this commandment which I command you this day is not too hard for you, neither is it far off. It is not in heaven, that you should say, 'Who will go up for us to heaven, and bring it to us, that we may hear it and do it?' Neither is it beyond the sea, that you should say, 'Who will go over the sea for us, and bring it to us, that we may hear it and do it?' But the word is very near you; it is in your mouth and in your heart, so that you can do it" (Deut. 30: 11-14).

The law is that which so pervades reality and is so internal to our existence that to receive the law is not to receive something new. It is something that is rather *recognized* as having always been present to us in some form. And it is a truth that is present to all people, even as creation itself is present to all people. Hence, Paul quotes a part of Psalm 19 which reads, "Their voice has gone out to all the earth, and their words to the ends of the world." In the psalm he quotes, the words are preceded by, "The heavens are telling the glory of God; and the firmament proclaims his handiwork. Day to day pours forth speech, and night to night declares knowledge." But this is not literally speech, the psalmist says, because, "There is no speech, nor are there words; their voice is not heard." Yet this *is* the truth that goes "out through all the world."

If, by toleration, we mean a willingness to hear other traditions and to learn from them, then we find much in both the Old Testament and the New Testament to encourage such an attitude. The fundamental virtue from which this practice of toleration would come is the virtue of humility. In humility it is assumed that, even with our best efforts at understanding the things of God, we are prevented from reaching that sublime goal. We are prevented by our creatureliness and by our sinfulness. Therefore, it is a matter of grace that truth comes to us from many directions, even from people who are not Christian, and even from philosophies that are not our own. The conviction of the Christian is not that his theology has all truth somehow hermetically sealed and free from foreign influence. Instead, it is that one God created us all, that He reveals himself in the world He has made, and that for all people, God has been "clearly perceived in the things that have been made" (Rom. 1:20). But if the Christian tradition did not hold that truth is One, then it could hardly make sense of the incarnation of God in Christ; this conviction both places the Christian on common ground with all men, and separates them from all unbelievers. Christians both learn from and teach all others—not one or the other, but both.

Toleration in the History of the Church

For almost all of the modern period, the church enjoyed the luxury of relative isolation from genuine alternatives to Christianity. Its conflicts and its intellectual challenges consisted of variations within the Judeo-Christian tradition. One might immediately think of modern secular philosophies, such as Marxism and Communism, as implying precisely the contrary. These are, of course, atheistic and materialistic alternatives to Christianity, and the like of these and others have proliferated in the twentieth century. But I contend (and in doing so would find plenty of good company) that even these types of apparently anti-Christian ideologies are unimaginable apart from a generally widespread predisposition toward a Christian view of the world, with its eschatological expectation, its sense of progress as a historic phenomenon, and its sense of justice as the goal of humanity. One could not imagine that Marxism would arise spontaneously in a culture influenced by Hinduism or Buddhism, for instance. So, in spite of its internal contradictions, and in spite of the spawning of its rebellious children, the existence of a cacooned Western (that is, pervasively Christian) culture has prevailed for a remarkably long period of time.

That period of relative isolation is now quickly coming to an end. The ease of travel and communication puts us in touch instantly and continually with those of other traditions. Therefore, we have to go back to the earlier part of the Christian era, at least to its first thirteen centuries, to find examples of how the church responded to a world of intellectual and cultural plurality. While for most of the second millennium the culture of Christendom was relatively secure in its adoptive homelands, it appears that the first and third millennia will prove to be the times of testing in the crucible of plurality.

To discover how the practice of toleration was brought to bear at critical points in the early and middle ages of the church, we will briefly look at two examples of such a practice in the ancient church and then one powerful example in the medieval church.

Justin Martyr. The first is Justin Martyr (d. 165), a figure of critical importance in the second century church. He was a seeker after philosophical truth before converting to Christianity. He was born a

Greek in the Samaritan territory and as a young man traveled to Ephesus to study philosophy.[10] He was a philosopher by profession, and even after his conversion he continued to wear the *pallium,* the traditional cloak of the philosopher. His search for metaphysical truth led him first to the Stoics, and then, after brief encounters with a Peripatetic and a Pythagorean teacher, he turned to the Platonists. After an old man introduced him to the Scriptures, and told him that "only prayer could open the way to God," Justin became a Christian.[11] He insisted that the Christian faith represented the highest philosophy and the touchstone by which other philosophies might be judged.

To say that the Christian faith is the "touchstone" is immediately to identify the manner in which Justin's openness to other traditions is framed. His was not an indiscriminate openness such as modern openness often implies. He was quite critical of the pagan cult of his time, rejecting these as leading away from what is true and good. At the same time, he believed that the identification of Christ as the *logos* opened the way to understanding even pre-Christian philosophies as bearing a measure of truth. Just as the Hebrew histories and prophecies gave witness to Christ, he believed it likely that Socrates was a "Christian before Christ." As Henry Chadwick put it,

> Justin does not make rigid and exclusive claims for divine revelation to the Hebrews so as to invalidate the value of other sources of wisdom. Abraham and Socrates are alike 'Christians before Christ'. But just as the aspirations of the Old Testament prophets found their fulfillment in Christ, so also the correct insights achieved by the Greek philosophers reached their completion in the gospel of Christ who embodies the highest moral ideal. Christ is for Justin the principle of unity and the criterion by which we may judge the truth, scattered like divided seeds among the different schools of philosophy insofar as they have dealt with religion and morals."[12]

Justin Martyr is a major figure, exerting enormous influence in the direction of Christian thought. His example of a hospitable spirit in evaluation of pagan philosophies was not always followed; but he did influence a significant trend in the church, one that did indeed predominate through all of the first millennium and beyond. We see his influence in the *Plea for Christians*, written by Athenagoras of Athens, a work addressed to Marcus Aurelius and Commodus (177 A.D.). And we also see his influence in Clement of Alexandria, to whose example we turn next.

Clement of Alexandria. The *Oxford Dictionary of the Christian Church* says simply that "practically nothing is known of his life."[13] But Chadwick elaborates on this paucity of biographical detail by writing that "Clement's personal reticence allowed him to reveal little of himself, but his personal ideals are clear to see."[14] We do know that he was born about 150 A.D. and died in approximately 215. Beyond that, we know him principally by the enormous influence he had upon the thinking of the church.

Before his time many of the intellectuals of the day remarked upon the fact that Christianity attracted so many of the poor, and along with the poor, the unlettered. Christianity appeared to them a religion for the ignorant. Yet after Clement's time, the reverse seemed to be the case: it was the province of the intellectual elite in places like Alexandria, Athens, and Rome, great centers of learning in the ancient world. In many ways, the period from Clement to Augustine was *the* period of Christian ascendancy in terms of its effect upon the intellectual life of the emerging cultures of both the East and the West.

Clement's accomplishment was that he cured the church of its fear of pagan intellectual achievements. Like Philo on behalf of Judaism more than a century before, Clement incorporated the best works of Hellenistic literature and philosophy in his own Christian teaching. The writings of Clement that remain to us contain more than seven hundred quotations from an excess of three hundred pagan sources. At the same time, it is perfectly clear that Scripture was his authority, the source of true philosophy. His arguments would explore the world of Homer or Heraclitus, but then he would resolve the issue beginning with the words "it is written." Hence, his thought was hardly syncretistic. But it was synthetic: it was an approach that was open to the pagan writer and thinker. There was, for him, a "chorus of truth" upon which the Christian might draw. This multiple source did not replace Scripture, but it illuminated its pages. All philosophy, if it was true philosophy, was of divine origin, even though what we receive through philosophy, is broken and almost unintelligible. Appealing to 1 Corinthians 13:12, he allows for the fact that we see "in a mirror dimly." Yet there is an image there, however dimly seen.

All truth, after all, Clement would argue, is God's truth. In his *Stromata* (Miscellanies) he wrote, "they may say that it is mere chance that the Greeks have expressed something of the true philosophy. But that chance is subject to divine providence. . . . Or in the next place it may be said that the Greeks possessed an idea of truth implanted by nature. But we know that the Creator of nature is one only."[15] This Alexandrian tradition had enormous influence on the church. Christianity became not simply an alternative "philosophy" within a world market of philosophies, but it became the means by which the intellectual life of the Mediterranean world surpassed anything known before. Problems that naturally presented themselves in earlier systems of thought would now be seen in a new light. The advent of Christianity had not simply replaced other ways of thinking about the world, but it presented the world with possibilities that had never appeared on the horizon until Christianity appeared. Therefore, as has often been noted, we find a quantum leap in the possibilities within philosophy from the second century to the fifth. And with the rise of medieval culture, after the recovery of high culture in the West, we find in figures such as Anselm clearly a new potency in the efforts of philosophy. It was a recovery of powers that had not been known since the height of the classical period before Christ.

I would not want to give the impression (and many readers would recognize the error anyway) that a tolerance or openness toward the pagan culture was uniformly adopted in the church. A famous example of a dissenting voice was Tertullian, who objected to all this philosophizing by asking trenchantly, *"Quid Athenae Hierlsolymis?"* — What has Athens to do with Jerusalem? This skepticism with regard to the place of philosophy in understanding the Christian faith takes place throughout the history of the church. It reflects the Apostle Paul's well known warning that "the foolishness of God is wiser than the wisdom of men" (1 Cor. 1:22). Yet it would be in the thirteenth century, the high water mark by many estimations of the Christian civilization of the West, that the problem of relating Christianity to pagan sources of wisdom would find a most creative response.

Thomas Aquinas, Maimonides, and Alfarabi: Aristotle Rediscovered. The popular modern prejudice concerning the Middle Ages is that it was a time of deep superstition and determined rejection of anything unapproved by the church. Crusades were launched against the infidels, relics were objects of veneration and almost worship, witches and heretics were burned at the stake. Actually, in the sixteenth and seventeenth centuries, the beginning of modernity, never was there a time of more widespread superstition, interest in magic and fortune telling, nor was there ever a time of more destructive religious wars. And the witch craze in Europe and America was more pronounced than at any time in the past, including the so-called "dark ages."

That is not to say that such things did not happen in the medieval period. But it has been the genius of the modern Enlightenment that people remember only this and forget the overwhelming examples to the contrary. Especially have we been persuaded to forget that the intellectual life of the church was due in no small part to the exchange of ideas among Jewish, Islamic, and Christian scholars. In a wonderful brief study by Notre Dame professor David Burrell, C.S.C., entitled *Knowing the Unknowable God*, he tells of "how Muslim, Jew and Christian conspired to fashion a doctrine of God by transforming classical philosophy to display divine transcendence."[16]

He concentrates upon the mutual development of thought that takes place through three major thinkers of the Middle Ages: the Jewish thinker Maimonides, the Muslim Ibn-Sina (Avicenna), and the Christian Thomas Aquinas. "A central purpose of this study" he said, "has been to show how the received doctrine of God in the West was already an intercultural, interfaith achievement."[17]

The central figure in this study is Thomas Aquinas, whose reshaping of Christian theology and philosophy took place partly under the influence of major Jewish and Muslim thinkers. Had the study been more extensive, Burrell could have enlarged the cast of characters. Men such as Aquinas and Scotus were either directly or indirectly influenced by the tradition of the *Falasifa*, the Islamic philosopers. They knew the work of tenth-century Alfarabi, and thirteenth-century Averroes. Their interaction with the thought of Maimonides brought further developments in the later thinking of the Jewish thinker Gersonides (Levi ben Gershom, 1288-1344).

The significance of this for our own study of toleration is clear. There was, long before the Enlightenment, a tradition of openness—born of the humility that was counseled by Clement and others in antiquity—that helped to shape the direction of Christian thought and of Western culture. It was not, to be sure, the same doctrine of toleration that developed in such a distinct way in modern times, and which is the real object of our inquiry.[18] But it was a definite practice; and it was a practice and attitude that left the lines of communication open among believing and thinking communities. The distinction between that practice and the later doctrine will help us to isolate the peculiar features that give the later doctrine its unmistakable modern flavor.

The Doctrine of Toleration

By "doctrine" I mean to distinguish a particular teaching. That a teaching can be wholly and ludicrously detached from a practice is the stuff of proverbs in every age. And what a teaching intends can sometimes be quite at variance from what it seems to intend. There is, of course, the teaching of a skill, the teaching of knowledge, and the teaching of virtue. And it is in the teaching of virtue that the public realm, the commonwealth, has a particular stake. For it is by the virtues that are inculcated in a people that the authorities in the commonwealth find support. The Soviet Union, for instance, wished to teach its peasant farmers the virtue of selflessness and community spirit, which is to say they wished to root out their desire for personal property and hopes for private gain. The fact that such teaching was unrealistic and unnatural as an economic system soon made itself felt. Nonetheless, the virtue fit the nature of the regime, and this was (within the context) all important. Monarchies hope to inculcate the sense of filial piety and regard for rank, while democracies stress the virtue of personal and individual responsibility. The extent to which these regimes "work" will depend largely upon the extent to which these virtues exist among the people.

When the idea of toleration in its new form began to be used frequently, and in reference to some kind of public virtue, it became a kind of encapsulated speech about the values of a public weary of fighting over doctrinal differences. It was hammered out in the crucible of a continent ravaged by war, war waged ostensibly over Protestant and Catholic loyalties. When Pierre Bayle, John Locke, and others used the term its immediate background was the devastating Thirty Years War on the Continent, and the Civil War in England. The word bore the anguish of people who had seen their homes laid waste and their communities decimated by the terror of religious conviction that had taken up arms.

Before the word tolerance or toleration had ever been used in reference to public policy, it referred simply to the Latin idea of that which "may be borne."[19] It refers to the capacity to bear or endure a hardship or a pain. One might tolerate a certain medicine better than someone else would. In the inanimate realm, it refers to the capacity to endure stress or physical abuse without damage. The wings on an airplane will tolerate more stress than the metal stand of your living room lamp. In biology, an organism can tolerate so much cold and so much heat and beyond that it becomes ill and dies.

By extension toleration applies to enduring a wrong or an injustice. It implies withholding judgment or deferring action, enduring instead the assault upon one's conscience, the injury to one's pride, the affront to better judgment, the offending of one's taste, one's sense of decorum, or one's deeply held convictions. It also implies that by toleration a higher good is served, something judged to be still more important than the immediate recognition of these matters of conscience, pride, judgment, taste, decorum, or even one's deeply held convictions. One might hold, for instance, that the cultivating of a free society requires a certain latitude, for individuals and groups, in deciding even those values of aesthetics, morals, or doctrine that people are likely to cling to as their most fundamental commitments.

When we move to this moral, or aesthetic, or religious realm, however, we run into considerable difficulties in defining just what we mean by toleration. The obvious implication is that we might "bear with" sin, or ugliness, or theological error. But to say this much implies strongly a standard of moral behavior, a standard of beauty, and a theological doctrine that defines what it is we endure without complaint. Obviously, there is more disagreement over the precise doctrine of the Trinity than there would be over how much cold a human being can endure before freezing to death.

But even if the standard is impossibly imprecise and subject to broad disagreement, the idea of toleration at least implies the existence of a standard. It does not originally imply that differences in moral choices, for instance, are neutral. It implies, instead, that there is something to endure, something to treat with patience. Moral tolerance implies a moral path from which some of us wander, to be treated tolerantly by others.

Over time, of course, tolerance has come to imply a certain disparagement of standards, or at least standards other than those that bear directly upon the ideal of non-interference in the lives of others. For instance, consider the "Declaration of Principles on Tolerance" signed by the member states of UNESCO on November 16, 1995: "Tolerance is respect, acceptance and appreciation of the rich diversity of our world's cultures, our forms of expression and ways of being human . . . . Tolerance is not concession, condescension or indulgence. Tolerance is, above all, an active attitude prompted by recognition of the universal human rights and fundamental freedoms of others."

It is important to note that tolerance, in the UNESCO statement—a statement we can take to be fairly representative of the contemporary meaning of toleration—is the virtue of restraint. Persons, societies, and governments must allow, and not interfere with, "forms of expression and ways of being human." Its point of reference is "human rights" rather than the classical idea of the "good." The former asserts the freedom of individuals or groups and the latter puts forward an idea of that which is truly or universally human. To say that one is a negative expression of how human beings live together and the other is a positive expression is not simply to say that one is bad and the other good—it is descriptive of the relationship among people that each intends to promote. "Rights" describe something negative, the absence of something, namely the absence of interference. It is non-interference with the ways of others.

These rights are not unlimited. The UNESCO statement acknowledges that: "Consistent with respect for human rights, the practice of tolerance does not mean toleration of social injustice or the abandonment or weakening of one's convictions." But the language of tolerance necessarily provokes that good thing only by virtue of suggesting what must be left alone: "It means that one is free to adhere to one's own convictions and accepts that others adhere to theirs. It means accepting the fact that human beings, naturally diverse in their appearance, situation, speech, behavior and values, have the right to live in peace and be as they are. It also means that one's views are not to be imposed on others."[20]

The most obvious feature of this doctrine, as we see it taking form and defining itself in modern times, is that it is something that is applied to the community. This is a public doctrine, meant to be adopted by member states of UNESCO as ways of living together as separate political communities. And yet it is a concept empty of content. It neither prescribes nor suggests even one thing around which a community might join in common conviction or concerted action. It advises that they leave one another alone and (perhaps somewhat on the positive side) encourage others to live their lives without interfering with the ways of their neighbors.

In other words, this doctrine is not so much a prescription for community as a prescription for non-interference among groups, and at the far end of its logic, a kind of hardened individualism. When we look at it in this way, we have to be struck by the fact that such a doctrine is a peculiar thing to foster in a community, if, that is, community itself is of any importance. It appears, in a way, of course, to forestall conflict—on the strength of its counsel against interfering with the ways and beliefs of others. But more important, it is a community's antibody: it is a solvent that resists the glue of common conviction that holds people together. Communities are bodies of people who live in some kind of dynamic relationship with one another because they pursue common goals and thus hold common values. In order to do that, they also exercise some discipline upon members of the group. Cities have regulations and laws. Clubs may require attendance and a certain level of participation. Labor unions may require loyalty, dues, and a level of competence in a field of work. The American Bar Association imposes standards of competence and a code of ethics. Churches have classically been recognized as such, in part, because they impose discipline to aid in the perfection of the

Christian and to resist the taint of heresy and immorality. That which makes a group into a strong community is its adherence to a commitment potent enough to hold the members together.

Yet this doctrine resists commitments that would in any way be strong enough to form community. Furthermore, it is being put forward as a *public* doctrine, as a virtue that is suitable for the living of a community life. How shall we understand this seeming contradiction?

The answer might lie in our inquiring *what sort of community this virtue serves.* That is the question we will seek to answer in the next chapter. It is directed at a remarkable historical coincidence; namely, that the rise of the doctrine of toleration coincides with the rise of the nation-states in Europe, and that it remains a strong public teaching especially in those states where, as Hannah Arendt has stated it, they are burdened "under the monstrous weight of their own bigness," and there is consequently a need for a bureaucracy that can deal directly with individuals and not be hindered by the competing loyalties and authorities that create groups within the population. They can then act as an organization with clear lines of command, for "the bigger a country becomes in terms of population, of objects, and of possessions, the greater will be the need for administration and with it the anonymous power of the administrators."[21]

By looking into this apparent paradox, we might well discover the secret of toleration's modern character. And then, by the way, we might rediscover the character of a practice of toleration with deeper roots and with more promise for the healing of nations.

3

A Feeling of Uncertainty

It came burning hot into my mind, whatever he
said and however he flattered, when he got me
to his house, he would sell me for a slave.

John Bunyon

IN *Cosmopolis*, an essay on the "hidden agenda of modernity,"
Stephen Toulmin finds himself in agreement with John Dewey
and Richard Rorty that "philosophy turned into its 'modern'
dead end" as a result of the Quest for Certainty—a quest that began,
they thought, with Réné Descartes. Toulmin further questions why
this impasse should have taken place at just this time. Why was it that
in the first half of the seventeenth century the West should have suddenly turned its back on the tolerant humanism of Michel de
Montaigne and Francis Bacon? It was as if modern thought had begun in one direction and then suddenly shifted course.

Toulmin expands upon this line of thought by observing what he
takes to be a remarkable change of the intellectual climate during a
rather precise period of time in Europe. Montaigne and Bacon were
not concerned to eliminate plurality, ambiguity, or the lack of certainty that might emerge in their search for knowledge. Descartes,

on the other hand, coming on stage somewhat later, thought of skepticism as "destructive nay-saying." He sought instead a secure basis of rational thought. The period from 1590 to 1640 saw a move away from the humanist interest in rhetoric, in the particular and the concrete diversity of life, and in the transitory nature of things. The passion, according to Toulmin, was shifted toward formal logic, rather than rhetoric, general principles rather than the concrete particulars, and from the transitory to the "timeless, general, and universal principles." The obvious occasion for this shift was the general European crisis of the early and mid-seventeenth century, and especially the Thirty Years War which devastated central Europe. Under such conditions, Renaissance humanism, which had tolerated ambiguity, plurality, and uncertainty, was abandoned for the tight logic, the general principle, and the promise of certainty. The world in crisis demanded "abstract, context-free inquiries" with the promise of universal principles leading to certainty rather than ambiguity.

Dewey's thesis in his famous book *The Quest for Certainty* undoubtedly influenced—if not directly, then indirectly—Toulmin's reconstruction of intellectual history in the seventeenth century. Dewey argued that the tendency to prefer the abstract and the theoretical to the concrete and practical is motivated heavily by a desire to "escape from peril." Practical engagement with the material world is fraught with uncertainties. One never knows if the effort will prove successful, or just what might be the results. Intellectual activity of the purer sort, on the level of abstract theory, is often free from the obvious contradictions that come to light in practical work. Thomas Edison's light bulbs either worked or they did not, and his efforts were contradicted, according to the story, over nine hundred times. But Hegel's idea of history suffers no such indignities. Thus, the realm of theory escapes the slings and arrows of all but a few academic philosophers and is by far the safer. Therefore, Dewey maintains, the "exaltation of pure intellect and its activity above practical affairs is fundamentally connected with the quest for a certainty which shall be absolute and unshakeable." The preference for theory over practice, or as an activity that necessarily precedes practice, is for Dewey not a necessity at all but an "escape." And it constitutes a mistaken bifurcation of intellect and practice that goes all the way back to "something as remote in time as Greek philosophy." So, for quite a long time indeed, according to Dewey, the search for an immutable *telos* or goal in life— the notion of the Good—has stemmed not from the practical needs of human beings but from their emotional needs only: "As long as man was unable by means of the arts of practice to direct the course of events, it was natural for him to seek an emotional substitute; in the absense of actual certainty in the midst of a precarious and hazardous world, men cultivated all sorts of things that would give them the *feeling* of certainty."[1] Society needed, perhaps, the courage and confidence that such certainty provides, Dewey thought; but now the time has come to reclaim the natural connectedness of practical work and intellectual speculation. This means for Dewey no longer dividing the two and making abstract thought the undisputed guide for action in the realm of the practical.

What Toulmin added to this analysis is simply the historical occasion in which the need for escape from peril appears to have been particularly intense, namely, Europe in the early seventeenth century. One of the lessons that Toulmin draws from this sort of analysis concerns modern theology and ethics. "In the High Middle Ages," he writes, "Christian theology . . . was more relaxed and adventurous than it became after the late sixteenth century. Medieval theologians were spared the Vatican monitoring and censorship to which a Hans Küng and a Charles Curran are subjected today. Nicolas Cusanus taught doctrine for which Bruno was to be burned at the stake; Copernicus gave free rein to his imagination in ways no longer permitted to Galileo."[2] Then, he says, "from 1610 on, and most of all after 1618, the argument [between Reformation and Counter-Reformation advocates] became active, bloody, and strident. Everyone now talked at the top of his voice, and the humanists' quiet discussions of finitude, and the need for toleration, no longer won a hearing."[3]

Hopes and Fears

There is, of course, a compelling plausibility to the arguments of Toulmin and those of his predecessor John Dewey. One can easily imagine that the violent shock of events in the early seventeenth century fetched a reaction of intellectual and cultural rigidity. It is easy to conclude that tolerant openness was dangerous; this was no time for patient uncertainty or easy intellectual ambiguity. What dangers lurk in mystery! The light of logic can alone relieve the fear of dark corners in an unpredictable world. It is an understandable theory, but nevertheless wrong, I think. And ironically it fails from want of wrestling with the concrete complexities of a world that knew both fears and hopes—hopes in fact that were as high as the fears were deep.

For Toulmin, the motive for this sudden rigidity in modern thought was that dreadful fear that had come upon Europe in unstable times. Two problems, however, present themselves in response to Toulmin's reading. Both have a bearing upon the present investigation into the meaning of tolerance. The first problem lies in his understanding of modernity as caught up in rigid intolerance with only periodic times and occasions of relief. Just the contrary appear more likely. It seems indisputable that the seventeenth century is in fact the fountainhead of a new conviction with regard to toleration. And it is in modern times that the case is made, for the first time in history, that "toleration" is a necessary public policy. The arguments for religious toleration eventually cut a wide swath in public thought, stimulated by the writings of Pierre Bayle and John Locke. By the time of John Stuart Mill, the principle had broadened to include other forms of tolerance, especially in the realm of ethics. This latitudinarian spirit is further embodied, along with all of the ambiguity and mystery that Toulmin could wish for, in the romantic movement of the nineteenth century—yet this too was a part of modernity.

The second objection to Toulmin and Dewey's analysis will take longer to establish. The gist of my objection is this: What we find in the seventeenth century is not a rigidity based on fear (at least not as a primary motive) but a new opportunistic spirit motivated by the desire for power. What occurred in that period were surely the terrors of war, just as Dewey and Toulmin have seen. But more than that, there was a new sense of opportunity—unparalleled in any time since the rise of the Roman Empire—for the growth of economic and political influence.

The fears of the early modern times do play a role in the development of ideas, as I will show especially in regard to Thomas Hobbes. But the fears do not drive modern people toward philosophy, especially not in the sense of establishing first principles and final causes. In fact, it drives them in a very different direction, toward justifying and strengthening authoritarian regimes and giving philosophical weight to the organizing of society *against* the kind of speculation that had been the occasion for religious wars. Europeans were not taking refuge in theological refinements and metaphysical theories; they were fighting wars over them. Their attentiveness to arguments for toleration matched their weariness with war. Metaphysics had made people mad, it seemed. Furthermore, it had distracted them from opportunities to become rich and powerful enough to put an end to the "poor, solitary, brutish" life of the provincial peasant and city shop keeper.

An Age of Secular Hope

Rather than viewing the opening of the modern period from the point of view of its dangers (which were certainly real enough), we will look at these same circumstances from the perspective of the equally real, and perhaps more significant and rare, opportunities. Opportunities opened up to an unprecedented degree in the seventeenth century due to a number of factors: the collapse of ecclesiastical authority giving rise to political power unhindered by church constraints, and the availability of vast tracts of land and other resources formerly held by the church. These were accompanied by the expansion of trade opportunities in the Orient and in the Americas and the objective growth of secular political power due to new economic advantages and new social arrangements. War was a result, in part, of the polarizing and fragmenting of religious loyalties, and in part to the withering of ecclesiastical restraints, and in part the sudden rich possibilities for the extension of secular authority.

That new power must replace (or at least substantially displace) the traditional forms through which social authority had always been exercised. The growth of secular power is obvious. The attending need to displace a former authority is not so obvious, and yet critical. The new secular power could only be maximized when social loyalties focused on that new authority. For that reason, the principles that became widespread preoccupations of the new era were sovereignty and toleration. Sovereignty had to do with the assertion of the political power now possible on a wider scale, a political power that mirrored, in fact, the rich new economic opportunities. War that had broken out over religious rivalries stood in a double relationship to that new secular power: it was both the means by which a sovereign authority expanded its power, and it constituted the emergency that justified such power.

The newly discovered public voice for a policy of toleration—first religious toleration and later a more general social tolerance—was a necessary concomitant feature of the growth of sovereignty, the consolidation of the nation-state and the expansion of secular power as well as the growth of economic opportunity. The habitual contours of society—one might say its natural arrangement within the ebb and flow of informal authority—was a function of the family, the village, the locale, the trade association, and of religion. These sometimes smaller and always subtler arrangements of customary authority in society were always potentially in competition with the comprehensive political arrangements of the modern state. They were seen as natural obstacles in the project of erecting large-scale central administration, remote from local arrangements.

Toleration then became the means of diminishing lesser loyalties, by calling their moral authority into question; and, by thus compromising competing authorities, toleration cleared the ground for the broader, more formal power. It became the mother philosophy of the unarticulated society, the society without traditional contours of social arrangements, the mass society, the society consisting of individuals alone, individuals whose loyalty is focused on the new, remote, comprehensive authority of the state. It should be no wonder, then, that toleration is most valued in large-scale Western societies, where cultural conquest has been most successful and economic expansion most obvious.

It is in Europe and North America that sanctions against intolerance have been most pronounced—to such an extent that small, compact, and traditionally homogenous societies such as Japan in the East and Ghana in Africa find such fastidious attitudes puzzling and the overcautious speech of Westerners amusing. And it is in great Western universities like Stanford that "multiculturalism" has become a serious undertaking, leaving much of the rest of the world to wonder if our fear of difference has not driven us mad. At least such preoccupations on our university campuses have not so far convinced everyone that their motivation is true interest in another culture. Is it instead animated by the desire to obliterate distinctions, to make of society an unarticulated mass? Is it, most of all, a useful way to diminish the potency of the overlapping authorities (the authority of family and church being the most enduring) that give character and shape to a natural and spontaneous society but which stand in the way of a highly organized one? These questions become the more serious as we give thought to the development and present character of modern institutions.

The Economics of Toleration

To demonstrate the role of "toleration" in its modern form, I want to show how it stands in a parallel relationship to two other forces in early modern times that had similar effect. All three reduce the capacity of a culture to exert traditional authority. All three tend to neutralize traditional social arrangements, thus creating a society that no longer operates on the basis of interpersonal relationships, but on the basis of abstraction—that is, on the basis of rationalized categories. The personally neutral society is a society now conceived in abstract categories. That is to say, it is a social arrangement that operates between the two poles of the individual and the state. Mediating social aggregates are minimized: they are, for the most part, neutralized by becoming a part of the apparatus of government or by becoming privatized as a matter of significance only to the individual. The varied, subtle, personal, and therefore unpredictable is replaced by the general, the clearly defined, the impersonal or abstract, and therefore predictable. We find this modern development in at least three areas: economics, war, and (the subject of our inquiry) the doctrine of toleration.

In a lay sermon published in 1816, Samual Taylor Coleridge wrote of the connection between seventeenth-century philosophy and economic developments:

> The commercial spirit, and the ascendancy of the experimental philosophy which took place at the close of the seventeenth century, though both good and beneficial in their own kinds, combined to foster its corruption. Flattered and dazzled by the real or supposed discoveries which it had made, the more the understanding was enriched, the more did it become debased; till science itself put on a selfish and sensual character, and *immediate*

utility, in exclusive reference to the gratification of the wants and appetites of the animal, the vanities and caprices of the social, and the ambition of the political, man was imposed as the test of all intellectual powers and pursuits. *Worth* was degraded into a lazy synonyme of *value*; and the value was exclusively attached to the interest of the senses.[4]

The "modern" in modern economics is the tendency to free commercial operations from personal relationships. Nothing of this sort can be done absolutely, of course. But the direction was marked out as early as the seventeenth century, much as Coleridge insisted. For instance, commercial and banking practices changed in a way that tended to make wealth more mobile. The seventeenth century saw the real beginning of joint-stock companies. Previously, trade and manufacturing concerns were based in family ownership, or they were joint concerns that were both owned and managed by partnerships. The expansion of joint-stock companies, beginning notably with the English East India Company in 1600, meant that there was an effective separation of ownership and management. It became possible for large numbers of people to have a financial interest in enterprises for which they had neither talent nor inclination. Their interest in a business enterprise, in a word, became abstract. And it was represented in the most abstract way: by money, that universal commodity.

As trade became less localized, the role that money played in the economy was ever greater. Thus, banking and credit began to make an increasingly greater impact on the economy. The increasing demands on coin created a situation in which banks issued a kind of paper money consisting of bank drafts that were endorsed successively by each holder. By the 1660's the Bank of Stockholm was issuing the "first true bank notes."[5] Credit, paper currency, and metal currency all grew along with the increased demand for money to aid the machinery of the urban, commercial, and industrial economy, with credit and "bank notes" growing at the greatest rates.

As one follows the sweep of events from the fourteenth century to the end of the seventeenth century, there are at least two general changes in economic relations that become apparent. The first is the loss of a certain rootedness or concreteness of the economic system. A largely agrarian system depends upon the land. In truth, of course, no system is ever really detached from the mineral and organic resources of the land. Even a highly technical and electronically based economy such as we find in our current time is ultimately dependent upon the very concrete and local resources provided by nature. That much never changes. What does change is the representation of wealth, and with it the image of how one is connected to wealth.

But with the introduction of a fluid commodity such as money, that can at once represent grain, beef, gold, oil, the labor of farmers, the skill of craftsmen, the risk of investors, and the wages of workers, we find that the appearance of a localized and concrete *basis* for the economy begins to be lost. Things do become more fluid, wealth more portable, commodities exchanged at longer range. The presence of money and credit communicates human needs and the supply of commodities in an objective fashion and in a language understood instantly across cultural, national, and language barriers. It appears, in fact, that the economy itself is quite fluid, and it requires some mental discipline to trace the ebb and flow of money, labor, credit, and movable commodities back to the ultimate resources of land, air, and sea that remain—as they always were—the sources of wealth.

The other general change in economic relations that comes on with the seventeenth century's expanded use of money and banking is the growing abstractness of commerce. The lenders, the investors, and the money managers are increasingly operating at a distance from the shuttle of the loom and the smell of newly turned ground. The day to day fortunes of weather are critical to the farmer and the sailor, but to the joint-stock holder the days of rain or drought only eventually cast a shadow over the ledger. It would take the twentieth century to make the accountant's "bottom line" the expression for a kind of realism, but the process began in the seventeenth century when the abstraction of monetary wealth was so effectively separated from the concreteness of land, labor, and the daily trade.

There was never a time, of course, when there were not investors and lenders, and those who dealt primarily in money. The distinct change that occurred in the seventeenth century had to do with two developments. One was the vastly increased number of people whose connection to an actual enterprise—whether that be fishing, foreign trade, ship building, fabric making, or domestic commerce—was primarily that of the investor or the lender. The second development was the ease with which financial resources, belonging to one person or to a company, could be employed in a vast array of wholly unrelated enterprises. The diversity of enterprises was possible because the owner was no longer necessarily the possessor of particular skills acquired over a lifetime. The owner was the possessor of money or stock; as such the owners connection with each of the various enterprises was an abstract one.

People were no longer so inextricably identified with a trade, a skill, an art, a craft; their sole interest came to be one thing and one thing only. Their status in society had not to do with a role so much as with the idea of possession. And that possession was expressed abstractly—even if in actual fact it included lands and houses. It was expressed in the precise arithmetic of a monetary sum.

With fluid economy, and one that is less localized, Europe began to experience fluctuations in the economy that were international in scope. Economic downturns no longer were confined to England that had experienced blight last year or to Spain because of its drought. Instead, economic problems were telegraphed from one part of Europe to another and even affected the transatlantic colonies. The seventeenth century endured significant depressions every second decade, first in 1620, then 1640, and in 1664. These radical fluctuations, at a time when both great wealth and great loss were continu-

ally possible, added to the overall feeling of instability, of strange
vertigo of new political powers, of displacement and alienation, and
of grave dangers from wars and persecution that the denizen of the
seventeenth century felt.

The abstractness of the new Europe was driven, as we can see, not
so much by fears in this case, as by the new opportunities and the
newly realized hopes. But with the new hopes also came new fears,
just as the man of wealth fears losing what the pauper never dreamed
of having. Such hopes and fears lead often to war.

War and the Dismantling of Natural Social Arrangements

By definition, war disrupts society. Social habits established over a
millennium can be dismantled in a few days of warfare. Communication is broken. Populations take refuge among strangers. Crops
are abandoned. Settled life with its thousands of small obligations,
its predictable manners, its covenants, not to speak of its material
structure and accumulation, are lost overnight. Whatever reliable
social structures existed are disrupted and emergency measures take
their place.

On the other hand, war re-organizes everything according to a
logic of its own. Social arrangements take on a form entirely reflective of the imminently practical goals of war. Bertolt Brecht has a
certain Sergeant reflect on this principle in "Mother Courage and Her
Children," a play about the Thirty Years War:

> What they could use around here is a good war. . . . You know
> what the trouble with peace is? No organization. And when do
> you get organization? In a war. . . . How many horses have they
> got in this town? How many young men? Nobody knows! They
> haven't bothered to count 'em! That's peace for you! I've been
> in places where they haven't had a war for seventy years and you
> know what? The people haven't even been given names! They
> don't know who they are! It takes a war to fix that. In a war,
> everyone registers, everyone's name's on a list. Their shoes are

stacked, their corn's in the bag, you count it all up—cattle, men, et cetera—and you take it away! That's the story: no organization, no war![6]

From late in the sixteenth century until the last quarter of the seventeenth century, war was a constant threat to Europeans. The occasion for war at that time, of course, was every bit as ambiguous as it is today, and the reasons for fighting as varied as the contending parties. Thus, today historians fall into discussions about whether these were *really* religious wars. Of course it will not do to say *simply* that they were religious wars. There were, on the one hand, the age-old differences among ethnic groups, some hungry for land, some seeking to redress old wrongs, some defending ill-got hegemony. But there is also no doubt that a distinctive sixteenth-century development was decisive: the breakup of Christendom brought on by the Protestant Reformation, and although the wars following the Reformation were not always clearly religious in nature, the religious differences also succeeded in opening old wounds, giving new occasion for ethnic rivalry. There is no question, however, that these wars—culminating in the Thirty Years War (1618-1648)—were also intense manifestations of religious differences. Richard S. Dunn expressed the place of religion in these conflicts as follows: "During the 130 years between 1559 and 1689, Europe passed through a tumultuous and anarchic period of civil wars and rebellions. Each upheaval had its own distinct character; each had multiple causes. The one common denominator, which constantly recurred, was Protestant-Catholic religious strife." These thirteen critical decades included the French civil wars of 1562-1598, the Dutch secession from Spanish rule, the Scottish rebellion against Mary Stuart, the Spanish attempt to invade England in 1588, the Thirty Years War fought mainly in central Europe, and the Puritan Revolution of 1640-1660.

It was a churchman, Armand Jean du Plessis, Cardinal de Richelieu, who began a new policy, one that would help bring about the preeminence of the nation-state in a world where rival loyalties to church and clan, to personal alliances and to sacred orders, still carried political weight. He served as First Minister of France from 1624 to 1642. Taking advantage of the weakened condition of France's neighbors, he moved to strengthen the French state. "Under his auspices," Henry Kissenger explained, "*raison d'etat* replaced the medieval concept of universal moral values as the operating principle of French policy."[7]

In Richelieu himself, almost as a microcosm of formerly Catholic Europe, one can see a turn from the religious vision of society to a secular one, the pragmatism of power politics prevailing over the idea of the good society. First, Europeans had grown earnest in the midst of a sixteenth century reform, then they had grown fanatical, in time they grew cynical, and last of all they turn pragmatic. War had, for every good reason, engendered cynicism; but its final issue was a finely honed political instrument for the security of a nation, a nation now large enough to serve the new financial interests of growing and enormously profitable market enterprises.

The people, then as now, did not always share the benefits that accrued to the state. There were, of course, voices of dissent. Fenélon (1651-1715), archbishop of Cambrai, wrote to Louis XIV: "Your peoples die of hunger. Agriculture is almost stationary. Industry languishes everywhere, all commerce is destroyed. France is a vast hospital. . . . It is you who have caused all this distress . . . . Your victories no longer cause rejoicing. There is only bitterness and despair . . . . You relate everything to yourself as though you were God on earth."[8]

When Richelieu began this policy under the rule of Louis XIV, he had good reason to have grave concerns for the security of France. They were surrounded by the rival nations of the Hapsburg Empire, Spain to the south, Italian city-states in the southeast, and the Spanish Netherlands to the north. He succeeded in fending off the designs of the Holy Roman Empire, but he did so only by raising permanently the claim of the state over the claims of the church. His effort was to achieve a balance of power among contending states. To do that he knew that he must, in policy, be neither Catholic nor Protestant; he must be first and foremost a statesman of the French nation.

War brought about yet another important change in the nature of political associations. We are accustomed to thinking of the nineteenth and twentieth centuries when we consider the growth of bureaucracies as the machinery of state. Richard Rubenstein, for one, saw the extensive bureaucratization of Germany as a key factor in the Jewish holocaust of the 1940s. From within the bureaucratic structure, individuals could make discrete decisions that, in and of themselves, seemed innocuous. One, for instance, might make lists of Jews living in a given city. Another arranges train schedules for the maximum transport of prisoners to camp. (The bureaucrat's business is train schedules, equipment on the tracks, timetables, maximum load and minimum expense—never mind that the cargo is human and that the destination is Dachau. He is not responsible for that—only for the timetables.) Yet another orders the manufacture of Zyclon B. These and a thousand other tasks were, in themselves, not malignant. Thousands of bureaucrats are involved, none are committing atrocities; yet the sum of their actions made possible demonic cruelty. Only a relative few actually shot someone or forced them into gas chambers; yet millions were exterminated. The efficiency of the relatively abstract workings of members of a bureau made such a holocaust possible.

The growth of bureaucracies had their most auspicious beginnings, however, in the seventeenth century. In *The Pursuit of Power: Technology, Armed Force, and Society since A.D. 1000*, William H. McNeill sees a significant change after 1600 which he calls the "bureaucratization of military administration."[9] He perceives far-reaching consequences of the development of well-ordered armies and navies that came to view chain of command as all-important in the pursuit of the goals of war.[10]

The practice of military drill, perfected in the seventeenth century, is analogous to what was happening to society as a whole. Close formation in rank and file was not new, but the practice of daily drill and the kind of rigorous discipline with close attention to details of dress and manner created a military culture of an entirely modern cast. The French lieutenant colonel Martinet, whose name became synonymous with harsh discipline, was an early proponent of the new refinement of dress, manner, and speech.

Consider what happens under such training. An army acts as if managed by a central nervous system. Command and execution more perfectly match. More important, the huge mass of humanity that makes up an army, one formerly made up of differing classes, perhaps different races, certainly from different locations, and from separate religious sects (especially after the Reformation), is melded into an undifferentiated mass. The huge assembly of compatriots loses those older natural distinctions, and the members of the newly created machine of war are distinguished only by the artifice of military rank and military unit. An army, under the pressure of war, discovering the usefulness of "bureaucratized violence," becomes a microcosm of society, turning (much more gradually) from its sacred identity—from its blood, its soil, its temples, and its gods—to the secular exigencies of utilitarian purposes. And in so doing it operates with greater efficiency in pursuit of material goals, even when it remarkably loses its moral and spiritual character.

The new military efficiency made possible new political economies of scale. Armies were no longer readily abandoned after a period of conflict had ended. Louis XIV, ever conscious of internal as well as external threats, decided to keep a standing army perpetually in readiness for conflict. Expanding the government's hegemony over ever greater regions made the armies increasingly indispensable. Armies made the expansion possible, even as the expansion made the armies necessary.

The Neutering of Natural Social Groups

Spontaneous society, or natural society, is made up of myriad inter-locking and overlapping groups. The groups are constituted of fami-lies, friendships, voluntary associations, and what Bertrand de Jouvenel calls the "team of action," those we find ourselves with due to a common public task. Each of these social aggregates performs the function of passing on obligations, intervening in disputes, dis-tributing knowledge, enforcing rules, and providing a culture for the mutual expression of love and loyalty. Michael Oakeshott makes the point that a *free* society is made up of a great number of these asso-ciations, both large and small, functioning in more or less informal ways. A society that develops along lines of a strong central author-ity, however, finds itself in partial competition with these smaller and more local authorities. A totalitarian regime is by definition in the business of outlawing the spontaneous and the non-political—that is, that which has not been organized—until everything from art to religion is politicized or eliminated.

It would take almost three centuries for totalitarian regimes to make their appearance. But the trend toward political hegemony, and the tension that centralized governments experienced with the spon-taneous associations that Oakeshott saw as the mark of a free soci-ety, was already in evidence early in the modern period. Nation-states were necessarily faced with the task of asserting authority from re-mote centers such as Paris and London. Natural social groups, with their own informal lines of authority, must be partially, if not wholly, circumvented, or they must be rendered neutral, if the new state is to function most efficiently. The authority of these social groups is al-most always of a religious nature, and religion itself is prodigal in the formation of groups that take on a life of their own. Therefore, it would not be surprising if a public policy arose whose tone and in-tent corresponded to the new public need to clear the way for an overarching authority. The fact that a public case for a policy of toleration is made beginning in the seventeenth century and gains strength every century after that is most significant. For the reach of "toleration"—defined precisely as modern people alone define it—extends just so far as the new nation-state is making its appearance. Where one appears, the other appears; and where states grow strong, the insistence on toleration grows strong with it.

Thomas Hobbes gives us a massive amount of evidence of this very function. Although it is not he who makes the case explicitly for toleration, he is the one who shows the necessity for not interposing any authority between the sovereign (which can either be a man or an assembly of men) and the individual. There occurs a difficulty, he writes in *De Corpore Politico*, "which if it be not removed, maketh it unlawful for any man to procure his own peace and preservation, because it maketh it unlawful for a man to put himself under the command of such absolute sovereignty as is required thereto": "And the difficulty is this: we have amongst us the Word of God for the rule of our actions; now if we shall subject ourselves to men also, obliging to do such actions as shall be by them commanded; when the commands of God and man shall differ, we are to obey god, rather than man: and consequently the covenant of general obedience to man is unlawful." If there are differences between the state and the church, the matter must be resolved on the side of the state. He argues "that subjects are not bound to follow the judgment of any authorities in controversies of religion which is not dependent on the sovereign power." For "since god speaketh not in these days to any man by his private interpretation of the Scriptures, nor by the interpretation of any power ... it remaineth that he speaketh by his vice-gods, or lieutenants here on earth, that is to say, by sovereign kings, or such as have sovereign authority as well as they."[11]

What is clear is that, for Hobbes, there is no legitimate place for authority that overlaps or exists alongside that of the state. Hobbes's nominalist basis allows him no authority except that of the individual, and through the individual, the state. Other authorities are illusory or seditious: "For when Christian men, take not their Christian sovereign, for God's Prophet; they must either take their own dreams, for the prophecy they mean to be governed by, and the tumour of their own hearts for the Spirit of God; or they must suffer themselves to be led by some strange prince; or by some of their fellow-subjects, that can bewitch them by slander of the government." All power and right resides in the individual. By contract, this sovereign individual bestows powers upon the sovereign for the sake of securing a safe and commodious life. The powers thus bestowed create the commonwealth, that true and only Kingdom of God, which is an artifice of the society of individuals and their "mortal god."[12]

Bertrand de Jouvenel, speaking of the individualist "metaphysic" that made twentieth century absolutism possible, said "this metaphysic refused to see in society anything but the state and the individual. It disregarded the role of the spiritual authorities and of all those intermediate social forces which enframe, protect, and control the life of man, thereby obviating and preventing the intervention of Power. It did not foresee that the overthrow of all these barriers and bulwarks would unleash a disorderly rout of egoistical interests and blind passions leading to the fatal and inauspicious coming of tyranny."[13]

In Hobbes we find in precise form the motivation for a modern idea of toleration. The engraving on the title page of the first edition of *Leviathan* depicts a gargantuan figure of a man, with the crown of a king, bearing in one hand the sword of the ruler and in the other the crosier of a bishop, keeping watch over a peaceful city. The giant figure is, upon closer inspection, composed of a multitude of people who make up his body. This giant authority rules with the symbols of church and state and the two are no longer permitted to resist or correct each other. Theology has been set aside in the interest of the political task of ruling. Therefore, all groups, including the church, but not exclusively the church, are coopted into the general political enterprise. Groups no longer appear distinctly, only the multitude of individuals and the ruler himself.

The sense of vocation or purpose that animates all kinds of groups, but which in the church claims a loyalty that transcends other loyalties, is both necessary to social cohesion and, at the same time, an explosive ingredient. In the seventeenth century Europeans had reason to be impressed with its explosive powers and thought rather to build cohesion around more secular goals. The gains in material prosperity were impressive enough that such goals seemed quite enough to demand the loyalty, and support the cohesion, of restless modern people.

The aims of theology, and therefore of the church, were increasingly made out to be private rather than public concerns. The large state, encompassing more diverse populations—made the more diverse by divisions in the church—found commitment to a creed or a particular communion only made the task of unifying the people a heavier burden to bear. Toleration was a way of setting aside, as strictly private, the difficult metaphysical and theological dimensions of public life. For much of the modern period the strategy worked. There was a large residue of assumptions about the nature of human life and human destiny upon which the culture could unconsciously depend, and which had been placed there by a millennium or more of what Kierkegaard would call "training in Christianity." For the time being Europeans could ignore those deeper claims of human purpose that clearly had implications for life together and about which there was almost universal and silent assent. They could live a public life for a long time without having to revisit questions of public order, private morality, and the ideas of those forebears who were willing to take public life seriously as an arena of theological decision.

The question raised by the long course of modernity is this: How long can society maintain itself on this residue of a culture's fundamental commitments? Or more precisely: How long can it do so and pretend that the issues once fought out at the theological level no longer matter? How long can it pretend that the character and virtue of a people, that which makes social life commodious and predictable, can simply be taken for granted? The issues are set aside because they are difficult, and the parties supporting different views become disagreeable, and the opportunities for material gain are being missed, and besides that the huge conglomerate of the nation-state is simply comprised of too many diverse groups who will never find common ground concerning things that are so complicated and that arise from such deep commitments. Nonetheless, the issues of how we live together remain; and they are unavoidably theological in nature, even if the parties decide that there is no need for God and everything is permissible. That also is a theological statement.

The answer self-evidently brings into play some form of toleration. But the question we must answer is this: Will it be the older form of tolerant practice that allowed groups to exist, to live out their *telos*, their purpose and vocation—groups that overlap each other, and whose intricate interplay make possible a larger, open society? Or will it be the modern form of toleration, one that wishes to set aside serious questions of vocation and purpose, except as these relate to the individual? Will it be a form of toleration that, in effect, tolerates nothing except the individual and the state, giving free reign to the egoistical forces at either end of the spectrum?

The alternative is always possible. It is especially conceivable in today's world that the increasing alienation of individuals—once drawn tightly into the social structure of groups, of overlapping groups with a hierarchy of claims upon their loyalty, from the family to the guild to the church—finally undermines the cohesion of the large modern state, making it impossible to govern and emptying it of the cultural resources that make life together possible.

To answer these questions, and to think seriously about these alternatives, we must look closely at the form and the genesis of the modern idea of toleration.

4

Thomas Hobbes and the Fears of Modernity

Auctoritas non veritas facit legem.[1]

Thomas Hobbes

HOBBES SAID THAT HE WAS BORN "A TWIN OF FEAR." Under threat of an invasion brought by the Spanish Armada, Thomas Hobbes'ss mother gave birth prematurely on April 5, 1588. He long theorized that that his own timidity was a consequence of the circumstances of his birth. Moreover, the threat of war, the fearful occasion, and his own timidity seemed to foreshadow the adult Hobbes'ss discovery that it is in fear and uncertainty that the true motivations for human action could be found. In fear, and in the desire to secure power over the things we fear, do we find keys that unlock the true causes operating in human life and in the social order.

Hobbes was the son of a poor, barely literate country cleric. It seems that the elder Hobbes was not able even to maintain his modest position in the church: stories circulated that he spent too much time in the ale house and not enough time in his pastoral duties. After Thomas had already begun at Oxford, the father was disciplined for speaking ill of a fellow pastor named Richard Jeane. Later, upon finding his adversary at the churchyard at Malmesbury, he attacked Jeane and, according to a witness, he "followed the said Mr. Jeaine revyling him and calling him knave and coming neare unto him strooke him the saide Mr. Jeaine with his fiste under the eare or about the head."[2] After this incident, the elder Hobbes went into hiding. It is uncertain whether Thomas Hobbes ever saw his father again.

From this unpromising beginning, Hobbes rose gradually but steadily to a place of prominence in English public life. His education took place at Magdalen Hall, which was, in this early part of the seventeenth century, a center of Puritan thought and Puritan influence. He was an uninspired student, caring less for his studies in Aristotelian philosophy than in escaping to the bookstores and following his own inclinations by reading of the exploits of voyagers to distant lands. It would be his own travels, and his own encounters with the world of contemporary thought that shaped and guided his intellectual development.

The most fortunate early circumstance for Hobbes lay in his being recommended to the Cavendish family (pronounced "Candish" in seventeenth century England) by the president of Magdalen Hall as a tutor and companion to the eldest son of William Cavendish, Baron Hardwick (later Earl of Devonshire). Hobbes was only slightly older than his "pupil." In 1610 the two were sent by the Cavendishes on a grand tour of Europe, traveling together through France, Germany, and Italy. It was during this time that Hobbes was awakened to a new love for learning and developed a "fixed determination to make himself a thorough scholar."[3] In subsequent years he would make two other extended trips to the continent. At about age forty he fell under the spell of Euclidean geometry. The impression it made upon him is doubtless due, in part, to the fact that mathematics was not a serious part of learning in England until the seventeenth century. In his days at Oxford, Hobbes said, geometry was still thought of as a kind of exotic "Black Art." All learning, he thought, should be so logically and inescapably arranged, beginning with the most obvious axiom and proceeding to the more elaborate theorem. If geometry could capture the world of shapes in such a sure manner, then the same ought to be possible in the other sciences—even the science of individual persons and the larger society in which we live.

A second important influence upon Hobbes'ss thinking began to take shape during the tour of 1634–37, a tour in which his pupil was the third Earl of Devonshire, a youth of fifteen years. It occurred to Hobbes that the natural state of things is not the state of "rest" as the ancients had assumed but the state of motion. Without motion, he reasons, there is no sense of things, and without sense the world is in no way present to us. The fundamental reality is, therefore, the ubiquitous state of motion. He was no doubt partly influenced in his thoughts along this line by his meeting of Galileo in Italy. And the significance of this thought was further developed by his association with a Franciscan friar named Marin Mersenne who succeeded in bringing together a select group of European intellectuals. The experience of "Mersenne's cell" was more important to Hobbes'ss intellectual development, by his own testimony, than the university had ever been.

It is difficult to overestimate the importance of this change in Hobbes from a view of the world held by the ancients, one in which the natural state of things is to be in rest, to a view of the world in restless motion. The world for Hobbes and his successors was a world of no given order, but a world infinitely malleable. I will have more to say about this issue later, but suffice it to say now that among the earlier societies, whether in the West or elsewhere, things were thought to have their proper place. This was the meaning of the metaphor of rest such as St. Augustine used it in his famous line in the *Confessions* that "We were made for Thee, O God, and our hearts are restless until they find rest in Thee." Even more pointedly, Thomas Traherne illustrates the sense of this older idea of rest in his discussion of the importance of place. "That any thing may be found to be an infinit Treasure," he said, "its Place must be found in Eternity, and in Gods Esteem. For as there is a Time, so there is a Place for all Things. Evry thing in its Place is Admirable Deep and Glorious: out of its Place like a Wandering Bird, is Desolat and Good for Nothing."[4]

But in this new world, heralded in some important ways by Hobbes himself, there was no proper place, no proper order. Instead the world awaited an order created by accident or by the imagination and will of human beings.

The Restlessness of Early Modernity

One cannot forget the events of Hobbes'ss life, for his philosophy was in every way a response to the maladies of his age. Religious wars had been a present threat and a constant concern since late in the sixtenth century. The mutuality of medieval feudal arrangements were everywhere being replaced by more formal powers—in Britain, for instance, by the Stuarts' efforts to impose absolute monarchy by appealing to a theory of divine right. On the continent the Thirty Years War (1618-1648) demonstrated the destructive power of religious polarization seized upon by political opportunists. In England the Puritan Revolution and the Civil War dominated life in the middle decades of the century. The loss of the monarchy followed by Cromwell's regime, followed yet again by the restoration of the monarchy under Charles ii, kept the island nations in perpetual turmoil. The fears of 1588 pressed in on every side and in every form, making the strongest impression upon the active mind of Hobbes.

The seventeenth century was a time of remarkable achievement in European intellectual life. Hobbes'ss life ran alongside some of the most influential thinkers in modern times, whose framing of scientific and philosophical and moral questions have affected the last four centuries with no sign that their influence has abated. He is almost an exact contemporary of Réné Descartes, who was born eight years later and died some twenty-nine years earlier than Hobbes. As a young man he knew Francis Bacon (1561-1626), who did perhaps more than any other Englishman to propagandize the virtues of the scientific method, and whose philosophy remains to this day the popular notion of what is real science. John Locke was considerably younger than Hobbes, but because Hobbes lived to such an advanced age, their lives overlapped, and the productive years of Locke began in the last decade of Hobbes'ss life. Pierre Bayle, a profound skeptic and a champion of religious toleration, died two years after Locke and a quarter of a century after Hobbes.

Hobbes thought of his own philosophy as the rebirth of true philosophy, engaging all facets of existence with the methods of a science that reduced everything to a clear-headed analysis of its causes, including the motives of the individual and the necessary life of society. If the story is apocryphal, it nevertheless reveals something of Hobbes'ss sincere self-appraisal: it was said that he had first suggested, as an epitaph for his tombstone, the words "This is the true philosopher's stone."[5]

Hobbes work, although better known by its individual volumes, actually consists of two trilogies. The First is *Elements of Law, Natural and Politic* (1650), *De Cive* (1642), and *Leviathan* (1651). The other includes one of the works of the first trilogy, and would be listed: *De Corpore* (1655), *De Homine* (1658), and *De Cive* (1642). This body of work represents what Hobbes thought to be philosophy in the mode of reason, reason based upon the most fundamental evidence of our senses. It was no longer possible to think of philosophy in terms of traditional metaphysics with its appeal not only to the senses but also to the notion of a moral aim. Such philosophy, and it included all traditional philosophy, was "anthropomorphistic." A new philosophy must replace the moral element with modern natural science. This is not only a description of Hobbes's work and his intentions, but it is the root of the problem which incessantly presents itself in Hobbes. As Leo Strauss has put it, "by renouncing all 'anthropomorphisms,' all conceptions of purpose and perfection, [Hobbes] could, therefore, to say the least, contribute nothing to the understanding of things human, to the foundation of morals and politics."[6]

It is important to see, however, that Hobbes was not simply inadvertently missing the moral element in philosphy—the element of the "ought" directed to human self-conciousness. Instead, he thought that that element could be replaced, in fact must be replaced, by human intention, by the will. Michael Oakeshott saw that Hobbes is consistently rationalist. In fact, "philosophy for him is the world as it appears in the mirror of reason; civil philosophy is the image of the civil order reflected in that mirror."[7] But the reasonable form of civil philosophy, like the civil order itself, is an artifact: it is the willed creation of human beings responding to their own needs.

The Individual in Society

Two intellectual influences play major roles in Hobbes's thought and, more indirectly, in the reception of his thought by the larger English and European society. The first is Puritanism, and the second is what has come to be called "nominalism." Each contributes to the overall effect of Hobbes's understanding of the individual within the ordered society. To appreciate these two influences is also to appreciate the impact that Hobbesian thought has had, in its many forms, upon modern and contemporary social organization as well as political policy.

1. *Puritanism.* It might be more significant than commonly thought that Hobbes took his university studies at Magdalen Hall. This was a center at Oxford of Puritan sympathies. And for all his disavowal of positive influence from his university days, there are interesting parallels between Hobbes's theory of the individual in the social setting and the Puritan analysis of human ills.

While all normative Christianity teaches the fallen and sinful condition of humanity, the Protestant branch in the West placed heavy emphasis upon this point. To remember the sinfulness of man is warranty against the idolatry that develops around human institutions, places, and offices, or even against the shamanistic effect of words and rites. Calvinist Protestants had elaborated that teaching into a thoroughgoing doctrine of "total depravity." The idea of "total depravity" never meant, of course, that human beings were as evil as they could possibly be, but only that everything—even our good works and our best intentions—is affected by sin. At the heart of every human motive is an inescapable ambiguity. Therefore, in the Puritan mind, even the best intentions, undergirded by virtuous character, belie the dark nature of the human heart that is only cosmetically hidden by the outward respectable life.

Puritanism pushed this idea further in its attempt to save the church, and even society itself, from the inexorable consequences of human sinfulness. Their zeal drove them, at times, to trenchant criticism of existing orders and institutions, fueling the wish for deliverance from the effects of human depravity. Driven in this direction, they were tempted by the same dualism that Christians of all ages have entertained. It is a kind of gnostic style of theologizing that finds no good in the created order, in the human nature, or in the institutions arising in such a world. For the gnostic—and, one could almost say, for the Puritan—Christianity is altogether a theology of redemption without the inclusion of a theology of creation.[8]

The strongly religious and pious character of the Puritan movement partly explains the hostile reaction to Hobbes, who was widely known as an "atheist."[9] But Puritanism might also account for a subtle cast to the intellectual atmosphere that was, strange to say, hospitable to Hobbes's point of view. Especially was it a viable atmosphere for the view that human nature, in the state of nature, was so thoroughly vitiated that only by an extraordinary intervention could life be made tolerable. In Hobbes's system, the state of human beings in nature is one of constant warfare. At least it entails the vigilance and preparation for war, if not open conflict. This warfare proceeds from the simple consideration that individuals are only motivated by fear or aversion and that even the most highly vaunted charitable works can only be understood as elaboration upon what is essentially self-concern. Francis Hutcheson and others would later refer to this ethical system of Hobbes as the "selfish system." But its consequence was, in Hobbes's mind, the clear setting forth of cause and effect in human affairs. It was viewing the human condition in the light of "science." And the "science" he had in mind was of the variety later known as "positive science," one that took account only of what could be considered the value-free data from which one could rationally build to more elaborate theories, just as Euclid had done in geometry and as Newton was doing in physics.

If each person can be counted on to look after his own interests, then outside of the civil order with its institutionalized system of real and threatened retaliation, individuals live within a state of struggle. "Hereby it is manifest," said Hobbes, "that during the time men live without a common power to keep them in awe, they are in that condition which is called war; and such a war, as is of every man, against every man." In such a state of nature, with all men and women following their natural inclinations, "there is no place for industry; because the fruit thereof is uncertain: and consequently no culture of the earth; no navigation, nor use of the commodities that may be imported by sea; no commodious building; no instruments of moving and removing, such things as require much force; no knowledge of the face of the earth; no account of time; no arts; no letters; no society; and which is worst of all, continual fear, and danger of violent death; and the life of man, solitary, poor, nasty, brutish, and short."[10]

This exceedingly pessimistic view of the human lot, given his nature, mirrors the most extreme position of some Calvinists that the worth of the human being is in no way intrinsic but depends utterly upon God's redemptive purpose. For Hobbes also, the salvation of man from such a depraved condition as he would find himself in, if left to informal devices, can only be overcome by the intervention of a Power. And that Power is the sovereign power of the state. It reflects the human's rational response to his needs, and becomes to humankind a "mortal god."[11]

2. *Nominalism.* The first of the four parts of *Leviathan* is devoted to the science of "man," not man as found in any extant society—that is, in families, informal associations, and in groups of friends, neighbors, and coworkers—but man as an individual.

Hobbes's focus on the individual human being is a consequence of his nominalism. The beginnings of nominalism we usually associate with the scholastic debates of the fourteenth century. Yet it was Hobbes perhaps more than any other who brought nominalistic thought to the surface in modern discourse. In *Leviathan* he states clearly the main point of the nominalist position: "Of names, some are *proper,* and singular to one only thing, as *Peter, John, this man, this tree*; and some are *common* to many things, *man, horse, tree*; every one of which, though but one name, is nevertheless the name of divers particular things; in respect of all which together, it is called an *universal*; there being nothing in the world universal but names; for the things named are every one of them individual and singular."[12] Hence, if things generally are to be considered in their state as individuals, then humanity also discloses its reality only in the individual person. Even to classify someone as human, it follows, is a contrivance, a matter of definition. "This universality of one name to many things," he writes in *The Elements of Law*, "hath been the cause that men think that the things themselves are universal." The consequences are that human beings "do seriously contend, that besides Peter and John, and all the rest of the men that are, have been, or shall be in the world, there is yet somewhat else that we call man, (viz.) man in general, deceiving themselves by taking the universal, or general appellation, for the thing it signifieth."[13] This can, of course, mean that the definition of "man" is not subject to any necessity imposed upon the one who speaks the word. The definition might take the form, as in the case of some ghastly twentieth century experiences, of that which is willed or imagined. Thus the "Jew" is not a man, or the mentally incompetent is not a "man," or the old person who has outlived usefulness to the rest of us is not "human" either. This happens whenever the reality to which we point, when we use language, is not a necessary one but a matter of convention—of definition as a product, an artifact, rather than an attempt to describe the intelligible and very real world. As Richard Weaver has pointed out, the effect of the triumph of nominalism was to move the locus of our engagement with the world from the domain of the intellect to the domain of the will.

Hobbesian Starting Points

These two influences, the Puritan-gnostic distrust of nature, along with human nature and the nominalist reduction of reality to individuals and of society to individual persons, can be seen in a series of principles in Hobbes's writing that bear almost an axiomatic status, and that place the individual in society in a recognizably modern way.

1. *Philosophy is the science of reducing things to their causes and determining the consequences of causes.* The study of causes and their consequences is of practical value. In a world of endless effects and constant motion, one who knows the causes of things, or who can predict the consequences of given causes, is in a position of power. At this point the Hobbesian purpose for philosophy would remind us of Francis Bacon, *Scientia propter potentiam*—knowledge for the sake of power.

It should also remind us that philosophy for Hobbes is no longer a matter of speculation. Speculation holds up a "mirror," as it were, for the sake of contemplation. The science of Kepler or the philosophy of Plato might be seen in that light. The object is to change the "observer" and allow him or her to come into true and virtuous participation with the order of being. Hobbes's view of philosophy, on the other hand, is marked by the modern spirit. It is practical in its aim. It seeks power: but not the power of true participation; instead, the power *over* things. The change it seeks is outward, not inward. "*Science* [which for Hobbes is the same as philosophy] is the knowledge of consequences, and dependence of one fact upon another: by which out of that we can presently do, we know how to do something else when we will, or the like another time; because when we see how any thing comes about, upon what causes, and by what manner; when the like causes come into our power, we see how to make it produce the like effects."[14]

The idea of reducing everything to its causes goes back to the Aristotelian method of philosophy. But one of the most revealing things we can see about Hobbes (and through Hobbes about the modern habit of thought) is that, of Aristotle's four causes, he considers only two of these to be true causes. For Aristotle the four causes consist of:

Efficient cause—that by which something is done.
Material cause—that out of which something is made.
Formal cause—that into which something is made.
Final cause—that for the sake of which something is done or made.

Thus the carpenter's labor might be the efficient cause for a given house. The wood and brick is its material cause. The design or blueprint is its formal cause. And the fact that John and Mary need a house to live in, which constitutes the purpose for building the house in the first place, is its final cause.

A moment's reflection will reveal that certain kinds of knowledge rely heavily upon the idea of a formal and final cause. Religion informs us that existence has a given design, which informs the way we think about and act in this world. And a teleological religion such as Christianity informs us that life has a *telos*, a goal and a purpose. The language of religion and morality is heavily invested in the language of formal and final causes. But these are the two causes that Hobbes sets aside.

What we know, according to Hobbes, is only the motion of bodies. The body that strikes another or moves another is the efficient cause. And the body that is moved is the material cause. But these causes are considered after the fact, and, therefore, they are the only true causes.

Think for a moment about how this prejudice in favor of efficient and material causes and against formal and final causes affects contemporary conversation. Today, if I choose to talk about the purpose of a human being's life, the ultimate goal for which one lives, and therefore the way one "ought" to live, everyone will recognize that I am appealing to some kind of religious understanding. Suppose I am attempting to counsel someone who has gotten himself deep into the kind of infidelity that can destroy his relationship with his wife, lose the respect of his children, sever the trust of friends, and give him moreover a deep sense of having betrayed the best that he expected of himself. I might appeal to what I recognize, and perhaps the person also acknowledges, as God's command—a command based upon some privileged knowledge of the design for which we are made and the purpose toward which life aims. In this day, such an appeal will seem to many to be based on assumptions that are definitely arbitrary, a matter of personal opinion, a matter of personal preference, or perhaps a matter of convention, which is to say the more or less arbitrary habits of thought in a large group of people.

But if I would be convincing to my modern friend, and know that I am being convincing, I might appeal instead to some theory of "why" (by what prior cause) he acts in a manner that brings him so much pain. I might, for instance, explore the possibility that the problem lies in a genetic or a chemical disorder. On the other hand, I might suggest the possibility of a childhood trauma, a neglectful father, or an abusive mother. Psychological theories since Freud have been principally of this sort: they seek for causes and remedies in precisely the form that Hobbes thought of efficient and material causes. This is not to disparage modern efforts and modern remedies; it is necessary to look at these causes quite as realistically as the others. It is important, however, to highlight the *nature* of the modern cast of mind that has, for the past three hundred years, tended to find the causes as they are seen by Hobbes as more weighty—and, what is more, more practical.

Of course, *if* we could know what exactly it means to be human (that is, if we could know what is the nature or the idea of being human), or if we could know what is the end toward which a human being is placed into existence, then there is hardly any knowledge that could be more practical. But Hobbes and his modern successors have ruled out precisely that kind of knowledge—the knowledge of formal and final causes. When we remember the evolving idea of modern science, that science makes us the masters of nature, or the modern notion that knowledge is power, then we will also recognize that understanding the formal and final causes of things does not give us leverage over the world in which we live but is more likely to change *us*, so that we can participate in some true sense in the order of existence. Knowing the efficient and material causes of things, on the other hand, gives us the levers by which we change our world. So the difference is precisely this: that which Hobbes rejects, and along with him the modern world, is that by which we are ourselves changed; and that which Hobbes retains, in the order of causes, is that by which we change the world around us. The modern spirit is captured in this exchange, an exchange of humility for pride, participation in existence for power over existence. Hobbes's contemporaries sensed the meaning of this exchange and often expressed their foreboding. In the course of three centuries, we might have learned the *practical* effects of such an exchange and thus the illusion of Hobbes's notion of the practical.

2. *The individual's motives are governed by fear and (consequently) by the desire for power.* What can be said of the individual human being that throws light on his action within a society? That is, what can be considered at the level of a "cause"? In *Leviathan*, Hobbes moves to what he takes to be the most fundamental things that can be said about a human being as a body within the world of bodies. Motions are either vital or animal. Vital motions are involuntary movements, such as the circulation of blood. Animal motion is voluntary. Animal motions can be understood as a disposition, which he refers to as "these small beginnings of motion, within the body of man, before they appear in walking, speaking, striking, and other visible actions."[15] These discrete "motions," which he calls "endeavors," are, in turn, of two types: appetites and aversions. In other words, we are drawn toward something we desire, and we are repulsed from that to which we have an aversion. Very basic, as you can see.

From this beginning, Hobbes concluded that there is no just reason to deny to anyone what they desire; and, in theory, everyone has a right to everything. But, of course, everyone cannot have whatever they want, because the nature of society is that there are competing wants. The result is that "every one is at war with every one." Apart from the civil government there is necessarily civil war. And since in war there is much to fear, we act out of aversion to that which we fear. We seek to have power over that which prevents us from having what we want or to avert the threat of what we fear.

How, then, can we have some of what we desire (which Hobbes refers to as the "commodius" life), which is to say that we have the power to seek some things and avoid others? That, for Hobbes, is the fundamental grounding of government. By contract, we give up our power to take what we want (and have a right to in nature), giving that power to another. That one to whom we give such power is our sovereign, and it is by virtue of his power that we can live the commodious life.

Voegelin

3. *The civil order is an artifice; it is not a reflection, as it was for the ancients and medievals, of the metaphysical order of existence.* The function of myth among the ancient people—and even among modern people, though we often do not know we have myths—was to illuminate the nature of things so that human beings could live in community and in harmony with that nature. From Aristotle through the late medieval times, this was also the purpose of philosophy or science. With modernity things began to change drastically with regard to the purpose of science. Descartes said that science makes us "the masters and possessors of nature." No matter how preposterous that sounds after a moment of sober reflection, this was to become a characteristic modern disposition and an expectation that was not only taken seriously but opposition to which put one seriously out of step with one's contemporaries. The idea of limitless and uniform progress and the inexorable technological mastery of nature was hardly ever questioned. It was until relatively recently, and to a degree remains, our myth.

Looking back upon this profound change in attitudes toward knowledge, it is not difficult to see, by contrast, how traditional societies saw their communities as ordered intentionally to *reflect* reality. The purpose of all philosophy, including civil philosophy, was to aid human beings in adjusting themselves to the given reality in which they found themselves. But after Bacon and Hobbes, the purpose of knowledge came to be seen differently: to cause reality to adjust to human needs and wishes. "Philosophers have tried to interpret the world in various ways," said Marx, "but the point is to change it." Thus, *how* communities of men and women are to live together is not something to be revealed or discovered; it is a matter of the imagination and will. All that makes up social life, its morals, its manners, its laws, its authority, does not so much reflect a deep metaphysical reality as it does an imaginative response to the environment.

The best way to understand this, with regard to the law, is to contrast the modern view to the traditional view expressed by thinkers from Cicero to Shakespeare. For Cicero, the idea of law is not exhausted by the notion of "legislation." In terms of making laws, one might find quite different sorts of statutes from one city to the next, and from one part of the world to another. But behind this man-made law—the law of the senates and the courts and the petty magistrates—there is something both permanent and universal. Hence, as Cicero insisted, the law in Rome is really not unlike the law in Corinth. This law that is the same everywhere and in all times, though it remain unwritten and dimly seen, would later be referred to as the Natural Law, and man-made law as "positive law." The purpose of positive law, from Cicero on, was to reflect, however imperfectly, the real law written into Nature and the human heart.

That we have to some extent abandoned the former sentiment, the one that insists our inventions are responses within reality and not reality itself, was indicated as far back as 1838 in Emerson's address to the Harvard Divinity School. "Build therefore your own world," he said, "a correspondent revolution in things will attend the influx of the spirit. So fast will disagreeable appearances, swine, snakes, pests, madhouses, prisons vanish; they are temporary and shall be no more seen ... so shall the advancing spirit create its ornaments along its path . . . until evil is no more seen. The kingdom of man over nature ... a dominion such as now is beyond his dream of God."[16] It appears in remarks aired on turn-of-the-millennium radio. Dr. Joy Brown, radio psychologist, reported quizzing her professor who had said it was the business of the counselor to help their patients adjust to reality. "Whose reality?" she asked.[17] And, what is more, she assumed her twentieth century listeners would see the self-evident logic of her query, that the reality of one is not necessarily the reality of another, reality itself being *in* our minds rather than outside.

For Hobbes, at the beginning of the modern period, the civil order is, in a similar vein, an artifice. It reflects not the intelligible world and its order, but it reflects the willed order created out of consideration for human desires and aversions. When asking why "certain creatures without reason, or speech, do nevertheless live in society, without any coercive power," Hobbes replies, "the agreement of these creatures is natural; that of men, is by covenant only, which is artificial: and therefore it is no wonder if there be somewhat else required, besides covenant, to make their agreement constant and lasting; which is a common power, to keep them in awe, and to direct their actions to the common benefit."[18] Civil order (peace, that is, instead of perpetual war) is created only by an act of the human will and is maintained only by an act of will.

4. *Hence, the moral order is an artifice.* It is to avert a state of war that the civil order, with its governing sovereign, is created. Apart from this civil authority, everyone has a right to everything—in theory at least. The idea of distinct rights and duties, and the idea of right and wrong, consequently come into view only *after* the institution of governing power. It is the covenant among citizens that creates the agreed upon definition of rights, and it is from this covenant and its definition that rights of any kind proceed.

Now we see why Francis Hutcheson referred to Hobbes's notion of a morality as "the selfish system." Since covenant is based on what is good for the individual, and the moral notion of right and wrong proceeds from that covenant, then the whole complex of moral governance is, like government itself, an artifice. Covenants are essentially voluntary, Hobbes says. Even if coerced by conquest they are voluntary, because the individual and the community have agreed to the covenant as an alternative to being killed by their enemies. "As justice dependeth on antecedent covenant; so does GRATITUDE depend on antecedent grace. . . . For no man giveth, but with intention of good to himself."[19] True moral philosophy, he insists, is the science of laws built upon an insight into the interaction of human (that is, individual) appetites and aversions. "*Good* and *evil*, are names that signify our appetites, and aversions."[20] The ordering of those appetites and aversions, compromising a great many for the sake of installing a power capable of ruling the warring interests among people, is the first step toward establishing what is just in society: "For where no covenant hath preceded, there hath no right been transferred, and every man has right to every thing; and consequently, no action can be unjust. But when a covenant is made, then to break it is unjust: and the definition of INJUSTICE, is no other than *the not performance of covenant.* And whatsoever is not unjust, is just."[21]

As one can easily see, with Hobbes we have entered into a different world from that of Cicero or that of the Hebrew prophets. For with Hobbes it is positive law that constitutes the foundation of the moral system. The one thing and the only thing more basic is loyalty to the covenant—which is to say, loyalty to the sovereign. The Hebrew prophets, eight centuries before Christ, had succeeded in planting the seed of a new thought regarding political loyalties—that one owes allegience to God before the King and that the law of God was to be the rock upon which a King would either rule or have his rule broken. No longer was the *Melech*, or the Pharoah, that from whom the law eminates; instead, law was understood to be superior to the one who rules. Hobbes as much as anyone in the seventeenth century reversed that order. His Leviathan was the "mortal god" without whom laws mean nothing.

5. *The commonwealth must be large enough to secure safety or to pursue common advantage among the nations.* Hobbes gave voice to what was happening on the practical level. Large states were replacing smaller states; naturally, they were able to marshal larger forces on the field of battle. Hobbes makes no effort to make this fact appealing to

moral sensibilities. Notice, for instance, how easily he moves from the common goal of defense to the common goal of maintaining the authority of the sovereign, and then to the common goal of conquest and "booty":

> And seeing that mutual aid is necessary for defence, as mutual fear is necessary for peace; we are to consider how great aids are required for such defense, and for the causing of such mutual fear, as men may not easily adventure on one another. And first it is evident: that the mutual aid of two or three men is of very little security. . . . And therefore before men have sufficient security in the help of one another, their number must be so great, that the odds of a few which the enemy may have, be no certain and sensible advantage. [This great number must be directed] to one and the same end. . . . This consent (or concord) amongst so many men, though it may be made by the fear of a present invader, or by the hope of conquest, or booty [will not occur] without some mutual and common fear to rule them.[22]

The justification for the large state, therefore, is to secure the common defense, ensure concord under the authority of the sovereign, and to have advantage in conquest. Diplomats and leaders of large Western powers have been more circumspect in their language, it is certain. Rarely do they admit that the consolidation of power, and the advantages it brings, is so central a motivation. Hobbes was considerably less fastidious. No commentator on political goals has been clearer than Hobbes, nor more reliable in revealing the mind behind modern politics.[23] For Hobbes makes it transparent that the new principle of political order is not so much justice, or even peace, as it is the *libido dominandi* of the emerging modern state.

6. *The authority of the sovereign within the social order must be absolute.* In setting forth this principle, Hobbes was simply more plainspoken than his successors or even his contemporaries who held to comparable theories of authority. As a matter of political fact, Hobbes

and his contemporaries were living in an age given over to the rise of central governments, which is to say that other competing authorities—such as the church and the inherited nobility—stood to lose their traditional authority within the social order.

Donald Livingston, a leading expert on the Enlightenment, compares Hobbes's theory of unitary government to that of his contemporary Johannes Althusius, who wrote in favor of the modern federated system of governments.[24] In Hobbes, the line of authority must be direct and unambiguous. In Althusius's federated system, the authority of governing is divided and overlapping. Hobbes's system must be absolutely simple, like a bureaucratic chart; Althusius's system must be organic, like life itself in nature. For Hobbes, authority extends from the top down; for Althusius, the life of the roots nourishes the branches all the way to the top. In other words, unlike Hobbes, Althusius saw that social bonds arise spontaneously everywhere, each forming its own kind of authority, and that the political life of a society, when it is healthy, reflects that spontaneous, organic organization. Livingston points out that, in an Althusian theory, "political order is rooted not in egoistically motivated individuals but in social bonds and duties." Therefore: "sovereignty . . . is a symbiotic relation among . . . independent social orders. Each of these has its own telos—something of its own to enjoy and defend. Accordingly, Althusius defines political science as 'symbiotics.'"[25]

I introduce this comparison with Althusius in order to highlight the nature of the Hobbesian strategy in political order. He argues strenuously at every point that the lines of authority must lead to a governing center. The covenant made by the many with their sovereign is one of relinquishing their own power to exact justice from others. The sovereign is thus empowered to provide defense and to exact justice, and "those two swords are but one."[26] Hobbes makes no attempt to disguise that government is about coercion. Nothing that government does is done outside the brutal fact that it has been given the power to use violence against enemies without and lawbreakers within: "This power of coercion . . . consisteth in the transferring of every man's right of resistance against him to whom he hath transferred the power of coercion." In Hobbes's view, this transfer has either taken place or it has not—if it has not, then the door to civil war and unregulated violence is left open. The power of the sovereign must be uncontested: "no man in any commonwealth whatsoever hath right to resist him, or them, on whom they have conferred this power coercive, or (as men use to call it) the sword of justice."[27]

In *Leviathan*, taking his text from Genesis 3, Hobbes makes the point that it is no business of those not chosen to govern to make judgments of what is just and unjust. "Whereby it is clearly," he wrote, "though allegorically, signified, that the commands of them that have the right to command, are not by their subjects to be censured, nor disputed."[28] Hobbes's use of scripture is, of course, problematic. But his use of every device possible to make a single point is quite clear. Wars arise from divided authority, which will sooner or later be settled by resorting to arms. He makes his case not based on the notion of a just social order or a virtuous government; but he makes it on the grounds of a rational argument that governing is about coercion and the use of violence to keep authority in effect. Such an arrangement, furthermore, provides for peaceful and commodious life, one worth the sacrifice of individual rights to a central authority. "And though of so unlimited a power, men may fancy many evil consequences, yet the consequences of the want of it, which is perpetual war of every man against his neighbor, are much worse."[29]

Those of us accustomed to a democratic form of government may not recognize anything of this "Leviathan," this absolutist scheme of polity. But Hobbes would say that any outward *form* will do. The sovereign with such omnipresent powers might be a single monarch, or an assembly of men, or a democracy such as existed in ancient Athens. Nevertheless, the authority itself is single; everything is governed from a central point of concentrated power. The point, for Hobbes, was that the sovereignty itself, be undivided.[30] Even in a mixed government, with executive, legislative, and judicial functions, the apparent division must give way to the need for administrative simplicity.[31]

Hobbes is never more a master interpreter of the modern state than when he insists that the form of the state is one thing and its effect something else. Whether monarchy, oligarchy, or democracy, the undivided sovereignty tends toward absolute rule—a condition he thought both necessary and desirable. The Athens of Pericles, for all its democratic form, was in effect a monarchy. It worked well because the disparate ends of the demagogues were manipulated and employed by the subtle Pericles.

How else might one get by in a world of such fearful prospect, so prone to disaster, so indifferent to the happiness of human beings, who live as waifs in a hostile environment? It is a world that wants mastery. And the knowledge of it is by no means intended that we might love it, as St. Augustine said; but it is needed that we might master and possess it, as Hobbes's contemporary, Descartes, insisted. Hobbes took such a program seriously. So have we moderns, for the most part, for we share in the legacy of a man born the twin of fear.

5

Pierre Bayle and the Modern
Sanctity of the Individual

The inconstancy of human opinions and pas-
sions is so great that it might be said that man
is a small republic that often changes its mag-
istrates.

Pierre Bayle

I F HOBBES IMPRESSED UPON THE EUROPEAN MIND the logic of undivided sovereignty, Pierre Bayle—an unintended father of the Enlightenment—gained for Europe a new mindfulness of the solitary and inviolable soul. Between Hobbes and Bayle, two ends of the modern tightrope were held in tension. The modern high wire act could begin. At stake were the fortunes of powers elevated far above the common scene where parish and patrimony had represented the greater part of civil power, where both the individual acting alone, and central powers acting from afar, were only occasional players in the affairs of the community. The authority of one was too inconsiderable, and that of the other was too distant. The traditional powers in the civil order always stood solidly on the ground: for their authority, the authority of families and faiths, of friendships and collegial associations, was natural. They were not, as were the new states,

88

products of artifice and organization, of bureaus and more or less arbitrary positive law. It was unintentional, at least on the part of Bayle, but these dual emphases were the two poles that gradually formed the axes of modern society: one, a sovereign and central national identity, the other the solitary human being; the other, associations that lie between these poles, or that exist altogether apart from this axis, gradually fade from modern consciousness—not entirely, of course, for they are as inescapable as they are natural, but at least they fade increasingly from the discourse on society and its features.

It is well known that Bayle played a critical role in changing seventeenth-century European convictions with regard to the sovereign rights of the individual in matters of conscience. The object here is to explore a certain irony in what he championed. Although the traditional idea of the development of liberal democratic institutions is that they protect the individual from the overweening designs of the state, in fact, Bayle's case against persecution and in favor of protecting the "erring conscience" was not so much cast against the state as against the traditional social powers of the church and local communities. In terms of political theory, he was, in fact, an absolutist. His critique of Louis xiv's Revocation of the Edict of Nantes was not that the state had exercised powers it did not have, but in fact that the King failed to assert his royal prerogative against the church. The case of Pierre Bayle reveals much about the rise of a modern doctrine of toleration in concert with, and not opposed to, the rise of the European nation-state, which was seen as the means of liberation from the oppressive powers of groups that traditionally shared power with the civil government.

Life, Exile, and Struggle

The development of Bayle's defense of private conviction is best understood in the context of his life, his exile, and his conflict with both Catholic and Reformed leaders. Susan Mendus described him as a man driven by the need to arrive at an honest assessment of religious issues that threatened society all around him. Enormous energy, deep sincerity of purpose, and a profound wit characterized a thinker both troubled and committed. The principle issue for Bayle, for most of his life, was the friction between the majority Catholic population in France and the minority Protestant (Huguenot) population. During the early years of his life in France, religious freedom of a very limited sort was accorded the Huguenots under the provision of the Edict of Nantes. Yet there were restrictions even then. And as time went on, those provisions became more and more circumscribed, until finally Louis XIV issued the infamous Revocation of the Edict of Nantes in 1685. In the latter and most productive years of his life, Bayle was a refugee in the Dutch city of Rotterdam. Yet even there the long arm of religious persecution could reach out to him, causing him to pay dearly for religious conviction, if not in his person, then certainly in his family living still in France. He suffered the continued distress of an exile: alone yet subject to the pressures of a church which was not his own and whose powers resided in the homeland. Allowing for these circumstances, we begin to see clearly the angst he bore for the plight of the conscientious private life under siege by church authority.

Pierre Bayle was born in 1647 at Carla-le-Comte. His father, Jean Bayle, was a Protestant pastor, and his older brother, Jacob, was to become a Protestant minister as well. Bayle considered his education inadequate, particularly since his early years were largely self-guided. As a young man he had to wait for his older brother to finish before family finances would permit him to begin his schooling. When finally his turn came, one biographer wrote, "Pierre left for Puylaurens as if he were setting out for Athens in Plato's day."[1] His fellow pupils at this Huguenot institution of higher learning were, by now, four or five years younger than Bayle, and he felt that the standards were low. Hungering for greater challenges, he transferred, without his family's knowledge at first, to the Jesuit University of Toulouse.

Living in France, as a member of a Protestant family—that is, as a member of a minority religious group—Pierre Bayle learned early the issues that animated the vigorous debates between Protestant and Catholic. He learned these issues first, of course, from his Huguenot friends and relatives, and thus from the Protestant side. He also could not have helped becoming aware of the strong sentiment, making itself felt on both sides and in every quarter during those days, that Christians should find a way toward reuniting the church.

In Toulouse, however, under the influence of Jesuit scholars, he converted to Catholicism. After a year and a half, he returned to the Reformed faith. This early experience perhaps marks the earnestness with which he struggled with religious issues but at the same time provides insight into his growing uncertainty and skepticism at the prospects of resolving such issues. One can only imagine the young, earnest scholar who months before appeared at the door of a university that represented all that had oppressed his family and neighbors. Not only was it Catholic but Jesuit, populated by older and highly respected scholars armed with arguments of the Counterreformation. Bayle turned to them only because he was utterly intoxicated with the mission of receiving an education. And an education in that day meant, among other things, learning how to recognize which was the true church. A confident Jesuit scholar berated Bayle's Huguenot justifications for resisting the authority of the national church. Bayle, humiliated by losing the argument so ingloriously, nevertheless recalled that he had come to Tolouse to find the truth. And once he thought he had found it, even with such ignominy, he bowed to it: he was converted to the Catholic faith. Then, even as he returned to the Reformed faith, he did so as an outcome of the same tortured search for the true church.

Moreover, his uncertain beginnings in Catholicism and his subsequent return to Protestantism, his anguished attempt along with an equally anguished turnabout, marked him. The conscience could not be fully trusted. A strain of skepticism accompanied every decisive move of the human spirit, and only those with a touch of skepticism could be fully trusted. In his *Historical and Critical Dictionary*, Bayle wrote of Melanchthon that he was "naturally good-natured and pacific, possessed great intelligence, had read widely, and knew a vast amount." Further: "These characteristics, when found together, usually make men indecisive. A man of great intellectual capacity, backed up by extensive knowledge, rarely finds that all the wrongs are on the same side: rather, he finds strong and weak points in each party."[2] The struggle for the "true church" in his early years was later to result in his conviction that, from a purely human point of view, indecisiveness is appropriate. Amie Godman Tannenbaum observes, "thus, for a short period of time, Bayle had personally experienced the 'erring conscience' which would be the cornerstone of his doctrine of toleration."[3]

If his "erring conscience" made him aware of the need for tolerance, the means by which he arrived at a decision relied wholly upon individual reason. Rather than falling back on custom—of either religious persuasion—he desired through reason to come to a personal sense of the truth. Bayle's quest is a remarkably modern one. It is the lonely quest of the solitary seeker. In a way he belongs to Catholic France; and, yet again, he belongs to his family's Protestant heritage. He is suspended between the two, with nothing but his private wits to give him direction.

Bayle studied in Geneva beginning in 1670. There he began to appreciate the skeptic tradition of antiquity, a tradition that was to exert considerable influence throughout the seventeenth and eighteenth centuries. He saw this skeptic philosophy as a natural extension of the Calvinist conviction that God is rationally inscrutable. Two prominent thinkers in Geneva would help him to refine the relevance of classical skepticism to the Christian intellectual disposition and would have a lifelong impact upon Bayle: Jacques Basnage (1653-1733) and Vincent Minutoli (1640-1710).

From the year 1673, Bayle saw a series of rapid changes in his situation. At first he became a tutor to the son of an aristocratic Protestant family living some distance from Geneva. By 1674 he had moved back to France and to Paris. Again he took a post with a Protestant family as a tutor, only to find the demands upon his time and the restrictions imposed by providing all of the instruction for the children became too burdensome to allow other intellectual engagements. Bayle was encouraged and, in time, persuaded by his friend Basnage to enter the competition for a new chair in philosophy established at the Protestant Academy at Sedan. Bayle won the competition and in 1675 began his six-year tenure as a professor. Although financially he was hardly better off than as a tutor in Paris, in terms of prestige his stock had gone up considerably. Yet it was not to last. In spite of the Edict of Nantes, with its provisions protecting the Protestant minority, the French crown was intermittently and steadily placing greater restrictions upon the Huguenots. In 1681 the Academy at Sedan was closed by the order of Louis XIV.

Even before the outright Revocation of the Edict of Nantes, the noose was tightening around the necks of recalcitrant Protestants in France. Bayle at first considered going to England where the the reputation for hospitable treatment of Huguenots had grown. Instead, however, it was to Rotterdam that he fled, primarily because of prospects at the École Illustre. The school's name disguised the fact that this institution was inferior to a university. Nonetheless, Bayle flourished there for a time. A chair of philosophy and history was created for him. It was here that he would build his reputation as a writer and an illustrious thinker, and it was here, in Rotterdam, in the midst of the large French-speaking Huguenot community—a community of exiles—that he would spend, for the most part, the rest of his life.

As time went on, his ties to his homeland and the obligations that attended these bonds became weaker. Of course, most refugees still had family members in France, as did Bayle himself. Such continuing family ties make the refugee cautious, for the notorious criticism of the regime by the one living abroad can always be visited upon the still vulnerable loved ones at home. Such was to be the fate of Pierre Bayle, as events proved. Nevertheless, taking a period of exile in its broad sweep and its long-range effects, it tends to set the refugee free from the corporate bonds that characterize normal community life. As Bayle's biographer, Elizabeth Labrousse, said, "Exile notoriously makes a man aware of himself as an individual and gives him a sense of the relativity of things." "It was in this spirit," she wrote, "that Bayle, along with some of his readers and disciples, set off on a voyage of intellectual adventure, while the Refuge itself was . . . a place of cultural ferment from which at least part of the ideology of the Enlightenment was to arise."[4]

Under such circumstances, Bayle entered his most productive years. His first work was *Letter on a Comet* (1683), which was published anonymously. It was widely read and Bayle enlarged the letter for a second edition, changing its title to *Miscellaneous Reflections on the Comet* (1683). The text of the letter employed the device of having been written by a follower of Descartes to a Catholic theologian. The occasion was the appearance of a comet that was seen in the Northern Hemisphere during December of 1680. The writer argued that the custom of attributing supernatural significance to the appearance of a comet was virtual idolatry. In the course of the argument every kind of scorn is heaped upon the idolatrous practices of antiquity. Only thinly veiled in all of this is a by now customary critique of the Catholic Church among Protestants for its sacramental theology, its institutions, its holy sites, and its venerable relics.

The success of this publication was followed by the even more enthusiastic reception of *General Criticism of Monsieur Maimborg's History of Calvinism* (1683). Executed in the white heat of controversy, it was a reply to an ex-Jesuit writer of popular history who, in his polemical treatment of the history of Calvinism, blamed the Huguenots for the religious wars and for the general turmoil in France caused by religious division. The success of Bayle's reply was such that Parisian authorities felt compelled to burn every copy that could be found in the city. Bayle's books were accorded the honor of a public spectacle, presided over by the official hangman of Paris. Naturally, the event only succeeded in heightening curiosity, exciting for the anonymous author a certain esoteric celebrity, and increasing public demand for the book.

Again, as in the case of *Miscellaneous Reflections on the Comet*, Bayle endeavored to keep secret his authorship. Written anonymously, the book was published at Amsterdam, which was advertised as "Villefranche." He published under the imprint of "Pierre Le Blanc," but the actual publisher was Wolfgang. In spite of these precautions it became widely known that Bayle was the author of the controversial critique of Maimborg's popularized broadside against Calvinism.

Soon, that which Bayle had taken precautions against, befell him. He learned that his beloved elder brother, Jacob, had died. Eventually the whole story came to light. Jacob had been held in prison for five months; he refused to renounce his Huguenot faith; and it became evident from informants in Paris that he was arrested because his brother was the author of *General Criticism*. The cold cell, the mold encrusted walls, and the usual seventeenth-century prison filth finally took its toll. Jacob died in prison on November 13, 1685. Pierre could not help feeling that he was indirectly responsible for his brother's death.

By 1685, all of his immediate family in France had died. And in October of that year the Revocation was issued. These circumstances, as difficult as they were to endure at the moment, set Bayle free from any inhibition he might have otherwise felt to write, and to publish, and to oppose the French authorities as vigorously as he pleased. In the Netherlands, and with no remaining "hostages" in France, he was safe from their reach.

The next work of his to appear, *Philosophical Commentary*, was devoted directly to the issue of religious toleration. By June of 1687, all three volumes had been published. The full title also gives the work's argument: *Philosophical Commentary on the words of Our Lord "Compel them to come in," in which it is proved by demonstrative reasoning that nothing is more abominable than to make conversion by force, and in which all the sophistry of those who would do so is refuted, likewise the apologia made by St Augustine for persecution.* More than any other work, this one identifies Bayle as one of the early formulators of the doctrine of toleration that—with some important changes—became the touchstone of modern moral philosophy. To the extent that he argued simply against force as a means of conversion, his views would not have been especially new. But when he buttresses this argument with the idea that the individual conscience has a stronger claim upon the soul than any collective obligations, we have here the beginnings of genuinely modern mentality.

Up until this point in his publishing career, Bayle had written under pseudonyms and endeavored to disguise his authorship. In the case of the earlier writings, he did it to avoid reprisals against his family back in France. In this case, he was most likely avoiding open controversy with his erstwhile friend and mentor Pierre Jurieu. It was a conflict that had developed over time and the story tells much about Bayle's intellectual development and the world in which he lived.

He had met Jurieu at Sedan. The distinguished Reformed professor of theology was ten years Bayle's senior. Well established in the Protestant community in France, and later in the community of Huguenot exiles, Jurieu was evidently a man of independent means, which allowed him to accumulate a large library, certainly one of which his junior colleague might dare only to dream. At any rate, he became, during their tenure at Sedan together, Bayle's friend and mentor.

Things began to change, however, when they were both in exile in Rotterdam. The older scholar and Huguenot leader held to the hope that the situation in France would finally reverse itself and the Protestants would gain freedom from the persecution of the Catho-

lic majority. He even was given to publicizing prophecies and por-
tents that encouraged the hope that the exile from France and the
French "apostasy" would soon come to an end. Bayle would have
none of this. Such irrational demagoguery was, for him, intellectually dishonest. Furthermore, his experience of persecution had taken
him along a different path from that of his former mentor. He began
to believe that the just answer to the crisis did not lie in overcoming
the persecutors only to become *their* persecutors but in tolerating the
conscience of both Protestants *and* Catholics. Not only was it the only
way to restore the *status quo ante* of the Huguenots but if in principle
toleration is owed to the minority faith, then it must be accorded by
the minority to the majority.

Such sentiments were close to treason, if not to heresy, in Jurieu's
estimation. It was giving in to the false claims of a false church. And
it was doing so at a time when the Huguenots would best be engaged
in mustering all their energies and convictions in the overthrow of
the circumstances thrust upon them since the Revocation of the Edict
of Nantes, and even before. The problem with the Catholic powers-
that-be, according to Jurieu, was not that they did not tolerate Protestant faith but that they do not recognize its fundamental truth and
their own fundamental error. You do not make a place for error,
Jurieu argued; you eliminate it. For him, Bayle was not only sound-
ing an uncertain note just at the time the troops needed to be read-
ied for ultimate combat he was also planting the seeds of Protestant
heresy.

As a doctrinaire Calvinist, Jurieu stood against Bayle's arguments
on toleration for reasons similar to those of their mutual Catholic
opponents: Bayle was being fired upon by both sides. In many ways,
because Jurieu in the end could influence those upon whom Bayle
really depended, this coreligionist became the more dangerous enemy. But thanks to Jurieu, we see Bayle in a different light than we
might have. The convictions he finally settled upon found strong
opposition on both sides. He held what many today are calling the

"radical middle." Yet to say that alone puts Bayle—and the whole story of an emerging doctrine of toleration—in a false light. It is not that Bayle occupied a moderate position between the Jesuits and the militant Calvinists. It was that he located a new center of gravity for civil and religious responsibility, one that would prove to be the hallmark of modernity. This new center of gravity is no longer any particular public or private authority. It is, instead, the newly emerging notion of the individual—one might say, without exaggeration, the autonomous, the self-ruling, individual.

If the theme of the inviolable conscience of the individual is evident in *Philosophical Commentary*, it is also a major theme in Bayle's last and most famous work, *Historical and Critical Dictionary*. Made up of articles on biography, theology, metaphysics, and politics, the *Dictionary* eventually made of Bayle a household name in Europe, especially in French-speaking Europe. It was the only work published under his own name; and by the time this three-volume work was published, Bayle was already well known for his other (supposedly pseudonymous) pieces.

Individualism and Toleration

In the mind of Jurieu—Bayle's Protestant detractor—and in the mind of Catholic authorities in France who would dispute with him for quite different reasons, Bayle's argument for toleration was almost unimaginable. Bayle's point of view would eventually take root—it does not strike readers today as exceptional—but this would take time. For his detractors, Truth has rights that Error does not share. Bayle was undertaking the difficult task of showing that an "erring conscience" necessarily must be accorded rights. And this right of an erring conscience must be protected out of regard for the frailty of human reason. Such an argument was not unheard of, even at this time. In fact, in some passages of Thomas Aquinas, the argument is made that the person is to obey his conscience even when it errs.[5] But it is with Bayle that the idea of the private conscience becomes something of the hinge upon which public life is to turn.

Here is the center of Bayle's case for toleration. That which persuades men in common, namely reason, cannot be fully relied upon. Only that which persuades men privately, their own consciences, can issue in true religion. Of course, looking back on the historical setting that gave rise to this turn of thought, we can appreciate the fact that persecution and violence drove men and women to seek shelter in the private life. But now we must face the less immediate implications of the kind of fortification of privacy that takes place throughout modern times. If the inviolable private conscience alone can issue in genuine faith, then one must give free reign to conscience and not press too far the claims of community. Reason is, after all, a function that is public because it involves demonstrable processes leading to demonstrable proofs. It relies upon that which men and women receive in common, whether that be of the senses, of tradition, or of revelation. Reason can thus have its effect in public so long as there is a degree of like-mindedness regarding particular presuppositions. Along with this is the exercise of judgment, the critical function of reason that also is dialogical and public in nature.

What are the consequences of Bayle's conviction concerning the "rights" of the erring conscience? What happens if one believes, along with Bayle, that reason is unreliable and that conscience (while no less reliable) is at least the appropriate agent of genuine assent to the truth and its only valid judge? Since reason has a public basis and conscience refers fundamentally to private convictions, the consequences are not too difficult to predict. One leads in the direction of community, and the other abandons community. Reason begins and ends with what we have in common, while conscience may restrict itself to the insights and impulses of the private heart.

Of course, by "reason" here I am referring to the classical notion of reason in the tradition of Aristotle and Aquinas. That use of reason implies a commonality of things and experiences upon which we might base certain general observations. It assumes that our most basic perceptions of the world can be trusted and are verified by the experience of others. In a word, they belong to a community of human experience. By the same token, I am not referring to the distinctly modern sense of reason in the tradition of Descartes. That idea of "reason" some have characterized as autonomous reason. Descartes's contribution to the character of modernity was that he made reason something that emerges from private experience. I can only be sure of the fact that "I think"; and if I think, then I might recover the conviction that "I am." All of the world, all of those public things, can only be reconstructed and believed on the basis of this interior knowledge of the act of thinking. One can see from this that Bayle's direction in defending religious toleration harmonized with a new spirit in the world, one that would trust the private over the public. As we contemplate this trend together, I feel that I cannot evoke in the reader's mind often enough the thought that it is precisely along with this loss of confidence in the *normal* operations of public life that we see the simultaneous interest in shoring up the sovereignty of remote but overawing centers of power as a way of compensating for what is lost.

Bayle's approach, although he is said to be influenced by Descartes, is not truly Cartesian. His reconstruction of a disordered world depended upon two primary convictions: the distrust of reason as an ultimate arbiter of truth, and the primacy of faith. These are unlike Descartes's premises in that they are fideistic (relying on faith) rather than rationalistic (relying on reason alone). But they share with the Cartesian method the desire to ground convictions in the private rather than in the public experience.

Bayle's Distrust of Reason

As a general statement about the disposition of the Christian tradition regarding reason, it would be fair to say that Christianity does not exhibit perfect confidence in human reason. Reason relies upon its presuppositions, and those are affected by sin and frailty. In other words, they are affected by the fact of our creatureliness, our necessarily limited grasp of things. And these presuppositions are also affected by the way fallen people, incurably self-centered, wish to see the world. More often than not, reason merely aids perversity even while claiming to guard against it. Nevertheless, even while giving sin its due, classical Christianity appeals to reason and tends to consider it useful within proper bounds. St. Thomas Aquinas, for instance, would insist that there are things that we can say about God simply because we have a knowledge of the world through our senses and that knowledge can be extended through the use of reason. We can know, for instance, that God exists. Other things, and more important things, such as the attributes of God or the reality of the Holy Trinity, we know only because they are revealed to us. Nonetheless, reason has its place in the economy of God's way with human beings, and this was a matter not disparaged from the time of Anselm until the late Middle Ages.

It is important, however, to acknowledge that there is an element of skepticism and disparagement of reason or philosophy in Christianity as a whole, in order to understand Bayle's particular effect in the seventeenth century. This skepticism, from the time of St. Paul, surfaced from time to time. While some, like Clement of Alexandria, would practically baptize the ancient philosophers into the church, others like Tertullian would grouse, "What has Athens to do with Jerusalem?" And while Anselm of Canterbury would elevate the role of logic in theology, his younger contemporary Abelard would highlight the logical inconsistencies of church teachings and Scripture with his famous *Sic et Non*. It is not surprising, then, that in the Protestant movement of the late Middle Ages, which emphasized Revelation and disparaged the earlier Scholasticism with its rationalistic bent, we find a sustained critique of the idea that reason is a trustworthy arbiter of truth. The role that Bayle played was to carry that skeptical trend to some of its logical conclusions. Yet in doing so, he not only went beyond what any of the Reformers would have agreed to, but he led much of the European intelligentsia to explore the limits of skepticism.

Knowing, as we do today, the excesses of the so-called Enlightenment, Bayle would no doubt be horrified to learn that he is considered by many to be a father of the Enlightenment. He was a skeptic only to the extent that he saw in reason a barrier to faith. For him, reason pressed as far as it will go remains inconclusive. Life cannot ultimately respond to such an uncertain trumpet. It remains for the Christian thinker to expose the brittleness of reason in order to clear the way for the exercise of faith, which alone has saving value. That his famous *Dictionary* was filled with examples of the skeptical side of the intellectual process made it a treasure trove for the later European intelligentsia who wished only to expose the contridictions of orthodox thinking and of Christian apologetics. Yet, such a use hardly did justice to Bayle's own sentiment. He speaks in his article on Spinoza, for instance, of "people whose religion is in the heart, and not in the mind": "The moment they seek it by human reasoning, they lose sight of it; it eludes the subtleties and sophistries of their processes of argument; when they try to weigh up the pros and cons, they become confused; but as soon as they stop arguing, and simply listen to the evidence of their feelings, the instinctive promptings of their conscience, the legacy of their upbringing, and so on, they are convinced by a religion and live their lives by it, so far as human infirmity allows."[6]

The Protestant emphasis upon faith and the Bible did not consistently or intentionally diminish the place of reason, but that was its tendency from Luther to Calvin to Beza and beyond. The result is often the astonished realization among historians that what was started by a cadre of European intellectuals gives rise in later years to thick-headed anti-intellectualism and vulgar irrationalism. However that might be, early Protestants frequently found themselves allied with secular skeptics in evoking the spirit of ancient philosophical skepticism. The school of thought most frequently referred to is that of the Greek skeptic Pyrrho.

Pyrrho, Bayle tells us, "everywhere found reasons for affirming and for denying; and this is why he suspended judgment after having carefully examined all the arguments pro and con, and always concluded that the matter should be looked into further."[7] Suspension of judgment was the key. The Pyrrhonian doubt was founded upon the inconclusiveness of rational arguments, making doubt in the sphere of philosophy the only intellectually honest position. Pyrrho's acting out of his convictions make for humorous reading and Bayle did not credit the stories that "Pyrrho did not prefer one thing to another and that neither a chariot nor a precipice could ever make him take a step forward or backward and that his friends who followed him around often saved his life."[8] He did believe, however, that "Pyrrho's indifference was astonishing. He did not like anything, nor was he ever angry about anything. No one was ever more completely persuaded than he of the vanity of things. When he spoke, it did not matter to him whether anyone listened or not; and even if he saw that his audience went away, he nevertheless continued speaking. He kept house with his sister and shared even the smallest household chores with her."[9]

The effect of Pyrrhonism upon Bayle was not, however, the suspension of judgment. For Bayle, there were two sides to the skeptic philosophy, one for which the Christian might be grateful and the other that posed a danger to any constructive thinking. On the one hand he praised the facility the Pyrrhonists had for calling attention to the weaknesses of natural reason. But, on the other hand, to be frozen in indecision can never be a good thing. The Christian, of course, appeals to faith. Faith breaks the deadlock of indecisive reason and calls to action.[10]

For our purposes in assessing the long-term influence of Bayle, it is more important perhaps to see how he made the argument against any kind of certitude built on the foundation of rational thought. The act of faith is divorced from the world of objects and evidence, from the common appropriation of things through the senses, from the community of men and women, and from the necessity of mutual obligations. It is a leap in the dark in the most absolute sense. Nothing defines isolation so much as "darkness." In the darkness we are alone with our thoughts and our senses. In the light it is assumed that we have the capacity to share things in common; we are no longer alone, we are in a world obviously peopled, we are in a community of sight and sound, of conversation and interaction. Bayle's faith is one that operates only when the community is stripped bare of reason, of reliance on the senses, of meaningful interaction (because we do not know for certain, do we?) that we are all making reference to the same things in the world which we might have formerly thought we inhabited in common. Now let us see how this affects his argument on religious toleration.

Individual Conscience and the Public Nature of Truth

From the time of St. Augustine forward, it was common to call upon the parable of the "Great Banquet" in Luke 14 to justify persecution of unbelievers and heretics. The parable tells of a banquet for which the invited guests all declined their invitations for various reasons. The irate master of the feast ordered his servants to "go out into the highways and hedges and compel them to come in, that my house may be filled." In Bayle's day, it would have been a point of agreement between the Calvinist Jurieu and the French Catholics who persecuted Calvinists that the true church (whichever it might be) is justified in "compelling" others even by force of government edict, and hence by threat of violence, to join it. The broad agreement on this point, even across otherwise impenetrable theological boundaries, gives us some sense of how new Bayle's approach was at the time. While it seems perfectly commonplace to us in the twentieth century, it was hardly so in the seventeenth.

Bayle could have argued, as Locke did, that while faith is a worthy goal it simply cannot be compelled from without, and that the very fact of compulsion makes the profession of faith false. Bayle, however, went beyond the mere inefficacy of the attempt to convert through force. He argues instead that the effort to cause a person to violate his own conscience—even though he might be in error—is itself evil. What makes a human action good or evil is not the mere act, but the disposition of the heart from which the act originates. Man looks upon the outward things, but God looks upon the heart. The act itself might be guided by an erroneous conscience, but nevertheless one that intends to do good in obedience to God. Better, Bayle would argue, to preserve the rights of the good conscience than to suppress the conscience and compel the action. For who would dare say that the outside authority is a more sure guide than the sincere conscience?

As an example he speaks of two men who are approached on different occasions by a beggar. One, not for altogether charitable purposes, gives the beggar some money. Perhaps he wants to rid himself of the nuisance as soon as possible; perhaps he wants to appear charitable to the community or to himself. He cares little whether his action confirms the beggar in his dependence and in his wasteful, lazy habits. The second man, however, refuses the beggar and sends him away with insults. He recognizes, in doing so, that he might actually do more harm to the beggar by giving him a coin than by withholding it.

Bayle points out that the second man actually engages in less error. It is clear that he violates the law of charity by "rudely rebuffing a poor man."[11] But however grievous might have been his mistake (and Bayle admits that he has done wrong) in using harsh words when kind words might have been better, or in judging the beggar a rogue when in fact he was a god-fearing unfortunate, this error is not on the same plane as a conscience which has as its fixed purpose rebellion against God. It is on this level, and not on the level of occasional actions, that the sin against God is productive of yet more evil.

If this is the case—if the heart must be taken into consideration in judging the gravity of evil—then the effort to compel a person to act against his or her conscience cannot but be the greatest evil. It is to thwart that very faculty that is responsible to God for the production of good and the avoidance of evil. Bayle draws from this observation, six principles. Notice that each one draws us deeper into the notion of individual sanctity of conscience:

1. That the intent to disobey God is a sin.
2. That the volition of disobeying the fixed and immutable sentence of conscience is the same thing as willing to transgress the Law of God.
3. Consequently, that whatever is done against the dictates of conscience is a sin.
4. That the greatest turpitude of sin, all things being equal elsewhere, comes from the greater knowledge one has that one sins.
5. That an action which would be incontestably good (giving charity, for example) if done at the direction of conscience, becomes worse by being done against its direction, than another done according to the direction which would be incontestably sinful (as reviling a poor man for example) if done against its direction.
6. That doing a thing we call evil to conform to a conscience which is in reality erroneous, renders this action much less evil than another action which we call good, done against the dictate of conscience supposedly conformed to truth.[12]

Then he writes, "From all these principles I legitimately conclude that the first and most indispensable of all our obligations, is that of never acting against the promptings of conscience, and that every action done against the lights of conscience is essentially evil."[13]

Bayle was, it is fair to say, focused on the evils of his own time and not those in our time. In the seventeenth century, the dignity of the individual conscience hardly constituted an excessive preoccupation. It was assumed almost everywhere and among all peoples that one of the necessities of community life was the establishment of religion. It was a community issue, not an individual one. Hobbes, as we have seen, certainly subscribed to the conventional wisdom of his time on this matter. And even Locke, as we will see later, considered that within reasonable bounds individuals might decide religious issues for themselves, but that did not include the choice of being a professing atheist or a practicing Catholic. Bayle opened doors that neither Locke nor Hobbes had entered; he opened the way to making the private conscience the supreme arbiter of matters of conscience. In doing so, we might say, he prepared the way for troubles that perhaps he could not have anticipated—troubles that did not become fully apparent until late in the nineteenth century. They are troubles that the twentieth century reaped in full fury: the maelstrom of societies governed by the impulses of private lives, the deceitful skill of demagogues, and what one author called "the triumph of vulgarity."[14]

In order to properly estimate both the importance of Bayle and the part he played in bringing on what I have called a "maelstrom," we must at least mark our place in our own times, understanding him partly in view of what has issued from this great emphasis upon the individual conscience. In so doing, we might well see Bayle differently, although we must necessarily judge him charitably. No one, lately, I think, has expressed this development more eloquently than Robert Pattison. He sees in the twentieth century how popular tastes and private impulses, unrefined by reason or aesthetic sense, egged on by the demands of mass market and the politics of democracy, has swept aside the higher disciplines of reason and taste:

That vulgarity should free itself from the limits prescribed for it by culture and set up on its own is an idea almost unimaginable before the modern period. The kingdom of Refinement views the prospect of an independent republic of Vulgaria with unalloyed contempt. In Vulgaria's democracy, cultivation would compete with unskilled labor. Public men with a taste for contemplation would be driven from office and replaced by noisy partisans of transient factions. Noise would be the legislated medium of all business, public and private. Special machinery would be installed in homes and public places to insure that no vestige of tranquility could flourish. The transcendent forces of religion would be given the choice of conforming to the noisy sensationalism of vulgar ideology or disbanding their congregations. The media would be controlled to assure the steady flow of rabble-rousing facts and the suppression of reasoned reflection. Science would be harnessed to quell any lingering desire for solitude by providing technologies to involve the population in ceaseless movement and acquisition. License, which is unbridled activity, would flourish. Morality would be swallowed up in the orchestration of sensations. Culture, where it had not disappeared, would become the object of indifference or derision, and education would teach meaningful skills for the practical life. Civilization would pulsate briefly in the throes of anarchy, lapse into the paralysis of overindulgence, and pass finally into the void beyond mind, taste, and decency. In short, a vulgar nation would be America—land of democracy, television, fast foods, cars, computers, high school, sexual liberation, Jerry Falwell, and *The National Enquirer*. But above all, land of rock 'n' roll.[15]

Christopher Lasch was more sanguine about the chances of democracy in his book *The True and Only Heaven*. His main concern was that the ideology of progress—the notion that things inevitably get better and better—wedded to democracy results in the false expectation that there really are no limits that might be theoretically imposed on the impulses and desires of the individual. At least the American middle class, and especially the lower middle class, has held to the classical sense of limits along with their optimism. He cites thinkers as varied as Reinhold Niebuhr, G.D.H. Cole, Josiah Royce, and Martin Luther King who embody this sense of restraint against the impulses of popular passions. "What these thinkers shared with each other and with their predecessors," Lasch wrote, "was a sense of limits."[16] Nevertheless, the "dominant current" in modern life is identified with this individualism and its acquisitive rights, innocent of any "sense of limits." Whether the moderating sense of limits or the unmoderated individualism would gain the upper hand was, perhaps, the most important cultural question in the later years of the twentieth century.

Harry Blamires noted that in the twentieth century, the voices that have been most effective in raising a protest against totalitarianism have not been Christians. But though they have recognized the threat posed by totalitarian ideologies and all-powerful national regimes, they have generally failed to see that social bonds, other than those of the state, are a great guarantor against tyranny. Instead, they think in terms of autonomous individual freedom, unfettered by *any* authority associated with any social entity whatever. "We sense deeply," he said, "the chasm between the church and the secular world when those secularists who speak idealistically of freedom reveal that they have in mind, not just the renunciation of dictatorships and other repressive agencies, but also the rejection of bonds and obligations such as those constituted by marriage, the family, and all social hierarchies."[17]

Now, returning to Bayle, we might ask the question, "Did he say all that might be said about the importance of private conscience in moral and religious decisions?" To his credit, he was seeking an antidote to the particular brand of chaos he found in his own world. The maneuverings of various ecclesiastical and governing powers to establish *their own* doctrine or practice had resulted in war. Using violence to establish the right to say "I am in the right and you are in the wrong . . . is throwing the world back into a chaos more frightful than that of Ovid."[18] But he seems not to anticipate the sort of disorder that might occur when private conscience is placed above the wisdom of the community.

He does not consider, for instance, one possible conclusion one might draw from his insight into the "erring conscience." If our insight into the truth of things is imperfect, one might ask, why leave it dependent upon the narrow thread of individual judgment. May one not assume that the wisdom of the extended community, fed by a thousand streams of memory, by the habits that have accumulated over several millennia of trial and error in community, might be more reliable. One need not assume the community is infallible—that it does not sometimes go far astray. Individual experience and insight is necessarily shallow; it is only the latest accretion on the surface of time. But the individual that is rooted in the memory and customs of a community has a better chance of understanding his situation.

David Hume, who was also deeply affected by Pyrrhonian skepticism, and whose philosophy first and foremost excluded the possibility of reducing everything to its fundamental causes, did take the route that Bayle missed a century earlier. When it becomes apparent to the "true philosopher" (by which Hume meant one no longer under the illusion of his own powers of autonomous thought) that the skeptic's position is the only one that can honestly be attested, then there is the possibility of falling back upon the guidance of "custom." In fact it was never tradition and custom that Hume warned against, nor was that the object of his skepticism. Donald Livingston notes that "Hume is at pains to show that this act of doubt is not directed to natural beliefs about the world but to higher-order acts of autonomous philosophical reflection which pretend to be totally emancipated from custom."[19] Yet it is in "autonomous reflection"—the individual judgment—that the modern age has placed its confidence all the more as time has gone by. In doing so, we have treated the door opened by Bayle and his Enlightenment successors as the only realistic way forward. To rely upon tradition or "custom" is retrograde and unprogressive. It was, moreover, the loss of nerve. As Kant expressed it, the very meaning of the Enlightenment was to "have the courage to use your own intelligence!"[20]

As in the case of skepticism, individualism draws its strength from Christian and Jewish sources. The prophetic movement of the eighth century before Christ began an emphasis upon the obedience of the individual to the revealed law, which constituted the individual's expression of his participation in the community, a community based upon a covenant with God. During the Babylonian exile and Jewish existence under the Persians, the loyalty of the individual to the covenant of community (always expressed in terms of ritual, but more importantly in terms of loyalty to a righteous code of conduct) became a critical issue. Life under Greek oppression once again called into question the survival of the community, a survival that depended largely upon the choice made by individuals. Gradually, as the focus continued to be placed upon the life of the individual, it became apparent that the justice of God—the great affirmation of eighth century prophetism—could not be defended on an individual basis. There were those who were rewarded for their righteous lives and those who were clearly not, and there were those who lived unjust lives and prospered all the same. How could the justice of God be defended? It could not, of course, unless this life proves to be only a part of the picture. The resulting doctrine of the resurrection of the dead and the individual judgment of the just and the unjust added immeasurably to the sense that the individual possesses a dignity altogether apart from that of the community. In the eighth century, one would say that the whole idea of the "saving" work of God applied to the nation itself, not to the individual. It was Israel that either survived or failed to survive, and it was the salvation of the community that was at stake. By the close of the second century, the religious concern of the prophetic movement had clearly shifted from the community toward the individual.

Christianity only intensified this emphasis. The central doctrine of the Resurrection, along with the idea of drawing out of the gentile nations a "new" Israel and the eschatological emphasis upon the destiny (rather than the origin) of peoples, served to continue this shift from the community to the individual.

Bayle the Christian believer, as well as the non-believing radicals of the Enlightenment that followed, drew from this Judeo-Christian tradition. There were, however, some important distinctions to be made between developments in secular thought and the original trajectory of the prophetic movement, through Christianity, out into the gentile world.

The individualism of Judaism and Christianity was messianic, constituting out of the redeemed persons a new community. The dignity of the individual arose from the unmerited grace of God the Creator and Redeemer. The community itself bore witness to its own transcendent reality, and its source, which lay not in itself but in the Spirit of God who gives it life. It was to be eschatologically realized— that is to say, realized as the goal of history rather than within history. At the same time, the community was given form within history as the incarnate presence of that which would find its true form at the end of history. As such, it bore witness in the present, fallen age to the saving intentions of God.

In the seventeenth century, on the other hand, a secular version of this idea of the dignity of the individual began to take form. Incrementally, the sense of an "alien dignity"—Luther's term to describe the fact that human dignity is not inherent in the human being but is only real by virtue of God's creation in His image, God's sustaining love, and God's intention to save—was replaced. It was transformed into a notion of intrinsic worth based upon the supposed competence of the individual human being to reason, to create, to love, to fashion the world in *his* own image.

The idea of a new community was not absent from this secular vision, though at first glance it might seem to have been. But the community for which this liberated and competent individual existed was now no longer the Kingdom of God or the church. Instead, the individual lived in relationship to the state, the newly arising bureaucratic and centralized state, the state permanently organized for war, the nation-state with its remote center of power and its command structure. It was the new entity that, in its most extreme forms, could only consider the authority of natural groups, based on regional and family affiliations, its competitor.[21] And above all, in the seventeenth century, the state recognized the church as its rival which must either be mastered in public or quarantined to the private sphere of life. In England, the remedy for religious discord was the former; in Luther's Germany it was the latter. But no one could lose sight of the fact that the new authoritarian state and the transcendent authority of religion were necessarily rivals. As long as both claimed some portion of public authority, there would always be tension over where one's authority ended and the other's began. Few were as clear as Hobbes on this issue; but the tension was unmistakable, even in Bayle.

The Scandal of Sovereignty

There is no reason to suppose that Bayle's protection of individual rights cannot be applied against the meddling of a secular state as well as the ambitions of zealous clerics for religious orthodoxy. Historically, it was the latter and not the former whose interests were represented in religious persecution and who sought to bring sanctions against those who refused religious conformity. In the case of France, especially, the church sought the complicity of the state in enforcing orthodoxy and outward conformity to the disciplines of Catholic Christianity. With the intervening three centuries, we are likely to dismiss the urgency of Bayle's plea for religious liberty. Doubtless, we are not likely to be as acutely aware of the barbarity which accompanied the persecution of Huguenots in sixteenth- and seventeenth-century France, and hence his passion strikes us more as something quaint. The blame for these enormities he laid at the door of the church primarily. He blamed the state only as a weak accomplice that had not found within itself the courage to resist the agenda that, after all, belonged legitimately to the church alone—and not to the state. In this connection, knowing as we do the subsequent story of the expanding role of the state, we must now take note of a central paradox. In fact, this paradox touches upon the thesis that we have tripped over from the beginning. To say "tripped over" here is not accidental, for the paradox constitutes a scandal in the original sense of the word—something one might stumble over, something that prevents the complete coherence of an intellectual position.

In what sense is this paradox a scandal?

Bayle argues for toleration, especially in reference to religious persecution. But one must remember that the issue of ethical or moral toleration is not totally absent from Bayle's thoughts, even if he himself is not making a point of the connection between toleration in religion (a seventeenth-century concern) and toleration in the realm of morality (a concern explored by Voltaire, John Stuart Mill, and the Marquis de Sade, but which really comes into its own as public policy in the twentieth century). Recall that Bayle's most telling illustrations of the sanctity of the individual conscience happen to concern the ethical (not strictly theological) choice of the giving of alms to the poor.

Whether regarding religion or, more properly, ethics, Bayle's argument seems to be ranged *against* the power to rule (or overrule) the conscientious choices of individuals. The logical extension of this argument might be something like the present-day libertarian position in American politics, the idea that government has a minimal role to play and should not interfere with morals or religion as long as these have no bearing on the control of violent crimes, fraud, or national defense. Yet what we find in Bayle is not an argument against the powerful exercise of the same sovereignty that had crushed the Huguenot community, sent him and his coreligionists into exile, burned his books, and brought about the imprisonment and death of his brother. Instead, we find that he defends the idea of political sovereignty, even of royal absolutism.

Bayle's essay on Hobbes in his *Dictionary* is complimentary in the extreme. In spite of the fact that Hobbes thought the sovereign should determine the faith of the commonwealth, a position that should have alienated Bayle, he praised Hobbes's argument for a strong monarch. He especially admired Hobbes's scientific approach to social issues, calling him, "one of the greatest geniuses of the xviith century."[22] While taking some mild exception to Hobbes's views, especially regarding the establishment of religion, Bayle affirms that "the love of his country inspired him with the design of that work [*De Cive*], and ... he intended by it to undeceive his countrymen with respect to the false principles, which produced there a horrible contempt of the royal authority."[23]

In his comments on Hobbes, it begins to emerge that Bayle's animus against tyranny in religion is much more directed against the church than against the state. In support of his favorable estimation of Hobbes, he quotes a contemporary writer who says that in *De Cive*, Hobbes "for ever destroyed the doctrine of the lawfulness of subjects conspiring and rebelling against their sovereigns, and the monstrous opinions of dethroning and executing of princes: restoring to the civil powers those rights of which they had been robbed by Ecclesiastics in the ages of ignorance, and heroically subduing that cruel hydra of the sectaries, I mean the boundless liberty of conscience."[24]

Here we come close to touching upon the dilemma that I mentioned: the scandal of absolutism that appears in the midst of a strong inclination toward toleration. Would not Bayle himself be numbered among those "sectaries"? Granted the situation in France was distinct from that in England, but in any case the Huguenots had more in common with English Puritans who deposed the king than with the royalists, at least theologically. Yet obviously the argument of Bayle was directed more against specific threats to religious freedom— threats which he took to be religious and clerical in nature—than it was against the accidental instrument of the oppression. In France, of course, that was the regime of Louis xiv. Elizabeth Labrousse is undoubtedly correct in saying that Bayle's argument was not against the authority of the sovereign but against the sovereign's permitting himself to be unduly influenced by the church. Thus, "Bayle sees absolute monarchy as signifying the supremacy of the civil power and its independence from religious authorities, specifically the national clergy and the Vatican."[25]

Labrousse would have done well to acknowledge that this is a powerful tension, if not an outright contradiction, in Bayle's thought. She resists this conclusion. What she does show, however, is that, in Bayle's mind at least, the convictions regarding absolutism on the one hand and toleration on the other are related. They are drawn from the same animus against the *non-governmental* authority of the church when it exercises political influence: "Nor is Bayle's praise of absolutism at odds with his championship of toleration. He interpreted the Revocation as an indication not so much that Louis xiv was exercising power despotically, as that he was failing to enforce his absolute authority: it was the action of a bigot under the thumb of his confessor, not that of a king making his own decisions. In any case, Bayle was only being realistic in refusing in the light of history, to believe that religious pluralism was possible in France on any other terms than under the aegis of undivided royal authority."[26]

The Cunning of Toleration

I have called attention to the relationship between the rise of the nation-state and the sudden prominence of a modern doctrine of toleration. There seems to be a contradiction here: at one and the same time there arises a doctrine of a strong state and the liberal notion of a free individual. It stands to reason that, to the extent the state is strong, the individual is less free; and to the extent the individual is free from social obligations, the state is thereby weakened. But Bayle provides us with a way to understand this mysterious development of modern thought. When Bayle spoke of oppression, he had in mind the kinds of oppression from which the individual might be liberated *by the state*. And if the remedy proved more oppressive than the cure? Such a question apparently did not occur to Bayle in quite that form.

What Bayle does remind us of, inadvertently, is that the individual might feel less threatened by the powers of a remote center of power, than by neighbors, local guilds, the obligations to feudal clans, and the ever present authority of the church. Certainly, it appears that Bayle felt that Huguenot freedoms over against the authority of the Roman Catholics in France might have been guaranteed, rather than threatened, by a strong, authoritarian state. In the twentieth century we might call these entities "mediating institutions," because on the scale of authorities in our life they stand somewhere between the individual and the government. In Bayle's world, these social entities had much greater authority than they do today. Furthermore, their authority was exercised quite often without any reference to the state. There was certainly not the sense that they derived their power from the state, and it was never a certainty that the state could intervene between the aggrieved individual and, say, the church's bishop or the local clan chief or baron.[27]

So what we find in Bayle is the willingness to sacrifice religious authority to the growing authority of the state, for the sake of rescuing the dignity and freedom of the individual. This process has continued to such an extent that the various groups, along with their own systems of authority, have been swallowed up by the state.

F. H. Hinsley thinks that this growth of central government authority was a necessary evolution in modern society. Nevertheless, he described perfectly what has happened, reminding us that it has not always been the case that political communities were identified with the centralized state. Overlapping authorities, most of them arising naturally out the existence of distinct groups within society, once made up the patchwork of a political community. Now, either by evolution or revolution, attempts have been made "not merely to narrow the gap between the community and the state, but to obliterate the distinction between them."[28]

In order for this to happen, it is expedient for the individual to feel a lessened obligation to these natural groups and to identify more strongly with the centralizing state. The result of this "rationalizing" tendency in the growth of bureaucratic power is the homogenizing of society. Rather than articulated hierarchies and complex associations, society becomes a "mass society"—one whose form is imposed from above. Society is less and less articulated along lines of social groups formed by kinship, locality, and faith, and it is made up instead of individuals who relate directly to the bureaucratic organization of this larger political entity. They might then be identified with "parties" whose purpose is to influence or seize control of the state, but in this case they are all the more absorbed into the centralizing process. The only authority left, and the only one worth identifying with, is that of the state.

There is more to the distinction between the state and the mediating groups, or the "natural" groups, than at first meets the eye. The difference hardly consists of the observation that, within a nation, the one is large and comprehensive while the other is small and specialized. The most important difference is that natural groups are essentially spontaneous; they might be intentionally organized, or even heavily burdened by a bureaucratic structure, just as the church often is both large and bureaucratic. But they are essentially spontaneous in that they would exist whether or not they were organized. Get rid of bureaucracies and you still have religions and families.

One cannot say the same for the state in its modern form. It is essentially organized; it is in no sense spontaneous or natural. The people who identify with one another in some historic and national sense can survive the collapse of the formal apparatus of the state. This we have seen happen numerous times in the twentieth century alone, even in the past decade. However, if a people were to rid themselves of the bureaucracy organized among them, then they *do* eliminate the state, root and branch. Yet a part of the power of the reified state is that its comes to be identified with a community of people.

The difference between the two—the reified state and the natural community that exists in and through a number of overlapping groups—has nothing to do with size or comprehensiveness. In fact, looked at from one perspective, the church is larger and the family is more comprehensive. The difference is such that the two are inevitable competitors. The spontaneous life of the family or religion resists organization. And the organized, rationalized state finds the spontaneous loyalties within families and religions inconvenient to organization. Ever since Solomon attempted to reorganize Israel along administrative districts, cutting across the boundaries of tribal lands, it has been recognized that the organized state wishes to diminish the role of natural social bodies.

Dietrich Bonhoeffer experienced one of the worst of the twentieth century's efforts to impose state political rule. His resistance was met by the full power of the state to impose its penalties. He was imprisoned and finally, in April of 1945, executed. In the midst of this German crisis, Bonhoeffer was writing his *Ethics*, a work written in secret and only published after his death, in which he deals with the antagonism between what he calls the "natural" and the "unnatural."

The unnatural is that which is organized and unduly resists the authority of the natural:

> Some entity within the fallen world posits itself as an absolute, declares itself to be the source of the natural, and thereby disintegrates the natural life. There now begins a struggle between the unnatural and the natural, in which the unnatural may for a time forcibly prevail, for the unnatural consists essentially in organization, and the natural cannot be organized but is simply there. It is possible, for example, to organize the undermining of children's respect for their parents, but respect for parents itself is simply practiced and cannot by its very nature be organized. For this reason the natural may be temporarily overcome by the unnatural. But in the long run every organization collapses, and the natural endures and prevails by its own inherent strength; for life itself is on the side of the natural.[29]

Here we see why magnifying the individual is important to any philosophy that tends toward the expansion of the state. Left to himself or herself, the individual naturally gravitates toward the bonds of affection, common experience, and common interests that create groups within society. The group, or groups, communicate to the person a sense of place and purpose, a complex of ideas through which to view the world, so that one might properly identify both the self and others. But if those bonds are weakened—if for instance the individual comes to suspect that the disciplines imposed by the association are fashioned merely to manipulate him and diminish his claims upon life, and if he then resorts to the more formal and alien powers of the state as his remedy, that individual, thus liberated, becomes fit material for the organizing designs of the state.

Such was never Bayle's intention. It is fair to say that it was never the intention of Enlightenment thinkers in general who sought to discover a place for "self" apart from social groups. But the lesson of history is that many of the most important developments were unintended by-products of intentions that would one day be universally acclaimed.

6

John Locke and the
Politics of Toleration

The reason why men enter into society is the preservation of their property; and the end why they choose and authorize a legislative is that there may be laws made, as guards and fences to the properties [and] . . . to limit the power and moderate the dominion of every part and member of the society.

John Locke

THE PHILOSOPHER MOST PROMINENTLY ASSOCIATED with the doctrine of toleration is John Locke, the author of the famous *Letter on Toleration*, certainly the work on this topic most likely to be included in a list of Western classics. Next to *An Essay Concerning Human Understanding*, it was his most influential work, published throughout the world and in many languages within a brief time after its anonymous publication in Latin and after its English translation and unauthorized distribution by William Popple.

Born August 29, 1632, John Locke was the son of a village lawyer at Wrington in Somerset. He spent his early years in the midst of the turbulence of civil war and the protracted struggle between those loyal to the king and the forces of a radicalized Parliament. He was a pupil at Westminster School when Charles I was executed, the school situated close enough that the pupils might easily have heard the crowd that gathered for the execution on January 30, 1649.[1] During Locke's time at Christchurch College, Oxford, Cromwell was installed as lord protector, the Quaker James Naylor entered Bristol as messiah, Ireland was invaded by parliamentary forces, Cromwell died and was succeeded by his son, and the monarchy was restored under Charles II. It is no wonder that Locke said, "I no sooner perceived myself in the world but I found myself in a storm which has lasted almost hitherto."[2] More than one student of Locke has taken note of the similarity between Locke's account of his early life and that of Hobbes (born more than a half century earlier) who declared himself "a twin of fear" cast into a world of turbulence.

Writers on Locke have sometimes remarked that he was making the argument for toleration at a time when the idea had little currency. We know by now, of course, that John Locke was endorsing a doctrine that had increasing support and that he was joined by some of the most influential voices of the age. Pierre Bayle, as a notable example, was a contemporary of Locke's. Cromwell himself favored openness and hospitality toward the Jews, and there was a movement of some strength among the nonconformists in England—among the Independents, the Congregationalists, and the Baptists—for religious freedom. These groups all prescribed limits to toleration, as Locke himself did. But we find Locke not the lone champion of an unpopular idea but the respected spokesman for an idea whose time had come, and which by now was being well received in many communities and in some of the most powerful circles in seventeenth-century England.

Soon after his time at Oxford, Locke became a medical advisor in the service of Lord Ashley, later to become the first earl of Shaftsbury, a figure of considerable stature in the political life of England. Because of Locke's position as medical advisor, he also became the attending physician to Lord Ashley during a critical illness that required the removal of an abscess from the liver. Thanks to Locke's skill, Ashley's life was saved, and Locke's place in the family was more secure than ever. As it turned out, Locke remained in their employ, later becoming the tutor to the third earl. Partly because of Shaftsbury's prominence in the founding of the Carolina colony in North America, Locke became secretary to the Lords Proprietors of the new enterprise at Charleston and exercised considerable influence on the writing of the Carolina constitution—a founding document remarkably open to religious diversity (at least by seventeenth-century standards).

Locke: Absolutist or Liberal?

Until midway through the twentieth century, Locke's reputation rested almost exclusively upon his later writings. During the intervening three centuries little attention had been given to such works as *Two Tracts on Government*, *Essay on Toleration*, and three unpublished essays entitled "Sacerdos," concerning the priesthood, "Error," on the notion of religious truth, and "A Defense of Nonconformity." All except the last of these are dated in the 1660s, while the ones on which we depend for the traditional view of Locke as the "father of Liberalism" were published in the 1680s and 1690s. These later works include *A Letter Concerning Toleration* (1689), *Two Treatises of Government* (1690), *An Essay Concerning Human Understanding* (1693), and *The Reasonableness of Christianity* (1695).

It would be natural, of course, to take these later writings as indicative of Locke's mature thought and, therefore, as more representative of who, and what sort of thinker, Locke really was. Such, as a matter of fact, is the state of conventional wisdom on the matter for most of three centuries. Readers have almost always understood Locke to be a thinker of liberal persuasion, opening the way for the new political regimes that were to come into existence in Europe and

America. In these later writings we see Locke defending the individual conscience against an established religion, defending the individual against government intrusion, and defending freedom in areas of moral and speculative opinion.

Locke's earlier writings prove something of an embarrassment to those wishing to preserve Locke's liberal reputation in an uncomplicated way. It was formerly thought Locke was innocent of the absolutist intentions of thinkers like Hobbes, but now it seems that he did very much agree with Hobbes, at least during a considerable span of his career. Was he a political absolutist who then changed his mind? It seems that the majority of Locke scholars, but not all, come to that conclusion.

Those in the majority follow the course of events in Locke's early career, taking into account the influence of the powerful earl of Shaftesbury. In 1660 the monarchy was restored under the reign of Charles II. The absolutist position would then have been well received. In 1666 Locke meets Lord Ashley, the future earl, and the next year joins Lord Ashley's household in London as personal physician. By the early 1670s, with Ashley being named earl of Shaftsbury and appointed lord chancellor, we find Locke moving in circles close to the king, and the king favoring religious toleration as a means of tempering religious conflict. In the meantime it becomes known that the King's heir, his brother James, has converted to Catholicism.

What ensues is known as the Exclusion crisis, the effort to exclude James, duke of York, from succession to the throne. Shaftsbury sides with the exclusion party and is subsequently charged with treason. He is acquitted, but in the continuing crisis, with his life in danger, flees along with his family and Locke to Holland. Shaftsbury dies in exile in 1683, and Locke remains in Holland until after James II is overthrown and William of Orange comes to the throne in 1689, after what is known as the Glorious Revolution of 1688. In the course of this crisis and exile, we find Locke moving away from the absolutist position and taking up the cause of toleration favored by

Shaftsbury and, as it happens, the new regime. If this is the explanation of the changes in posture we find in Locke's writings, then we are left with a rather tidy story of how events conspired to make of Locke the famous theorist of liberal political theory.

Robert P. Kraynak raises doubts that such a clean break with the past can actually be seen in the movement toward toleration. He gives instead a very different explanation, helping us to see Locke's thought more in terms of a development, even a natural development, than that of a reversal. I will now trace the steps of his argument, and then show how other features of Lockean thought tend to confirm Kraynak's assessment of Locke's metamorphosis.[3] Finally, I will indicate some other aspects of Locke's position that place him well within the trend we have seen taking place in the seventeenth century—the trend we have noticed coming to the surface over and over again—that of linking state sovereignty to individual rights.

First, Kraynak calls attention to what has seemed so to puzzle contemporary scholars since these early writings came to light. Especially troubling is the *Two Tracts on Government* (1660 and 1662), in which it becomes clear that Locke was an "authoritarian," rather than a "liberal" in his view of public order. These early *Tracts* were written to uphold the authority of the "supreme magistrate" over matters of religion, especially in what was known as *adiaphora*, the indifferent things (as opposed to essential and necessary things), in religion. Toleration is hardly in view in this writing, and when he raises the issue in 1667, in *An Essay on Toleration*, he clearly takes a position that is at variance with his famous *Letter Concerning Toleration*, two decades later. "That whole trust, power, and authority of the magistrate is vested in him for no other purpose but to be made use of for the good, preservation, and peace of men," he writes, in answer to the claim of some that they should have "liberty of conscience" in matters of religion.

As puzzling as this seemingly remarkable change is to contemporary scholars, Kraynak finds it remarkable that they do not consider the possibility that there is a deeper, underlying principle to which Locke is perfectly loyal: "They have not considered the possibility that absolutism is the original form of liberalism." One can, of course, accept at face value that since liberalism defends the individual from encroachments against personal freedom that it has no interest in, and in fact is antagonistic toward, the power employed by government. Kraynak believes that not to examine such a premise is naïve. If control of a political crisis is the aim of a policy, government might well benefit from a strategy that takes on the role of liberator.

Next, he examines Locke's view of the problem of social order, as reflected in his political writings both early and late. For Locke, as we have also seen in the case of Hobbes and Bayle, as well as many other thoughtful people of the seventeenth century, "religious sectarian warfare is the fundamental problem of politics." Locke concludes, from his analysis of that religious conflict, that the desire of the clerical class for power led it to prescribe certain doctrines and practices, including ceremonial ones, in order to exclude the pretensions of dissenters. The church is in a position to exclude some, include others, and in general manage society as the dispenser of salvation or damnation.

The key point is that the priests, who developed out of that simple faith taught by Jesus, took it upon themselves to teach and to regulate that which was better understood as a covenant entered into by God and the individual. Thus having insinuated itself into matters of personal religion and morality, "from the earliest days, the church used the defense of orthodoxy as a pretext for controlling the state and civil magistrate." It was, then, the assumption of Locke—and to one degree or another, the assumption of Enlightenment thinkers, especially those Leo Strauss would call of the "radical enlightenment"—that the political disorders of his time were largely attributable to the political ambitions of the various sects. It was further their assumption that this ambition stemmed from the nature of clerical institutions as they developed in history.

The Protestant reformers questioned the orthodoxy of the established church and created widespread disorder by insisting, through various sects, on establishing new bases of orthodoxy and thus securing their own power politically. At the same time, implicit in the Reformation was the freeing of the church from "priestly orthodoxy" and securing instead liberty of conscience.

The background of the Reformation and the ensuing wars clarified the problem for Locke. Orthodoxy was employed by the state to bring order, but now orthodoxy was an uncertain touchstone. Locke found that this new circumstance called for rethinking the role of the state in regard to religion. If one cannot be certain of what is right in matters of religion, and one does not wish to endure the tumultuous conflicts arising from many religious opinions, then two options present themselves. One option is "secular absolutism, in which the state establishes a religion but makes no claim it is the true religion." This was Hobbes's solution, and it became in essence the option first taken by Locke. The other option is liberal toleration. In this case, religion is no less subordinated to the state: it is relegated to the sphere of the private life and prevented from having meaningful political influence because "the disestablishment of religion deprives them [the priests] of all pretexts for interfering in politics." The change that students of Locke have noticed, and puzzled over, as they have compared the early writings to the later, is a change in strategy, as Kraynak sees it, and not a change in "purpose and principle."

Both ways that Locke adopted as he continued struggling with this problem have a common underlying conviction. It is futile, he contended, to try to establish the "true" religion. Furthermore, all warring parties in the struggle to establish what is true have some merit in their argument. For that reason, society must abandon any hopes of establishing truth through the state sponsorship of a given orthodoxy, and it must abandon the suppression of false religion. In the beginning, Locke avoided this problem by calling for the establishment of a "positive" religion, and by the end, he wants to relegate all religious questions to the non-public realm of the private conscience. The two approaches "differ, according to Locke, only as strategies in the political management of religion."

Sovereignty and the Private Realm

Kraynak's thesis raises some important questions about Locke's central purpose in arguing for toleration, questions which he goes far toward answering but which will bear further fruit. The first question is why did Locke reject the imposition of religion as an answer to the dilemma of social conflicts that are spurred on by religion?

The advantages of imposition are quite obvious. First, it settles the question of religion. Second, religion then becomes an ally to public order instead of an irritant and a threat. Kraynak observes that two models of the imposition of religion were available in Locke's England. One was Hobbes's secular absolutism in which the magistrate decides the issue of religion. Hobbes would argue that there are no distinct "indifferent" things at issue in religion, for since the central thing in both religion and the civic life is "peace," then that is the central and necessary thing for both the magistrate and the church. All other things are, beside this necessary peace, "indifferent." The other model is Hooker's idea of a christian commonwealth. Hooker insisted that the state impose the true religion for reasons that are necessary to the health of the nation, but it is nonetheless obligated to use prudence simply because it cannot dictate the beliefs of the private conscience. So, as an internal analysis of the relationship between Hobbes and Hooker, the two views are precisely opposite. But from the outside, and according to the formal structure of the two, they are quite alike. In a word, their respective arguments are opposite to one another, but the outcome looks to be quite the same. Therefore, Locke can actually combine the two, arguing as Hooker would, yet accomplishing what Hobbes had in mind. The "necessary things" of religion are reduced to a minimum, and the more they are reduced the more they approach the Hobbesian position that only peace and order is the central issue: "It is not surprising, then, that the theoretical argument which Locke uses to justify the magistrate's power are the Hobbesian ones for absolutism."

There are reasons, however, that Locke comes to the conviction that absolutism and the imposition of a positive religion will not work. It will not work principally because human beings are inclined to believe the claims of religion that they have adopted on the basis of reason and conscience. The magistrate's arbitrary imposition of religion is an affront to the human pride. In his *Essay on Toleration* we see him beginning to probe in that direction when he states that it is human nature to "preserve the liberty of that part wherein lies the dignity of man, which could be imposed on, would make him but a little different from a beast."[4]

In what Kraynak refers to as a "proto-Kantian" view of human nature, Locke avoided both Hobbes's cynicism and Aristotle's idealism with regard to human motivation. Instead, he concluded that men naturally tend to be *partial* to their own convictions because they have come to them in their own way. Further, this partiality is not to be despised, because it represents the human beings' "sense of dignity as a rational animal." It is this psychological insight that opens the door from the absolutist position of Hobbes to the tolerationist position of Bayle. Locke did not defend his findings on toleration on the basis of truth, or on the basis of justice: he defended them on the basis of pragmatism. If one aims at peace and an orderly political life, in a world where the universal claims of truth and justice are both weightier than life itself and irresolvable, then the prudent man resorts to that which is possible.

But the pragmatic option is not completely satisfying. There remains the stubborn conviction that truth and justice are worthy of sacrifice, while the pragmatic half solution is a mere postponing of the inevitable reckoning with what is finally true and what is finally just. If conscience is private and limited in its demand, while the true and just are public and universal, then the private must reconcile itself to the public, not the other way around. But, Locke saw, along this path is not ultimate peace, but unending conflict.

His solution was to define religious faith, and the truth of religion, as a truth confined to the "private and superpolitical concernment between God and a man's soul."[5] In that way, public matters might be harmonized through a broad commonality of interest. Private beliefs, on the other hand, that had proved to be impossible to resolve and so troubling to public order might be resolved in the realm of the private. Reducing, as far as possible, the legitimate realm of religion to that of the private life reduces the opportunities for conflict (at least on religious issues) in the public sphere. What is left to discuss in the public arena, therefore, is not the common good that creates society at the level of common affections and common goals, but merely the resolution of differing material interests.

The distinction is not, simply speaking, one of public and private. Religion is not reduced to the private realm, for it is public in its aim. It results in public worship and public practices. In that respect, both the church and the state have a public role in the order of the civil society. The genius of Locke is not that he strictly divided the public and private between the state and religion; the real effectiveness of his argument lies in the idea that the respective interests of the church and the state differ in their point of origin, one private and the other public. The state receives its authority from public necessity. In *A Letter Concerning Toleration* he stated it this way: "The commonwealth seems to me to be a society of men constituted only for the procuring, preserving, and advancing their own civil interests. Civil interests I call life, liberty, health, and the indolency of body; and the possession of outward things, such as money, lands, houses, furniture, and the like. . . . Now that the whole jurisdiction of the magistrate reaches only to these civil concernments; and that all civil power, right, and dominion, is bounded and confined to the only care of promoting these things."[6] The church arises from the necessities of private conscience and the soul's salvation: "A church then I take to be a voluntary society of men, joining themselves together of their own accord, in order to the public worshipping of God, in such a manner as they judge acceptable to him, and effectual to the salvation of their souls."[7] And, moreover, this is an outward manifestation of something which of necessity originates inwardly: "True and saving religion consists in the inward persuasion of the mind, without which nothing can be acceptable to God."[8]

Kraynak's thesis, as we have seen, is that Locke found in toleration a strategy that does not endanger absolutist aims of the secular government and, moreover, that this reveals Locke's more fundamental concern. Now, if we stopped at this point, as Kraynak does, we might conclude that Locke was some sort of skilled hypocrite. His appropriation of Hooker's language with its religious piety, while all the time arguing Hobbes's analysis of society and pursuing Hobbesian goals would then be a subterfuge that could hardly have been innocent. And yet the evidence of Locke's sentiment, expressed not so much in his published as in his unpublished writings, hardly supports this conclusion. What Kraynak's argument fails to do is explain Locke's frequent and effective use of the Christian faith to reinforce his strategy. Eric Voegelin completes this picture by showing how Locke's reliance on reason—that is, autonomous reason, unencumbered by the intellectual tradition of the Christian West—makes use of the authority of Christianity. That Christianity serves an instrumental purpose does not mean that, in Locke's mind, it is invalid or even that it is subordinate to reason. Instead, Locke attempts to make reason the touchstone upon which divine revelation can be tested. And this is where Voegelin's insight begins.

In the *Essay Concerning Human Understanding*, Locke refers to reason as "natural revelation" that constitutes a part of God's beneficent provision for humanity and "communicates to mankind that portion of truth which he has laid within the reach of their natural faculties." This view, as Voegelin observes, is harmless and could even be taken as a bit of Thomistic theology. But then Locke continues in a manner full of novel possibilities: "Revelation is natural reason enlarged by a new set of discoveries communicated by God immediately, which Reason vouches the truth of, by the testimony and proofs it gives that they come from God. So that he that takes away Reason to make way for Revelation, puts out the light of both, and does much the same as if he would persuade a man to put out his eyes, the better to receive the remote light of an invisible star by a telescope." Voegelin concludes from this that "Reason is made the judge of the truth of Revelation."[9] In Locke's view, reason is considered a faculty like eyesight. Some eyes are better than others, but they all function alike, and they all register the immediate sensation of light upon the lens and the optic nerve. Before Locke, "reason" described only a more or less effective relationship with a reason-producing environment that includes not just facts (like the light from a star) but an intellectual tradition and affective habits on both the personal and the social level. In Locke's view of reason as a simple faculty, Voegelin says the connection with faith that created this affective and intellectual tradition is lost, and "the experiences that give meaning to the symbols of myth and religion are lost." Thus "Reason has become an autonomous, natural faculty."[10]

This rather truncated idea of reason makes it possible to view Christianity in a new light. No longer is Christianity representative of complex experiences that illuminate the order of being, experiences that give rise to a tradition of thought, feeling, and practice that develop into ever more complex and powerful forms, giving rise in turn to social life and institutions heretofore impossible. Instead, Christianity is composed merely of those events and words that comprise the "facts" of its beginning. For Locke, it is an attempt to restore the "legitimate nucleus" of Christianity. For Voegelin, however, it explains why Locke considers seventeen centuries of cultural development expendable without regard for any of its intrinsic value and without any effort to make critical judgments of any part of it. And it explains why Locke considered it possible to start over again with primitive history. By this method, "when Locke approaches Christianity he makes a tabula rasa of Western history." It compares with his attempt in the *Essay Concerning Human Understanding*, in which he had "swept aside all earlier metaphysical efforts and started philosophizing from scratch."[11]

Complexity or Confusion?

There is no doubt that Locke had a profound influence on the founding of late seventeenth- and eighteenth-century political institutions in Britain and America, and upon philosophy and political theory throughout the West. The originality of what Locke, along with Hobbes previously, had created—a matter of lasting influence—was underscored by Francis Fukuyama in a striking passage from *The End of History and the Last Man*:

> Contemporary liberal democracies did not emerge out of the shadowy mists of tradition. Like communist societies, they were deliberately created by human beings at a definite point in time, on the basis of a certain theoretical understanding of man and of the appropriate political institutions that should govern human society. While liberal democracy cannot trace its theoretical origins to a single author like Karl Marx, it does claim to be based on specific rational principles whose rich intellectual ancestry we can readily trace. The principles underlying American democracy, codified in the Declaration of Independence and the Constitution, were based on the writings of Jefferson, Madison, Hamilton, and the other American Founding Fathers, who in turn derived many of their ideas from the English liberal tradition of Thomas Hobbes and John Locke. If we are to uncover the self-understanding of the world's oldest liberal democracy— a self-understanding that has been adopted by many democratic societies outside North America—we need to look back to the political writings of Hobbes and Locke.[12]

It is generally thought that Locke's reliance on natural or autonomous reason was eclipsed in the nineteenth and twentieth centuries by varying styles of philosophical and cultural Romanticism. There is a sense in which secular autonomy leads inevitably to flights of romanticism and an exaggerated reliance on human potential such as one finds in Emerson. Who can imagine, for instance, *anyone* before the Enlightenment, with its insistence that "everyone should think for himself," saying what Emerson did in *Self Reliance*: "Society everywhere is in conspiracy against the manhood of every one of its members. Society is a joint-stock company, in which members agree, for the better securing of his bread to each shareholder, to surrender the liberty and culture of the eater. . . . Self reliance is its aversion. . . He who would gather immortal palms must not be hindered by the name of goodness, but must explore if it be goodness. Nothing is at last sacred but the integrity of your own mind."[13] There are still places in the world where this sort of sentiment would be laughed off the stage; nonetheless, it marks an unfailing characteristic of modernity with its stubborn individualism—an individualism that denies that men and women are everywhere embedded in society in a way that is altogether distinct from citizenship. So Locke is undoubtedly still with us, if not in the everyday philosophical expression, at least in our institutions and in our sense of the nature of community life.

Yet the issue of Locke's apparent contradictions and inconsistencies prevent us from gaining much confidence in the integrity of his system. It seems, on the one hand, egalitarian and, on the other, paternalistic; here it is liberal, there it regulates; it is either Protestant Christian or Socinian; either slyly sectarian or secular; either remarkably open to private choice or determined in its anti-Catholicism. What are we to make of these shifts and contrasting faces of Lockean political thought? Now that the world has before it the full range of Locke's writings, especially his political writings, students of Locke have interpreted his work in one of four ways:

1. From the 1660s to the late 1680s, Locke changed his mind, moving from an advocate of intervention by a Sovereign and a more or less authoritarian regime, to an advocate for government by consent, religious freedom, and equality of private rights.

2. Locke's true agenda is to be found in certain emphases which were consistent throughout his career, and the changes represent strategic repositioning for the sake of achieving those fundamental goals. Thus, Leo Strauss, taking a position similar to that of Kraynak's, contends that Locke is really a Hobbesian in both his view of human nature, with its consistent egoistic motivation, and in his political authoritarianism. Wilmoore Kendall found in Locke's "majority rule principle" the trick by which authoritarian rule is transferred from the monarch to the consenting people without risking the loss of governmental regulation and the private freedoms Locke asserted could be brought into harmony with civic order.

3. Locke's system is complex, some insist, and must not be reduced to "nothing but"—"nothing but the protection of bourgeois property," "nothing but Hobbesian authoritarianism more pleasingly put forward," and so on. The virtue of Locke's thought lies in its hold upon a reality that inevitably embraces contradictions because the needs and desires of the individual are fundamentally in tension with the needs of the community. Charles Monson Jr. maintains that "Locke's theory is so complex that writers can assert a variety of principles as basic—and with sufficient ingenuity find justification for their interpretations."[14] Defending what he calls the "traditional interpretation" of Locke as the classic of liberalism, Monson holds that "one does not need to be particularly astute to discover inconsistencies, for when statements originating from different basic concepts are laid side by side, incompatibilities become evident. Locke's theory requires both obedience to the state and the right to revolt: consent v. freedom. He relies upon majority rule, yet affirms the inalienability of an individual's consent: equality v. consent. It is no wonder,

then, that some writers have concluded that Locke is 'a blundering incompetent' or 'a man whose problem exceeds his powers.'"

4. Eric Voegelin may well exemplify the object of Monson's complaint against those who see Locke as "a man whose problem exceeds
his powers." Voegelin detects a deep-seated philosophical confusion
in Locke's approach. For Locke, "the implications of the new meaning of Reason are obvious, and the further course of disintegration
that will flow from it is inexorable. The title of Reason from now on
covers a highly explosive combination of elements. The principle
ones are the following: (1) the historically accidental body of
civilizational values that emerges from the century of the Puritan
Revolution and Newtonian physics, (2) the apparatus of critical
method in philology and history as well in the experiment and logic
of science, and (3) an act of faith that erects these values and methods into absolutes."[15]

Locke recognizes the breakdown of the sources of civil order and
the loss of spiritual authority. He is "in search of an authority for what
he considers the doctrine of Christianity [in *The Reasonableness of
Christianity*] precisely because the institutional organization of this
authority is gone."[16] But what happens in the course of his attempt
to restore Christian authority is that "he decides that Christianity is
identical with what he personally thinks and can understand." Thus
a solution is found: "the church must back with the authority of Christ
the reason of Locke."[17] In comparing this with an earlier era in which
civilizational crisis is faced in Hellenic society, Voegelin refers back
to his treatment of Plato's ideas which had lifted discourse to a new
level in Hellenic civilization. Then he says, "But Locke is no Plato."
Such a philosophical feat was "not within the range of his personality."[18]

Locke follows a primitivistic impulse; that is, when the sources
of thought about social order fail, or become too weak to exert a
shaping influence on society, the temptation is to reach back to an
earlier time to regain one's orientation. In the more secularized en-

vironment of the seventeenth century, the most readily available source of spiritual guidance was no longer the living mystery of Christian existence illumined by the evangelical logos, but simply the Bible, raw and uninterpreted. Voegelin saw this as inadequate to the task of restoring a Christian community that was now seventeen centuries beyond its primitive beginnings.

Even apart from his understandable efforts to restore some measure of authority, Locke has habits of thought that undermine the task he has taken on, says Voegelin. "A study of Locke as a thinker would have to explore the vast shadowy field of half thought that surrounds the rather small nucleus that in itself is not too clear. His mode of philosophizing was characterized by a good deal of whim. Spurts of irritation by contemporary evils would push his thought in a direction he would not have moved, could he have seen the end of the road." Men such as Locke "who have the happy gift can indulge in irresponsible *boutades* of thought, can produce considerable havoc and misery, and can nevertheless sincerely protest that their intentions have been misunderstood when the mischievousness of their indulgence is held up to them." So Voegelin's summary judgment was that "He had neither the strength of the mystic who would make the mysteries luminous by reenacting the religious experiences they symbolize, nor the courage of the philosopher who would let himself be carried wherever his thought led."[19]

Locke's Bipolar Disorder

There is yet another possibility. It emerges in the light of Locke's weak analysis of society: his failure to take account of the full range of realities that make up the concrete existence of any society of any size. It is a failure that was especially tempting in a time of the rise of the nation-states and the bourgeois desire to relate to that entity as individual stock holders in a joint-stock company, without the complications brought on by other, and less formal, social groupings. This failure of perception does not, of course, reflect the real life of men and women, where both biological and social necessities exert their unremitting powers, and where there is the constant creation of the tender bonds of family, friendship, collegial relations, and families of faith. The failure occurs instead at the level of conscious reflection upon the nature and shape of public life. Myths do not have to reflect reality in order to have their effect upon life; that is why the pre-Christian Greeks discovered the necessity to subject myth to a test of critical judgment, thus freeing themselves from the influence of the myth.

In modern times it is perfectly possible to think that social life takes place primarily between the two great poles of the individual and the state, and that all else is merely exterior to those primary realities. Yet that does not make it so. Nevertheless, the vision of a bipolar existence exerts its influence and has exerted its influence considerably since the seventeenth century. It is no good complaining that no adequate theory of society leaves out the obvious connections that almost every one of us take to be the most important in life and that press upon us with more weight than any other: our family, our faith, our friends, and our colleagues. These groups are real and weighty, but they are simply not a part of the architectonic vision of modern society, one that we think suspends itself between two solid piers, the state and the self.

The inconsistencies that plague students of Locke seem to lie neither in his own inadequacies (Voegelin) nor in a hidden agenda (Kraynak and Strauss). Instead, the constant difficulty that Locke encounters lies in the fact that he attempts to describe a world that does not exist, a world that forms itself around two contrary poles, that of the state and that of the individual. It is a bipolar vision of society, fatally simplified because it neglects the social reality that lies about us on every hand: a world of multilayered associations, most of which are not organized and formal, as is the relation between citizen and state, but which are spontaneous, organic, ever changing, and evolving, calling upon spiritual energies that are deeper than citizenship can ever hope to imitate.

In Locke's *Second Treatise of Civil Government*, his principal work of political theory, he writes consistently as if the relationship between the *individual* and the *commonwealth* were the only relationships that mattered so far as political theory and policy are concerned. He takes note of smaller associations, but only as they figure into the evolution of this grand arrangement between the individual and the state. He writes, for instance, on the "beginning of political societies":

> Thus whether a family by degrees grew up into a commonwealth, and the fatherly authority being continued on to the elder son, every one in his turn growing up under it, tacitly submitted to it; and the easiness and equality of it not offending any one, every one acquiesced, till time seemed to have confirmed it, and settled a right of succession by prescription; or whether several families, or the descendants of several families, whom chance, neighborhood, or business brought together, uniting into a society, the need of a general, whose conduct might defend them against their enemies in war ... made the first beginners of commonwealths generally put the rule into one man's hands.[20]

Nonetheless, Locke fails to consider seriously that men and women are only to be found in society and in associations that can hardly be described as governmental in nature. They are, instead, according to him, "by nature all free, equal, and independent." Association, with its authority, its laws, its taboos, and its mutual obligations and attractions, count for nothing in calculating the shape and the authority structure of a given society. Though some are based in biological necessity (families) and others in locality or consanguinity, or common tasks, the association Locke focuses on is subject to the will of those in contract. Society, in this view, is not based upon accidents of birth or providential circumstances that are *given*, instead (if one can believe the myth) the association to which we *really* belong is one we have *chosen*. For the association that counts is made up of freely assenting individuals who make up the commonwealth. To say that they are "free, equal, and independent" is to say that "no one can be put out of their estate, and subjected to the political power of another, without his own consent."[21] The creation of the community is altogether seen as a transaction between individuals (one might justifiably say "property owning individuals") and the state. This is quite different from Althusius who, as we have seen, considered the commonwealth a complex community of interlocking associations, governmental as well as non-governmental, formal as well as informal, given as well as chosen. For Locke, "that which *makes* the community, and brings men out of the loose state of nature into one politic society, is the agreement which every one has with the rest to incorporate and act as one body, and so be one distinct commonwealth."[22]

How could Locke respond to the idea of federated associations such as we find in Althusius? In this earlier model of the commonwealth, which had its influence well into the modern era, including the federal system of states in America, Althusius conceived of all associations (not just individuals) as contributing to the nature and shape of the larger commonwealth. The theory did not leave aside the family, or the professional association, or the church. For Locke, however, it is clear that "federation" occurs only in the contract made among individuals and between the individual and the state, or between sovereign governments. When he distinguishes the legislative, executive, and federative powers of the commonwealth, he means by "federative" the power to act on behalf of the body politic in foreign relations. "So that," he writes, "under this consideration the whole community is one body in the state of nature in respect of all other states or persons out of its community."[23] It is easily apparent that what Althusius meant and what Locke meant by federation were quite different. For one, political bodies of all sizes and types constitute the commonwealth; some of them—the church, for instance, or the family—might well transcend the commonwealth. For the other, only the organized state acts as a political body. The notion of community in this latter view, Locke's view, is simpler: it takes into its vision only citizens of a state. It fails to consider that the role of citizen barely touches the surface of a person's deepest and most significant relationships. One is more likely, for instance, to change citizenship from one country to another than to be dissociated from one's family or one's faith. For the emerging liberal idea of citizenship, however, even the family seems to have no other reason for being except to produce and raise to maturity individuals who then become (by their freely assenting will) citizens of the state.[24]

The Political Theology of John Locke

The vision of society that John Locke has articulated (and which Francis Fukuyama says Locke has, along with others, invented) hinges, interestingly enough, on a theological point. It has to do with his treatment of revelation, as a source of the social order, over against the newly emerging idea of Reason.[25] Emphasis upon reason did not begin, of course, with the seventeenth century. Beginning in the twelfth century, with Anselm, and extending throughout the Scholastic period of church history, reason and its power to order experience was quite central to the development of Western society. But throughout, the prevailing note was that given by St. Anselm: *fides quarens intellectum*, faith in search of understanding. First, reason relied upon that which was revealed. Second, but important, it relied upon that which was known through the senses. Third, reason operated upon a foundation of tradition: that arduous development of thought that had extended humanity's grasp of those things known by revelation and through the senses. Reason thus involves dialogue, with revealed knowledge, with sensed reality, and with the accumulated experience and wisdom of generations.

What was different about the Enlightenment sense of reason? When we use the term "autonomous reason" to describe the modern era's peculiar idea of the rational process, we do not imply, of course, that they calculated that reason starts from nothing and operates on its own. Reason is a secondary activity: it must have something furnished to the mind first, then reason responds to what is given. In that sense, the Enlightenment view of reason, which is to say the modern view of reason, is no different from that of the medieval Schoolmen or from that of the ancients. What is different is both *what* is furnished to the mind and *how* one comes by it—the nature and source of the raw material to which reason reacts. For medieval Christian thought, the "given" consists of the three things—revelation, sense experience, and tradition—that connect the human being to the world. These relate the thinking human being to what is present (experience), what is past (tradition) and what is the meaning of things, or one could say the eschatological aim of things.

As matters developed in the Enlightenment era, the material to which reason responds is one of two things. For Descartes and his followers, the firm ground of reason began with an awareness of the distinction between the self and the world; and this awareness begins with the narrow point of self-awareness: "I think, therefore I am." All else can be doubted, but the world will be reconstructed rationally from this meager point of reference. That was the approach of the Rationalists.

The Empiricists (notably, but not all, from Britain) resembled, in their approach, the Aristotelian. They assumed all knowledge enters the mind through the senses. There is no innate knowledge (Locke), and we are capable of calculations based upon efficient cause and material cause alone, not formal cause or final cause (Hobbes). This is hardly an adequate explanation of either rationalism or empiricism, but it is enough to suggest what these two have in common and what distinguished both of them from earlier philosophies.

What distinguishes the earlier and the later philosophies is also what distinguishes the modern period from all preceding history. The Cartesian philosophy and the Lockean, as examples, depended fundamentally upon that experience which is available to all human beings everywhere. Everyone thinks, and with that they experience the same as Descartes. Everyone absorbs the data of their senses, just as Hobbes and Locke do. Not everyone becomes a philosopher, of course, but theoretically the fundaments of philosophy are available to everyone on the same terms.

Earlier philosophies, to one extent or another, depend upon experiences that are *not* available to everyone, which are in fact available to very few. For Plato, only a few become philosophers and upon them the rest are dependent for understanding the right order of the soul and of the city. Aristotle was not so hierarchical in his outlook as Plato, but by the sixteenth century Aristotelian thought had become so authoritative that the effect was a dependence upon a single philosopher, even though he had been interpreted by a cadre of Muslim, Jewish, and Christian scholars. Besides this, from the beginning of Christianity's broad influence upon Western culture, revelation began to be a decisive factor in shaping philosophy. Revelation is nothing other than the idea that truths important enough to determine the ordering of the soul and the culture become known to us through the rare experiences of a very few members of society over a long period of time. It is a tradition, or a custom, of the most refined and rare type. But the implication is clear: because of these few and these rare, the rest of us come closer to understanding the purpose, the nature, and the shape of life. What this earlier view of philosophy, including that influenced by revealed theology, brings to us is the notion that the many depend upon the few. Philosophy and its benefits is understood in terms of community. In Christian thought the same effect is reflected in the Pauline doctrine of the *charismata*, gifts acquired by a few for the benefit of the many.

The modern empiricists and rationalists did not find their basis in the contribution of the few over a period of time but in the universally accessible experience of thinking and sensing. Philosophy, on this model, does not theoretically depend upon community, for every person has access to the very things that makes any person a philosopher. Of course, no one expects everyone to be a philosopher; but perhaps the more salient point is that, for the modern person, the notion came into vogue that for any philosophy to have legitimacy it must only be *founded* on that which is the experience of all. Locke's *Essay on Human Understanding* is introduced by Locke as taking up an issue of interest to a group of gentlemen of his acquaintance—not philosophers, nor specialists of a theoretical sort, but simply men of the world and of general acquaintance with ideas. This stands in marked contrast to the ancient and medieval philosopher who was free to call upon sources that simply *could not* be verified by just anyone.

Leo Strauss emphasized that the medieval Enlightenment (by which he meant the time of the revival of Aristotelian philosophy from Avicenna to Maimonides to Aquinas, and which he uses as a term of contrast with the *modern* Enlightenment) was marked by its esoteric nature, which is to say a few philosophers would suffice for any community, just as would a few physicians and a few lawyers and a few master builders. Vocations that actually *contribute* to the life of a community are practiced by the few for the benefit of the many. But "the modern Enlightenment was essentially *exoteric.*" We must take note of the fact that "the modern Enlightenment, as opposed to the medieval, generally publicizes its teachings."[26]

Let us attempt to parse the difference between these two visions of philosophy and of community life. In the first place, the earlier idea of philosophy presupposes and builds upon the existence of community. For the later view, community might be the topic of philosophy, but one hardly understands the community as dependent upon the philosopher, nor the philosopher as servant of the community.

Each person is *theoretically* his or her own philosopher. Society is an indiscriminate mass as far as much of modern thought is concerned. It is not a community articulated into a body with interdependent members, a community which in fact benefits from the very distinct and varied *charismata*, but a group of individuals equally endowed (if not with talent and wit) at least with the access to the raw stuff by which the community understands itself.

The modern vision, as one can easily see, is one that tends toward an unarticulated citizenship. And that is the same as saying that people are no longer so bothered by those "tender bonds" which Tennessee Williams once thought so inimical to self-realization. Especially as regards those matters of refined thought and sentiment upon which the order of a society depends, it is, so to speak, "every man for himself." Kant's dictum, "Have the courage to think for yourself," frees men and women from the ordering and restraining power of custom, tradition, and transcendent law. It also frees them from each other.

Locke's toleration plays a part in giving birth to an unarticulated society, a mass society. Toleration in its modern form is the solvent that dissolves the bonds of interdependency. It therefore makes society fit for the "new" ordering and regulating powers of the state. Locke, as Voegelin admits, knew that the old sources of social order had evaporated and England was in need of principles of peace fitted for new times. Early he detected the problematic role played by religion, but also its essential role; and at that time the answer was authoritarian rule. Later, he thought that if religion were given its proper role in shaping the individual for citizenship, and government its proper role in shaping the life of the commonwealth, without one intermixing with the other, then all would be well. Issues of the soul's salvation would not interfere with the pursuit of public order (or common "wealth") and government would not (except in the case of Catholics and atheists, neither of whom could be trusted) interfere with that progress of the soul.

And for a while, we must say, Locke's new principles appeared to work: America seemed to benefit by them. Maurice Cranston observes that "Locke's foreign admirers who visited England soon after his death—people such as Montesquieu and Voltaire—were impressed by everything they saw—the freedom, the toleration, the good sense; they found us uniquely 'a nation of philosophers'." "We do not hear such compliments today," he continues. Of course, now we (on both sides of the Atlantic) have the considerable inconvenience (in truth, a powerful advantage) of speaking from the perspective of a thoroughly secularized public order and thoroughly individualized (which perhaps is to say "isolated") modern souls.

To learn where we have begun to drift off course is not to regret the entire journey. Distance, nevertheless, gives us perspective. Now we might see, and fully appreciate, the long-term consequences of a society in which individuals come to think of themselves as free of every bond and every obligation except that of the state. Locke's generation could not have appreciated where the trend would finally lead us. Nor could the Americans of Hamilton's generation, nor the Germans of Bismarck's. They still lived, at that time, off the potent residue of a fully articulate culture, one in which the rich associations that make up a people and impose their peculiar disciplines were still doing their work of giving a cohesive shape and texture to a nation's life. They had not yet been weakened by the egoistic strains of individualism or by the overbearing power of a Leviathan acting through courts and legislature and executive to politicize the whole of life.

7

The Triumph of Toleration

W HAT HENRY KAMEN WRITES close to the end of his book *The Rise of Toleration* is, in a very fundamental sense, quite true, though not entirely:

> By the middle of the seventeenth century the greatest exponents of toleration had had their say. W. K. Jordan claims with justice that "the theory of religious toleration stood substantially complete in 1660." The liberal Calvinists in Holland, the Latitudinarians in England, the colonial pioneers in America, had together formulated a set of principles which were not appreciably enlarged upon in the second half of the century. The fact that only a minority of people actively supported toleration, and that the principles drawn up by religious leaders were seldom put into full effect by politicians, as of minor consequence. Governments and governing classes are invariably behind the times in their political philosophy, and it was enough for the moment that in the West as a whole the most prominent theorists were in favor of toleration.[1]

The trajectory of toleration was still to be worked out, and its story far from completed. The ship had been launched, but it was not yet on the high seas, and by the end of the seventeenth century there was still no way to guess whether the theory would even be seaworthy. There were in fact some important changes, or one might better say developments, that would take place by the middle of the nineteenth century. And the real test of the formulations of Locke and Bayle, especially as these regarded not only religious liberty but moral diversity, would come in the twentieth century.

Good judgment in political theory—as well as in the theologies and philosophies that nourish it—I take to be a matter of following trajectories to their likely end. When critical faculties of a culture operate in a healthy manner, its philosophers and its theologians (its fundamental critics) are always adjusting the vision of that culture, pushing and coaxing it in a direction that keeps it from steering against the rocks. It is no wonder that Pierre Bayle was more impressed with the dangers of state-sponsored religious orthodoxy than he was that of unbridled individualism, or that Thomas Hobbes and John Locke felt more the need to avoid sectarian strife than either an aggressive state or an impotent church. The cost of religious bigotry had been enormous in their world, even as it has been well rehearsed in ours. And the liberating of individuals from an oppressive state of affairs that bred conflict on every hand was certainly an appropriate task for the social theorists of that day. Nor has that day ever left us. They perhaps cannot be blamed for not predicting what fury the privatizing of religion and morality would unleash upon the world, or how ineffectual would be a later nominally Christian culture against the new moral challenge of quasi-religious ideologies in the twentieth century. It is for us to view the trajectory and assess its eventual outcome. And to do that we must take our place, as we have begun to do, alongside the "founders"—with John Locke in particular—and mark where their theories of sovereign states and sovereign individuals have taken us.

An Evolving Dogma

I have made the argument that what emerges as "toleration" in modern times, especially since the early part of the seventeenth century, is a modern doctrine. As a doctrine, it is a teaching that has gained a certain place in the social communication of values, and it calls for a certain practice of civil attitudes and restraints, but it is not the practice itself. The *practice* of toleration, or of what we would now call toleration, is distinguished by the fact that it reflects an older view of social existence. In this chapter, I wish to make that distinction as clear as possible by following the evolution of the doctrine from Locke down to the twentieth century.

I believe it is possible to see the Western idea of tolerance—especially religious toleration—as affected by the successive rise and fall of two contrasting sentiments rooted in very old and stubborn ideas about the human condition. On the one hand, the classical idea of decorum and the Christian idea of grace imply limits to human powers—limits in the face of which a person is persuaded that nature must be disciplined or supported from the outside. On the other hand, there is the contrary sentiment that neither nature nor supernature poses barriers to the human spirit. The ancients would recognize this latter disposition in a variety of Gnostic speculative schemes. The modern romantic would share this disposition. The romantic spirit is one that looks forward to progress and expects good things from the uninhibited unfolding and full expression of human nature.

It would be a mistake to think of the former of these sentiments as pessimistic and the other as optimistic. The Christian or the Aristotelian can be perfectly optimistic, in fact wildly optimistic, about the general situation of the world and its ultimate course and yet still admit that men and women have their absolute limits, whether in knowledge, power, or imagination. Aristotle, for instance, held that human happiness and human excellence coincided, so that to pursue the good is also to pursue that which makes one happy. So also did Christians believe in this divinely ordained coincidence that makes virtue both possible and profitable in terms of ultimate human destiny. One can hardly argue that this is a pessimistic view of life, for while holding to human limits, it is nevertheless breathtakingly optimistic. Thus, men and women are called to observe those limits (the classical disposition) or to call for help from the outside (the Christian disposition) as the way toward human excellence and happiness. The characteristic virtue of such a disposition is humility, and its opposite is hubris (among the Greeks) and pride (among the Christians).

And it should not be surprising that those who think most about power and progress—the Hegelians, the Nietszcheans, the transcendentalists, and the romantic pantheists of various sorts—often start with an optimistic view of man that is swallowed up in a pessimistic view of the world. The heroism comes to take the form, in its most apocalyptic visions, of some type of Götterdammerung. Michael Bakunin (1814-1876), for instance, a Russian anarchist of extraordinary talent and intelligence, saw the key to a better life in a total rejection of everything the culture had to offer, including its moral order. In the throes of Europe's mid–nineteenth-century revolutionary fervor, Bakunin thought the true democratic revolution required "a total reversal of the state of the world."[2] The nineteenth- and twentieth-century calls for revolution often could hardly be distinguished from calls for self-immolation, sometimes based upon the superstition that out of the utter ruin of the old world would come the new order. As Louis Aragon put it:

> The blue eyes of revolution
> Shine with a necessary cruelty.[3]

The distinction between an older vision of life that gave rise to a practice of toleration and the newer vision that helps to formulate a *doctrine* of toleration can naturally be detected, if we do our investigation skillfully, in the use of language to describe toleration at or near the beginning of the modern era. That sounds complicated, but in fact it should not be at all. It is a matter, as I see it, of listening closely to one of the major figures that we associate with the early idea of toleration and comparing him with one who came along after the process of state building had further shaped social life. Ideally, these two figures would be from the same country, so that we would be comparing two distinct points on the line of political development. And ideally, these would be far enough apart—at least a century—so we might detect whether their differences in language were merely accidental or, in fact, revealing of a process over a period of time.

What I would expect to find is that, first, the idea of religious toleration at the beginning of the modern period, reflected in the American Constitution, for instance, and in constitutional principles of European nations, while openly confident in the competence of the human conscience, was still largely anchored in a Christian vision of human experience that can only be fully understood as encounter with the divine. Second, I would then not be surprised to find how, using the same word "toleration," a parallel vision of humanity has been projected into discussions of community life. It is one that attaches itself to some of the early features of the dogma, yet has succeeded in divesting itself of the kinds of restraint that were still obligatory in the seventeenth century. And third, I would expect to find that the later concept of toleration replaces the former one. In this exercise, we would find that there are actually in use two very distinct meanings of the one word "toleration." And the difference is that the doctrine of toleration has eclipsed the earlier, more naïve, sense in which the term was used.

Two figures, John Locke (1632-1704) and John Stuart Mill (1806-1873)—two Englishmen separated by more than a century, both of whom are prominent in the development of the idea of toleration—are just what the investigation calls for. Are these two champions of toleration indeed speaking the same language when they defend toleration? If there are significant changes in what they mean, and if the shadow of an earlier tradition still falls upon the earlier writer, then we cannot help but conclude that subtle but very definite changes have taken place in the idea of toleration. Further, they help us to understand how one word with the appearance of bearing a linguistic and philosophical tradition can come to mean two very different things. The term as it is used in the era of Locke is found in Mill's time almost freed of its earlier inhibitions and, like Icarus, winging its way to the sun. Not only does it alter its definition, but the differences in these concepts portend very different ideas of public life and very different approaches to public policy. A third philosopher—this time an American, John Dewey (1859-1952)—shows the further progress along a road that after Mill is clearly distinguished from the earlier sentiment with its definite Christian context.

Lockean Toleration

We have seen that the idea of religious toleration did not begin with John Locke, though he is often credited with the articulation of that public policy as it came to assume a certain form in the modern West, and especially in North America. By the time Locke wrote his famous *Letter Concerning Toleration*, the notion that religious toleration should replace sectarian conflict in Britain was already widely accepted. Yet, in the seventeenth century, there was reason for a new sense of urgency for reasons that we have already explored: the specter of sectarian war, regicide, exile, tyranny, and the steady suspicion that there would never be any end to all this. The Glorious Revolution of 1688 brought to an end yet another dangerous period in the political events of England brought on by a struggle over sectarian differences. And now there were new lands to be settled across the Atlantic and hence new policies to be considered for a new world and a new start. Locke himself had already, since the 1660s, been caught up in colonizing prospects, serving as secretary for the Lords Proprietors of the new colony of Carolina. Though the extent of his influence is debated, it is undoubted that he had a major impact upon the framing of the constitution of the new settlement on the North American shores. We see his hand especially in the formulating of policies of religious toleration. In this constitution, *The Fundamental Constitutions of Carolina*, dated 21 July 1669, we find one hundred and eleven items or paragraphs. Of those, fifteen (86-100) deal with religion. The beginning and the end of that section of the document illustrate for us both Locke's commitment to toleration and his sense of its limits. By this we see that Locke is indeed a man of the modern era, in that he is open to toleration, but that he still builds upon an older vision of the political order. That he still maintains something of that traditional vision is seen in the first provision of that section (89): "No man shall be permitted to be a freeman of Carolina, or to have any estate or habitation within it, that does not acknowledge a God, and that God is publicly and solumnly to be worshipped." And like a matching bookend, the last item in that section reads: "No person whatsoever shall disturb, molest, or persecute another for his speculative opinions in religion or his way of worship."[4] When we examine his habits in speaking of religious toleration, Locke paved the way for thinking in distinctively modern ways. But at the same time, we find him not fully forgetful of the earlier sentiment that makes the religious expression of a given society indispensable to its existence.

In the last chapter we attended to those features of Locke's thought that were taken up in the trends of modern thought—his Enlightenment side. But he also maintained a traditional and more or less orthodox side. Whether that revealed more practical prudence or genuine conviction has often been discussed; but few find evidence that he was *not* a genuine believer and a sincere member of the church—even if in the last fifteen years of his life he was theologically a Socinian.[5] His retention of those older habits of thought that were the basis of a substantially Christian vision of society is evident more in the rhetoric he feels compelled to use, at times, than it is in the main flow of his thought.

We begin with some central elements in his argument for toleration. For Locke, there is "absolutely no such thing under the Gospel as a Christian commonwealth."[6] The matters which the Gospel intends to influence are beyond the reach of the coercive powers of the state. Not only is Locke considered by many to be "the most influential philosopher of modern times,"[7] but he is the author of the most influential single document on the theory of toleration, the *Letter Concerning Toleration*, which was published in 1689. In this famous "letter" he puts forth three arguments against the idea of governments attempting to govern matters of faith.

First, the "care of souls is not committed to the civil magistrate, any more than to other men."[8] It is not committed to him by God, nor can it be committed by the consent of the people, because no one "can so far abandon the care of his own salvation as blindly to leave the choice to any other, whether prince or subject, to prescribe to him what faith or worship he shall embrace."

In an age—our own—tutored under the traditions of liberal democracies, the statement seems little more than common sense. Yet behind this statement is a very lively debate about the nature of society. Is it to be seen on the order of a family, with the king having responsibilities analogous to a father's? Or is society built upon contracts freely (although perhaps tacitly) entered upon by individuals. The first concept places more responsibility upon those of rank and office in a commonwealth to oversee the religious welfare of their people and their subjects. Those with hereditary title are likely to be strengthened by such a view. The second concept is more harmonious with the ambitions of the rising bourgeois population, with their positions and powers based upon individual accomplishment and material acquisition. One view is clearly more corporate in nature, and the other is clearly more individual in its focus. Thus, we see that

Locke's views were harmonious with the liberal tendency of his age. He argued, for instance, against the patriarchal view of government that was implicit in the idea of the divine right of kings. For Locke, the modern state could no longer be viewed on the model of a family with its implied heirarchy and its responsibility for the full range of needs experienced by the individual. At the same time, he disagreed with the authoritarian vision of the modern state that was found in Hobbes's *Leviathan*.[9] Nevertheless, he still has little in common with the romanticism of later spokesmen for toleration such as Rousseau; and he retains much of the Augustinian respect for a soul made in the image of God.[10] So the individualism which his view expresses has more in it of a sense of the sacred bonds of the human soul than the secular autonomy of the individual such as one would find in writers of the radical Enlightenment.

Second, he argues, " the care of souls cannot belong to the civil magistrate, because his power consists only in outward force; but true and saving religion consists in the inward persuasion of the mind, without which nothing can be acceptable to God." The magistrate can impose penalties to enforce law, but "penalties are no way capable to produce . . . belief."[11] So it is the ineffectiveness of the magistrate in producing belief that, for Locke, argues for toleration. As the first point rests on the inviolability of the human soul and its competency in matters of religion, so the second point apparently argues from the importance of producing "true and saving religion" in the individual.

Finally, given the "variety and contradictions of opinions in religion," and the fact that governments are divided in these matters as much as in secular matters, salvation would then not answer to the faith of believers but to the chance that one's own government is right—and that, by the same token, other governments are wrong. In a word, salvation would come as an accident of birth.

One can quickly note the principal features of Lockean toleration. First, toleration stands as a restraint against the misguided use of force. It admits the ludicrousness of a forced religious faith: "A sweet religion, indeed," he says, "that obliges man to dissemble and talk lies, both to God and man, for the salvation of their souls."[12] Second, it is thereby a defense against persecution—a matter that is decisive in distinguishing Locke's variety of toleration. Third, toleration serves the interest of truth, a truth only apprehended by reason, assisted by revelation, and attained by faith. Fourth, toleration is made necessary by the frailty and inadequacy of human reason, clouded and rendered unreliable by sin.[13] Fifth, toleration is as an expression of humility.

It has been argued, and I think reasonably, that Locke's concept of toleration is grounded in a "late medieval nominalist repudiation of the Platonic and Aristotelian epistemology of the chain of being."[14] The result of this epistemological change is that a sense of cosmic order, which is articulated in a hierarchy of civil and religious authorities, to which an individual gives fealty, is also modified. Social arrangements instead reflect the inviolability of conscience and the moral responsibility of the people. The result is a contractarian theory of political order that was not unlike that of Hobbes, was to be expanded by Rousseau and Kant, and has had a major influence in Western thought and political practice. Yet even with contractarianism's nominalist tendency, it had not altogether abandoned a sense of universal truth. Therefore, the individual responds to a truth which is only dimly perceived and imperfectly grasped but which lies, nevertheless, beyond and outside the individual. Tolerance arises, then, from the tentativeness and imperfection of human reason, from the incompetence of the state to choose for the individual, and from the ultimate responsibility laid on the individual because of conscience. But it does *not* arise from an optimism regarding human society or institutions, nor from a sense of the unfolding competence of individual choices.

Tolerance, in this case, acts fundamentally as a *restraint* upon the power, hubris, and the imagined moral competence of the state, or of society, as it exerts authority through any number of authoritative associations. As Bertrand de Jouvenel reminds us, *every* group possesses a certain system of authority. Yet Locke also maintains that tolerance itself must be restrained. Without law, imposed by the State, there is no liberty worthy of human life; instead "wherever law ends, tyranny begins."[15] For this reason Locke concludes that toleration could not be extended to atheists. The very existence of society and a civil order requires adherence to oaths, bonds, covenants, and these presuppose a belief in a God who holds men and women accountable. Therefore these promises that form the very mortar of civil life "can have no hold upon an atheist."[16]

The fact that the Lockean idea of religious toleration exercised a primary influence upon constitutional traditions in the United States need not be rehearsed here. With some important modifications—Jefferson and Madison wanted to extend toleration to Catholics and atheists—the argument of Jefferson for the Virginia article on religious toleration was largely commentary on Lockean principles.

As I have suggested already, Locke introduced what his world took to be new ideas but using an old rhetoric. Here, I have underlined the features of Locke's thought that will help us to understand the subsequent evolution of toleration. In the nineteenth century, a very different idea of toleration was projected upon this view introduced to us by Locke. This later view actually constitutes in a way a development of the idea of Locke; but the change is so profound that we would also have to say that it constitutes a new definition. The newer use of "toleration," in fact, becomes the dominant definition in the modern West. And though it grows out of the older use of the term, it actually comes to eclipse the earlier understanding. The result is important. The operative language of toleration embraces a concept that acts not as restraint against moral presumption but actually becomes the engine for social conformity.

Mill and the Utilitarian Virtue of Toleration

The further development of the doctrine of toleration is most expansively articulated by John Stuart Mill. The primary text of his doctrine is the essay *On Liberty*. The influence of this book on European and North American ideas of tolerance is difficult to exaggerate. Ruth Borchard recalled that Mill himself considered this his great work, "likely to survive longer than anything else that I have written": "It was translated into nearly all living languages, read by men of all nations, colours, creeds. It is still one of the great torches of Western civilization. It was forbidden, burned by totalitarian regimes of all kinds, read secretly, reprinted, brought out triumphantly upon the downfall of a tyranny—*On Liberty* lives on as Mill had foreseen."[17]

John Stuart Mill was most influenced by his father, James Mill, who sought to educate his son by the most stringent and thorough methods. Devoid of popular superstitions, Mill would be reared a nonbeliever and free thinker. Through his father, he was under the influence of Benthamite utilitarianism until he broke with it in his youth. This episode of youthful rebellion was justified by the younger Mill on this basis: one could not, he argued, appreciate the complexities of reality from the extended application of a single idea. His early criticism was similar to that of Hume who saw a single focus, elaborated to explain the world, as the very mark of a false philosophy. It is a very great irony that Mill later formulated *On Liberty* according to a principle "every bit as single-minded and simplistic as Bentham's."[18] He recognized the power of a single, simplified formula to sweep aside the complexities of social conventions and institutions and to mark the way toward reform. Mill himself referred to *On Liberty* as "a kind of philosophic text-book of a single truth."[19] Gertrude Himmelfarb points out how remarkable is his conversion from a Macauley-like critique of single-mindedness to the bare-bones simplicity of his famous 1859 essay: "The key words bear out the single-mindedness of the doctrine: 'one,' 'sole,' 'only,' 'absolute.' The entire argument hinges upon them; they appear in almost every sentence. There is 'one' principle, the 'sole' end, the 'only' purpose, and the 'only' part of conduct'; the principle governs 'absolutely,' and the independence of the individual is 'absolute.'"[20]

In one paragraph of the introduction to *On Liberty*, Mill states his thesis, using all of these single-focused expressions:

> The object of this Essay is to assert one very simple principle, as entitled to govern absolutely the dealings of society with the individual in the way of compulsion and control, whether the means used be physical force in the form of legal penalties, or the moral coercion of public opinion. That principle is, that the sole end for which mankind are warranted, individually or collectively, in interfering with the liberty of action of any of their number, is self-protection. That the only purpose for which power can be rightfully exercised over any member of a civilised community, against his will, is to prevent harm to others. His own good, either physical or moral, is not a sufficient warrant. He cannot rightfully be compelled to do or forbear because it will be better for him to do so, because it will will make him happier, because, in the opinions of others, to do so would be wise, or even right. These are good reasons for remonstrating with him, or reasoning with him, or persuading him, or entreating him, but not for compelling him, or visiting him with any evil in case he do otherwise. To justify that, the conduct from which it is desired to deter him must be calculated to produce evil to some one else. The only part of the conduct of any one, for which he is amenable to society, is that which concerns others. In the part which merely concerns himself, his independence, is of right, absolute. Over himself, over his own body and mind, the individual is sovereign.

In many important ways, Mill's idea of toleration appears to be—and in fact is—a continuation of the Lockean tradition. The empiricist confidence in reason is still present. The inviolability of private moral conscience in matters of private concern appears to be an extension of Locke's thesis that matters hinging on belief and conscientious private choice (that is, religion) cannot be effected by collective coercion. Locke was concerned with the wasteful and destructive conflicts arising from antagonistic religious opinion; so was Mill. Locke argued, "If any man err from the right way, it is his own misfortune, not injury to thee."[21] Mill wrote, "The only part of the conduct of anyone, for which he is answerable to society, is that which concerns others." Differences emerge, however, when we draw out two distinct aspects of Mill's concept of toleration.

First, while Locke addresses the impracticability of coercion in matters that he judges to be inherently private, he does not so much argue that this, in itself, is a positive good; it simply will not work. Mill speaks of the religious wars for mostly rhetorical purposes, while the conflicts were actually a danger to life and limb in the time of Locke. Mill, instead, speaks for the positive benefit of individual liberty. Locke had in mind measures against the disruption of order; Mill had in mind the fuller enrichment of society through the unpredictable inventiveness and imaginativeness of individuals. For Locke, the idea of protecting the individual's rights is prophylactic; for Mill, it is generative. Some argued at the time that Mill's concern for protecting individual eccentricity was hardly a timely warning. Macauley said that Mill "is really crying 'Fire' in Noah's flood." How can one bother about threats against individuality in an era of "phrenology, clairvoyance, spirit-rapping, Comtism" and the like.[22]

Mill argues for "the fullest liberty of professing and discussing, as a matter of ethical conviction, any doctrine, however immoral it may be considered."[23] Society benefits from originality, energy, free choice, the unpredictable variety of individual preferences. Custom and convention are necessary, but they also endanger and stifle the creative energies of human ingenuity and experimentation. "He who lets the world or his own portion of it, choose his plan of life for him, has no need of any other faculty than the ape-like one of imitation."[24]

He contrasts this view of variety and energy, experimentation and choice, to the Calvinist emphasis upon obedience and its warning against the sin of "self-will."[25] Whatever other exception might be taken to the Calvinist vision of life, we should take note that Mill's critique mainly serves to set him at odds with a view of life in which human experience constitutes an encounter with the divine. Calvinism belongs to that species of theology in which life is understood as dialogue—real living is, in Martin Buber's words, in meeting.[26] Or to use the language of Gerhart Niemeyer and others, life is understood as a participation in reality, a participation that is informed by a sense of the sacred. All of these expressions underscore the over-against-ness of humanity, the dialectical give and take of communion with a world that is *other* than self. Relationship—or to use the Johannine touchstone, love—is at the heart of this vision of life.

Mill's contempt for the Calvinists, then, accurately reflects that his understanding of human experience is almost the precise opposite of one described with words such as "encounter," "dialogue," "meeting," "relationship," and perhaps even "love." For Mill, reality is continually unfolding, a development inherent in the potentials of persons. He finds agreeable the formulation of Wilhelm von Humboldt, whom he quotes in a epigraph to the essay: "The grand, leading principle, towards which every argument unfolded in these pages directly converges, is the absolute and essential importance of human development in its richest diversity."[27]

It is worth considering why Mill has so little sympathy with injunctions against self-will, why he seems to see little danger in presumption and much to be avoided from the "Calvinistic theory" with its "narrow theory of life" producing the "pinched and hidebound type of character."[28] Custom and restraint are indeed necessary for the sake of "character," that is, giving shape and direction to these forces of development. But the better part is force, not restraint. "'Pagan self-assertion' is one of the elements of human worth as well as 'Christian self-denial,'" he writes. "It may be better to be a John Knox than an Alcibiades, but it is better to be a Pericles than either."[29]

The genius of society lies in individuality. While society dreads and attempts to suppress the "wild" and "erratic"—those who "break these fetters" and become an object of scorn for those who would reduce them to commonplace, "much as if one should complain of the Niagara river for not flowing smoothly between its banks like a Dutch canal"—its progress nevertheless depends upon it. "Individuality," Mill writes, "is the same thing with development."[30]

The other aspect of Mill's thought that helps us distinguish his view of toleration from Locke's has to do with his appeal to truth as the aim of toleration. Herbert Marcuse has reduced Mill's thesis to the following formula: "The *telos* of tolerance is truth."[31] But what is this truth toward which the liberated energies of individuality are addressed?

Immediately we are caught short by his use of the word truth. It seems that individuality, even to the point of eccentricity, is to be restrained by no fetters whatever so long as no harm is inflicted on others, and so long as it respects the distinction between the private and public realm. Now it would seem that toleration and individual liberty is subservient to something, and that something is "truth."

Others have questioned whether this is not a major fissure in Mills alleged pursuit of a single truth.[32] I will not add to what has already been said by others. But we are moved closer to an understanding of his specific use of the expression, "pursuit of a single truth," when we know that it serves a higher purpose; it is instrumental in the pursuit of truth and, therefore, has a utilitarian role. It is powerful, as he often describes it. But power, tied to some purpose, makes it a virtue within the canons of that system of ethics. Libertarian toleration is a strategy, a pragmatic virtue—and we cannot fully discern its nature unless we discover the constellation of values it serves. We undertake next to clarify that constellation of values and that "truth" which is the *telos* of a utilitarian idea of toleration.

Progress, Persecution, and Toleration

At this point I want to hold in view, though since it seems to be a matter of growing awareness I should not have to explain it at length, the idea of a powerful modern myth: the myth of progress. Christopher Lasch's *True and Only Heaven* is a compendium of the evidences, and implications, of a social phenomenon that is no longer in doubt. Earlier contributors to this understanding include Eric Voegelin and Gerhardt Niemeyer.

What should impress us is that the idea of progress works upon us as a myth—not precisely as a dogma or a doctrine that must be consciously inculcated in society, but as an experience of life out of which we unconsciously live. The idea of expressly comparing "one's own age with former ages," said Mill, had become only in his own century an inescapable mental habit.[33]

It is not difficult to see why this metaphor of progress has been so powerfully persuasive since Mill's time. The rapidly growing powers of science and technology have, beyond doubt, made the deepest impression upon our sense of history as well as our notion of how we relate to nature. The movement of society from one technological marvel to the next has been rapid and overwhelming in its social impact. True, it does not encompass all of life: it has not noticeably carried with it any elevation of the arts, manners, or morals. A case might be made that it has brought about their rapid decline in some areas. Nevertheless, the impression of inexorable movement forward pervades everything; it rules especially our language about society and history.

I wanted simply to touch upon this well-known modern emerging self-awareness before we ask once more what "truth" it is that Mill's tolerance will serve. For what we will find, in contrast to Locke, is decided emphasis upon a process: "It is proper to state that I forego any advantage which could be derived to any argument from the idea of abstract right, as a thing independent of utility. I regard utility as the ultimate appeal on all ethical questions; but it must be utility in the largest sense, grounded on the permanent interest of man as a progressive being."[34]

Note the disparagement of "abstraction," the grounding of ethics in utility, and the defining of humanity as "progressive being." All of these seem far removed from the Lockean sense of the human responsibility before eternal truth (necessarily an abstraction), a responsibility of such high order that it cannot be settled on the basis of society's interest (that is, it responds to things of value in themselves, *not* to utilitarian interests) and therefore calls for restraint and humility (not overbearing optimism about human capacities). Seen in this light, there is no question that what Mill means by "toleration" has taken on characteristics foreign to Locke's principle. It has not altered, but has added to, the earlier impulse.

Mill's idea of toleration—in addition to its being a development of Locke's doctrine—attaches itself to another aspect of Enlightenment thought: this very myth of historical progress. In a manner of speaking, of course, there is no use arguing with a myth. It is not simply an explanation of life; it is the way we experience life—it is the point of departure for any explanation we might make. For Mill, development is not a matter of question, it is the point of departure. He argues, for instance, against a stifling adherence to custom by saying that for human beings to conform to custom "does not educate or develop in him any of the qualities which are the distinctive endowment of a human being."[35] Even Christianity is judged worthy to the extent that it once lay along the path of progress, but now one must beware of its retrograde possibilities: "For I believe that other ethics than any which can be evolved from exclusively Christian sources, must exist side by side with Christian ethics to produce the moral regeneration of mankind . . . . the interests of truth require a diversity of opinion."[36]

To draw out the distinction between these two ideas of tolerance, then, we might say:

1. Locke's toleration is essentially a negative thing—a check against the overzealous ambitions of society in an area where coercion plays no constructive part. Mill's toleration is essentially optimistic: it is the unfolding of possibilities in an incomplete world, moving toward some greater advance in the human lot.

2. Locke's toleration restrains human ambition in areas where values are transcendent (that is, they lie beyond utilitarian calculations of the magistrate). Mill's toleration becomes the strategy or the pragmatic virtue necessary to progress.

3. Locke's toleration still communicates a certain view of life as an encounter with the divine. Mill's toleration communicates a world of immanent potentiality.

4. Locke's view restrains sin; Mill's view restrains restraint. Locke fears the seduction of power that says "We would be as gods." Mill, on the other hand, weighs the importance of the human role in self-creation. "Among the works of man," he says, "which human life is rightly employed in perfecting and beautifying, the first in importance surely is man himself."[37]

Finally, we must note that toleration is about persecution. The phenomenon of persecution has been illuminated in recent years by René Girard's study of the historic accounts of persecutors and of myths based on collective murder. Among the phenomena that have consistently attended persecution has been the circumstance of a crisis characterized by loss of distinction. Society at peace articulates its values and its sense of reality through manners, morals, customs, traditions, and an almost intuitive sense of the interrelationships of persons within that society. Crisis is occasioned by the loss of this ability to articulate the distinctive actions of sacred and secular, of father and child, of men and women, of leaders and the led. Violence becomes random and senseless. "Every man does what is right in his own eyes."[38] The reaction attempts to recreate order, often by attacking the most obvious sign of disorder. As a means of reasserting order in the midst of a devastating and overwhelming social crisis, society selects its victim. The victim might be, and often is, innocent. But it nevertheless bears the signs of the disorder that plagues society. He says a great deal more about the role of violence in the establishment of order. I will not follow that lead here except to point out when we are speaking of coercion and tolerance, we are also speaking at some level about the threat of violence and the restraint of violence.

We must remember this when we think about progress, because progress as an organizing, or reordering principle, takes on the character of the crisis itself. The idea of progress—and our feeling for it—is borrowed, of course, from the Christian and Jewish sense of eschatological hope. But progress is incapable of communicating the same idea of an order of being because it does not correspond to a transcendent reality (or a promise), but it means the development of immanent possibilities—the principle virtue attributed to toleration since John Stuart Mill. At the same time, in the real world, relationships and covenants that do exist (and reflect a sense of order) are thrown into doubt because they have become subject to progress. They lose their reality, their value, because they will be outdated. When progress becomes its own goal, flux replaces logos and the crisis is complete.

Now, let me view an intellectual descendent of Mill's ideal, one who is closer to us and therefore makes us more aware of the presence of this view on our own time. The figure I have in mind is John Dewey, and along with him his disciples among American pragmatists. Dewey's is a system where growth or development has become the ordering principle—the proposed principle for articulating society's "truth," or its "values." The term "progress" by Dewey's time is studiously avoided and can only come back into the discussion where the text is carefully decoded to reveal the underlying myth.

Note, for instance, John Dewey's concept of the "goals" of society: "Not health as an end fixed once for all, but the needed improvement in health—a continual process—is the end and good . . . . Not perfection as a final goal, but the ever-enduring process of perfecting, maturing, refining is the aim of living . . . . Growth itself is the only moral 'end.'"[39]

Dewey does not mention, here, that the very idea of "growth," "maturing," "refining" and especially "perfecting" implies a before and an after, a lesser and a greater; it implies gradations and therefore implies a standard or goal. So, to say that "growth itself is the only moral aim" is only to say that the aim remains unannounced. Therefore, the second implication is that, apart from a stated aim, the only other possible standard is the power or impact of the action itself. It means, in the language of political action, that might makes right. For the judgement of a right action or a proper action can only be decided on the level of force, power and effect.

Only at this stage do we see that development as the basis of toleration invites, not toleration at all, but persecution. It becomes apparent that although the subject of an action may be obscured—there is in fact a subject. And if by the "success" or the pragmatic value of an action we mean that it serves the benefits that it intends, then we have only to ask the question: Whose interest? And if the answer is "Why, the commonweal!" or "the people," or "the whole of nature," we must still ask, within a pragmatic vision of the world, who precisely has decided what is best for the world. And we are necessarily given the answer "Whoever has the values that prevail!" In short, the whole issue is ultimately decided on the basis of a power struggle and the contest of wills.

Discomforting things begin to happen for the pragmatist, however, once questions like "whose practical interests?" are raised. In a puppet show the puppeteer must remain hidden if the show is to be at all convincing. Just so, pragmatists speak often in the passive voice. A pragmatist such as John Herman Randall defends his view against a "dualistic" interpretation of reality (one that espouses "heaven," "the supernatural," "God," "revelation") by saying that: "In contrast to this confusion of metaphysics and practice [moral law and ethical action], empirical naturalism insists that metaphysics is the account of what experience finds in nature [whose experience is not specified], and that practical philosophy is the account of what experience finds [the same lapse] to be good or sought for, to be bad and avoided ["sought for" and "avoided" by whom?].[40] Like the puppeteer, the subject of any action remains carefully concealed. And as for the purpose of the action—the goal, the *telos*—it appears when the show is over. Until that time, one could almost believe that the show *was* the purpose.

To continue in this analogy, the more spectacular the production the less we are likely to ask what Bertrand de Jouvenel asked when he posed the question: "Every year we can do more and more ... but what on earth shall we do?" Yet only when we ask that question will we reclaim tolerance as restraint against the presumption of power, and reject that tolerance that is only a clever new disguise for persecution and a new language for social conformity.[41]

8

The Shadow Leviathan

> *Compared with worship of the State, zoolatry*
> *is rational and dignified. A bull or a crocodile*
> *may not have great intrinsic value, but it has*
> *some, for it is a conscious being. The State has*
> *none.*
>
> —Dean William Ralph Inge

TOLERATION IS ABOUT *TELOS*. Otherwise, it has no meaning at all.

In speaking of *telos*, the idea of an end, a goal, or a purpose, we are tempted to use classical expression or normative Christian expression. Modern language about *telos*—that is, language that denies the objectivity and realism of moral purpose—must be practiced. For instance, I received a message from a colleague alleging that "*our* universe," by which he meant the universe that exists in the mind of Western university professors, "is orderly and has limits." It therefore causes us to adopt a certain set of moral values that others do not share. Now it does not easily come into peoples' minds, I contend, that when we are talking about the *universe*, that is, everything there is, that such a thing exists primarily in someone's mind, except as a kind of reflection. And it wouldn't immediately come into someone's thinking that the universe of a Taiwanese fisherman is any different from that of a Harvard professor, since after all we are talking about everything that exists including teachers and fishermen, Westerners and Easterners. I am not pretending that the issue is an easy one to address; but what I insist on is that to say the universe exists *primarily* outside our minds is more natural. That's why the modern way of talking about moral purpose takes practice, because it doesn't come to us naturally: it is not self-evident. Instead, it is the product of a culture; it has been cultivated and made habitual among us. So we use it especially when the subject of our moral discussions are not very important to us. We can urge someone to *clarify* their own values, whatever that means.

But when moral issues strike us as urgent, or when they regard our intimate life of the home, when they flare up before us as something dangerous and imminent, then we likely fall back on classical language about what is right or wrong. The point of reference becomes very "fixed" and stable and not at all subject to relative social needs. But when the emergency is over, people in our times tend to lapse back into the cultivated speech of modern moral discourse. It is a dangerous way to live. And we live in dangerous times.

What I am about to present briefly is not an especially modern view of moral theory, but we still understand it. In outline, it goes like this:

That for which human beings contend, when the stakes are highest, are those matters regarding the end or the goal of human existence. There can be more than one goal, of course, depending upon the nature of that for which we attempt to state the goal. In that I am a human being, I have a *telos*, a purpose, in common with all other human beings. It is a part of what it *means* to be human, in fact the determining part. In that I am a teacher, my occupation commits me to a goal that is common to teachers, but not to all human beings. In that *we* are a family, we share an end with other families, but these are distinct from the goals of an individual—distinct, but not unrelated to those goals. In that we are a community, a church, a trade association, or a political party, we have goals that are distinct from the individual and the family. And we may carry these goals all at the same time: my purpose in life attends the fact that I have several distinct roles. I am a husband, a father, a grandfather, a colleague, a citizen of Texas, an American, a Baptist, and a Christian. How can we be loyal to all those ends at once?

The ends do not all have the same weight because some are more inclusive and essential than others. Some have to do with temporary roles, others with roles I cannot divest myself of. Some I have in common with a few others, and others I have by virtue of the fact that I am a human being living in a created order. Some goals end in time and at least one is eternal. We therefore think of them as having a certain weighted order—a hierarchy. We may never arrive at a conclusive statement that expresses it adequately, but we can at least talk about the issue of a summum bonum—an all-inclusive good. And we necessarily do so—whether deliberately and consciously or not—because this guides us in our actions. We sense that time is not wasted when we do so. It serves us well in emergencies—and life itself is a kind of emergency, though we do not like to think of it that way.

The classical view of ethics and the normative view of Christian ethics presuppose the idea of the Good when making judgments about how to act. There is a necessary relationship between the idea of a "good," an ultimate or even a proximate goal, and the appropriateness of behavior.

The Rejection of Purpose

What has happened in modern thought, however, is that we have attempted to do without the notion of a goal as a point of reference,[1] what Aristotle would call a "final cause." In this study we have seen that, from Hobbes to Dewey, the idea of a final cause faded away. The world is explained by material causes (that out of which something is made) and efficient causes (that by which something is made), but not final cause (that for the sake of which something is made). Ever since Hobbes, the idea of *final* cause as indeed a *cause* has been doubted, or at least neglected.

This same idea is often articulated in terms of "motion." The biblical idea of "rest" contains within it the assumption that the motion of people and things and events anticipates a time of "rest," that is, a time in which their motion is complete. It is a way of conceptualizing that things and people have a purpose. Augustine's famous line about his own restless life in his *Confessions* reflected this strong biblical sentiment: "We were made for Thee, O God, and our hearts are restless until they find rest in Thee." This sort of metaphor makes sense in a world that believes things exist, that they are "set in motion," for a purpose. In that world, the language of purposefulness, moral responsibility, and moral choice comes naturally.

Recall, however, Hobbes's elation with the idea he had gained from his encounter with Galileo. The natural state of things is not "rest" but "motion"—all things are in motion, and this, not rest, marks the nature of the world and all things and people in it. This concept, as Hobbes realized, had profound political implications. If *rest* is not the natural state of things, and motion is, then there are no given purposes toward which the world or we move. The nature of things is not *given* and *discoverable*, or it is not something the true nature of which must be *revealed* to us, as every representative of Western culture from Aristotle to Thomas Aquinas assumed, but it is subject always to change. And if subject to change, it is malleable; and if malleable, then the world is essentially unstable. In that case, any order that exists does so either accidentally or because of the action of human beings upon things. Order is a product of the human will or it is projected upon things by the imagination. It is something we make or imagine but not something we find and participate in. As Thomas Spragens put it in his *The Politics of Motion*, a book on the thought of Thomas Hobbes, "A world of 'restless' motion which has no *telos* contained restless men who had no *summum bonum*."[2]

The characteristic feature of modern thought is this change in orientation. Hobbes's "discovery" that all things are in motion and that there is no such thing as a state of "rest" toward which all things move is almost laughable in its apparent naïveté. One wonders if Hobbes is faking an inability to comprehend subtlety, or if he is resorting purposefully to a kind of primitive adoption of literal language. In either event, he takes the metaphor of "rest" as a description of physical destiny. But the seriousness of his modern change of orientation is nevertheless real. If things have purpose—that is, they come to rest, have a destiny—then human beings have a theoretical task before them: they must come to *understand* in order to *act*. But if things have no inherent purpose, and there is no "givenness," and no meaning in using the term "good" besides what we voluntarily ascribe to it, then our attempts to understand might be considered as tactics in the strategy of coping with the world, but the essential thing is not to understand but to act. And this is what is characteristic of modernity: the shift from the intellect (as a means of understanding the world) to the will (as a means of changing the world).

Such a shift in intellectual commitment is not confined to the modern era, but it is repeated so frequently and attested to so regularly that we are right in ascribing to it a modern "feel." It always means the same thing, or nearly so. The late medieval triumph of nominalism over realism was just such a shift. To give up the task of understanding universals (held to be real by the realists) and to assert that universals or categories are what they are because we *name* them as such is really to say that the intellect is subject to the will. Close to the end of the period we call the Enlightenment, Kant summarized the meaning of enlightenment in an essay, "What is Enlightenment?" "Enlightenment is man's leaving his self-caused immaturity," he wrote. But what sort of immaturity? It was not lack of intelligence, but lack of will: "Immaturity is the incapacity to use one's intelligence without the guidance of another. Such immaturity is self-caused if it is not caused by lack of intelligence, but by lack of *determination* and *courage* to use one's intelligence without being guided by another. *Sapere Aude!* Have the courage to use your own intelligence! Is therefore the motto of the enlightenment."[3] The emphasis upon "determination" and "courage" are mine; it is clear that Kant is not placing his own emphasis upon the intellect, but upon those virtues associated with the will—the virtues of determination and courage. One might be prevented by lack of intelligence; but one is more likely to be prevented by failure of the will to no longer rely upon the thinking of others—that which is embedded in tradition, custom, the recognition of expertise. Therefore, Kant raises the call *Sapere Aude!*

Moving considerably forward, when we find Karl Marx laying aside the theoretical task of founding philosophy on economics, he says so explicitly: "The philosophers have only *interpreted* the world in their various ways; the point, however, is to *change* it."[4] This is Marx's famous "Eleventh Thesis on Feuerbach." Thus, for Marx, reality is neither an expression of a continuing existence, nor one of the emergence of history, but it is that which is projected upon the future by acting and willing human beings in the present. It is, in effect, manufactured out of the urges, the dreams, and the desires of the present. Naturally this has a profound effect on moral judgment which, as Gerhart Niemeyer wrote, "hinges [for Marx] not on a genuine discernment of actions and motives concrete that run counter to the good, but rather on Marx's inability or unwillingness to find in actual existence any kind of essential reality and his willful and fanciful construction of a reality apart from experience or memory."[5] The change is not always apparent in Marx, but it is consistent. While we inevitably, habitually, and naturally anticipate language that places discernment before action, the logic of this shift from intellect to will is that we place action and the will to action in a position prior to intellect. The world which we intend to discern is, to some degree, a world of our own making. We fall comfortably into the habit of speaking of possible realities rather than real possibilities.

John Stuart Mill gives witness to this same shift at every turn. In his book *Utilitarianism* (1863), he notes that "from the dawn of philosophy, the question concerning the *summum bonum*, or, what is the same thing, concerning the foundation of morality, has been accounted the main problem of speculative thought, has occupied the most gifted intellectuals, and divided them into sects and schools, carrying on a vigorous warfare against one another."[6] And after so many and long efforts, no resolution has come except when thinkers resort to the principle of utilitarianism.

And what is this "principle of utility"? For Mill, the answer defines the foundation of moral discourse:

> The creed which accepts as the foundation of morals *utility*, or the *greatest happiness principle*, holds that actions are right in proportion as they tend to promote happiness, wrong as they tend to produce the reverse of happiness. By 'happiness' is intended pleasure, and the absence of pain; by 'unhappiness,' pain, and the privation of pleasure. To give a clear view of the moral standard set up by the theory, much more requires to be said; and to what extent this is left an open question. But these supplementary explanations do not affect the theory of life on which this theory of morality is grounded—namely, that pleasure, and freedom from pain, are the only things desirable as ends; and that all desirable things (which are as numerous in the utilitarian as in any other scheme) are desirable either for the pleasure inherent in themselves, or as means to the promotion of pleasure and the prevention of pain.[7]

Mill is careful to say that when moral discourse finds its basis in happiness or pleasure, that does not commit the speaker to the lowest and most physical form of pleasure. Mill's critics would compare him to the Epicureans. He responded by defending the Epicureans as not quite what people often take them to have been. "To suppose that life," he writes, "has . . . no higher end than pleasure—no better and nobler object of desire and pursuit—they designate as utterly mean and groveling; as a doctrine worthy only of swine, to whom the followers of Epicurus were, at a very early period contemptuously likened; and modern holders of the doctrine are occasionally made the subject of equally polite comparisons by its German, French, and English assailants."[8] But it is not the Epicureans, he insists, that "represent human nature in a degrading light," but their critics. Human beings are not happy with a beast's life, and it is to that higher and nobler happiness that a human being aspires. The difference for the utilitarian is that they would not normally refer to the so-called "nobler" pleasures. Instead they think of the "higher pleasures"—such as the intellectual—as serving them better in terms of "circumstantial advantages rather than in their intrinsic nature."[9]

To say that something is right because of its contribution to pleasure or happiness, and wrong in that it detracts from pleasure and happiness would indeed place Mill in league with the Epicureans. But he distinguishes himself as a *modern* thinker, as one fallen under the spell of Enlightenment habits of mind, when he carefully defines that "greatest happiness principle" as subject to utilitarian purposes and *not* to some intrinsic value.

Mill hits an obstacle when it becomes apparent that, by the principle of utility, an act is right or wrong not in a general sense but only as regards its circumstance. When circumstances change, the ethic changes. Human beings, his critics say, are convinced something is right or just on the basis of a transcendent reality, not the shifting circumstances that allow an action to contribute to more happiness and pleasure. Furthermore, what it means to say that there is nothing "right" in a general sense is that fundamentally the intellect has no role to play in *guiding* the ethical process. It has a role to play in responding to circumstances, but there is no stable guidance it can give, when the purpose of moral action is to respond to the needs of the moment. In this case the intellect is led by the will—an unfailing mark, as we have seen, of the modern impulse.

Mill's reply seems continually to evade this essential point of conflict between himself and his detractors. Instead, he tends to comfort himself and reassure his readers with the fact that a transcendent point of reference does not always make a difference:

> The sanction, so far as it is disinterested, is always in the mind itself; and the notion therefore of the transcendental moralists must be that this sanction will not exist *in* the mind unless it is believed to have its root out of the mind; and that if a person is able to say to himself, "This which is restraining me, and which is called my conscience, is only a feeling in my own mind," he may possibly draw the conclusion that when the feeling ceases the obligation ceases, and that if he find the feeling inconvenient, he may disregard it, and endeavor to get rid of it. But is the danger confined to the utilitarian morality? Does the belief that moral obligation has its seat outside the mind make the feeling of it too strong to be got rid of? The fact is so far otherwise, that all moralists admit and lament the ease with which, in the generality of minds, conscience can be silenced or stifled. The question, "Need I obey my conscience?" is quite as often put to themselves by persons who never heard of the principle of utility, as by its adherents.[10]

Friedrich Nietzsche (1844-1900) likewise admits to the importance of meaning for human life—and at the same time the impossibility of its objective reality apart from human invention. Nietzsche would use stronger words than Mill, but he, like Mill, sees the necessity of goals drawing upon the human community's most creative resources. Because there is this initial necessity, and the feeling of that necessity, Nietzsche recognizes that human beings suffer and they seek to provide that for which they suffer the loss. But it was only those human beings with the highest awareness of this absence who give to life through their creative urges its meaning and purpose.

"Until the advent of the ascetic ideal, man, the animal *man*, had no meaning at all on this earth."[11] This desire for meaning explains both the human being's will to life *and* his will to death. Either life or death offer a purpose to which the will can be directed. And "man would sooner have the void for his purpose than be void of purpose."[12] What is this "ascetic ideal"? It is the accomplishment of *something* where there is *nothing*. It arises from the human being's "*horror vacui*," for which reason "*he needs a goal*"[13] But for Nietzsche that goal can only be created by the creative human being. His ideal is missing; it renders him ascetic, and it is the will, not the intellect initially, that comes to the rescue.

John Dewey saw clearly what was happening to moral philosophy in terms of the classical understanding of "ends" or "goals" of moral conduct. In *Nature and Experience* he wrote that in the Greek theory of value, things are intelligible because their true nature resided in objects that were their ends. Things that are continually changing, and have no final form, are not capable of being known; the idea of an end marks their limit, and allows them to be known and for human beings to say what is their nature. "The whole scheme of cosmic change was a vehicle for attaining ends possessed of properties which caused them to be objects of attraction of all lesser things, rendering the latter uneasy and restless until they attained the end-object which constitutes their real nature."[14] To *know* the nature of something is thus to know its end; and to know its end is to understand its action in history. Therefore, moral judgments can be made for the actions of human beings on the basis of the belief that we can know their highest end and the true good of their nature.

Dewey thought that the scientific revolution of the seventeenth century brought such a belief in these "occult" objects to an end: "Essences and forms were attacked as occult; 'final causes' were either wholly denied or relegated to a divine realm too high for human knowledge."[15] He exaggerates his case somewhat, although the tendency he detects is accurate. He covers himself by saying further on that "If ends were recognized at all, it was only under the caption of design, and design was defined as conscious aim rather than as objective order and architechtonic form."[16] Of course, the problem with that partial retraction is that that is all it ever was—and he seems to have temporarily forgotten that the mechanistic and impersonal view of the world came *with* the so-called scientific revolution and not before it.

Nonetheless, Dewey recognizes this loss of ends as a problem for moral philosophy. On what basis can one decide what is right, what is beneficial, what is demeaning, what is noble, and what is not? He sees the answer in an intermediate category of "goals" that emerge out of the conditions and opportunities of the time. These are not final and ultimate ends, but they are "ends-in-view." They are possible consequences that occur within given circumstances and become the objects of thought and serve for a time as guides in the moral process. They are distinguished from ends as they are used in classical thought in two ways: "They are not objects of contemplative possession and use, but are intellectual and regulative means, degenerating into reminiscences or dreams unless they are employed as plans within the state of affairs. And when they are attained, the objects which they inform are conclusions and fulfillments; *only* as these objects are the consequence of prior reflection, deliberate choice and directed effort are they fulfillments, conclusions, completions, perfections." Clearly the end-in-view is not a given thing, but an artifice. For, "a natural end which occurs without the intervention of human art is a terminus, a de facto boundary, but it is not entitled to any such honorific status of completions and realizations as classic metaphysics assigned them."[17] And just as clearly, Dewey follows the course which we cannot but think is inevitable. Once the possibility of purposeful action is abandoned—not just the possibility of *knowing* with any degree of precision, but the confidence that there are purposes whether or not we know them, and that they properly belong to the realm of the intellect and not to the realm of the will—then it becomes inevitable that the will rushes in to fill the vacuum.

Among late–twentieth-century thinkers, Michel Foucault clearly exemplifies the trend we have seen from Hobbes to the present. Only what we find in Foucault is that he adopts and clarifies the logic of the trend itself. Stanley Grenz has referred to him as "Nietzsche's truest disciple," which he undoubtedly appears to be since he makes explicit the meaningless of a life without the intervention of a will to power. For him, truth is not that which lies within the order of things, but that which acts upon things bringing the order which reflects the power that truth serves: "'Truth' is to be understood as a system of ordered procedures for the production, regulation, distribution, circulation and operation of statements. 'Truth' is linked in a circular relation with systems of power which produce and sustain it, and to effects of power which it induces and extend it. A 'regime' of truth."[18]

Unity and Power

In every case where there is a loss of confidence in the giveness of a *telos* in life, we find a corresponding need to make up for that loss. This is the same thing as the shift from the intellect to the will that we find taking place generally in modern thought. For Hobbes the absence of a final cause to which men and women might refer argues for the need of one whose own will becomes the authority that sets things in order. For Locke, the recognition that sense data cannot supply a governing purpose in life, and that therefore the human intellect is incapable of recognizing any such thing, means that one must now depend upon revelation. He thinks of this individually, not collectively or communally. To perform such a function, therefore, Scripture must be so basic in its teaching that every man and woman might interpret it by his or her own lights. For Mill, the principle of utility allows people to ascertain what *telos* might profitably serve their present circumstance. And for Nietzsche, the *telos* grows out of a basic will to power and in itself is a useful invention that serves the interests of that same will to power. The void left by the loss of meaning must be filled by the heroic use of imagination as an instrument of the will to power.

For Dewey, the end-in-view serves an instrumental purpose that makes sense within the context of a given state of growth in society. Recognizing that religious practice and discourse is the connection in which this *telos* is communicated, Dewey seeks to find its pragmatic substitute. "All religions," he writes in *A Common Faith*, "marked by elevated ideal quality, have dwelt upon the power of religion to introduce perspective into the piecemeal and shifting episodes of existence." He admits the function and its necessity, but not religion as its necessary source: "Here too we need to reverse the ordinary statement and say that whatever introduces genuine perspective is religious, not that religion is something that introduces it." This condition naturally arose from an awareness of forces beyond our control, which cause us to fear. Thus, "as the old saying goes, fear created the gods."[19]

One cannot miss how clearly this line of thought traces from the Enlightenment with its rebellion against a given order and the representation of that order in social institutions. Fear arises from being subject to powers beyond our control. Hence we ally ourselves with those unseen powers. But now is the time of emancipation from those old fears, for now mankind has come into possession of new powers and the shackles of his world's "necessary order" can be thrown off with the rise of a new humanity, a humanity with possession of its own faculties. The shift is complete. No longer dependent upon the task of "knowing" in order to rightly "act," one is now free to "act" and "make" and thus "possess" one's own world, one's own life. Dewey inevitably describes this shift, in *A Common Faith*: "With increase of mechanisms of control, the element of fear has, relatively speaking, subsided. Some optimistic souls have even concluded that the forces

about us are on the whole essentially benign. But every crisis, whether
of the individual or of the community, reminds man of the precarious and partial nature of the control he exercises."[20]

Life without Windows

We do not have to recite more instances than we already have to acquire a sense that the idea of a *telos* is not easily dispensed with. In
fact, it seems indispensable to the human sense of life. Yet the modern view of things has restricted us. For the sake of intensity and
control we have reduced our knowledge of things to a room with
objects all of which we can touch, taste, handle, and move. In such a
room, windows are a distraction; we cannot after all do anything
about the stars. They belong to a speculative order. So we commit
ourselves to living in that room, though we cannot help feeling that
life is more humane when there is a stream of light and a draft of air
from the outside. But who can prove such things? And what use are
they?

But if we did not sense such things, why would each of the thinkers we have named have rushed to remedy, as they see it, the impossibility of the classic view of a settled or fixed purpose in life? We
must look at this in yet another way, they each say. The real goal
emerges out of our power of invention, and we must invent. Why
must we invent? Why must we consider the end-in-view, and settle
for a contextual and situational goal? Why cannot we merely settle
for the truth—that there is no necessary *telos*, no real purpose? The
answer is too obvious even to need statement. We despair without
purpose! It is no longer possible to live as a human without a notion of what it *means* to be human.

Skepticism has been a healthy part of the intellectual armament
of Western culture from its earliest times. From the Reformation
through the eighteenth century there is considerable weight given to
the classical skeptical tradition and the impossibility of absolute cer-

tainty regarding those matters of greatest importance in human life. We have seen that Bayle, for instance, welcomed the skeptic insight as a way of casting a shadow on reason, thus opening the way for faith. For him, it was a way of refuting both the old Scholastic science and the new doctrinaire Calvinists, making space for the true Protestant reliance upon belief. Locke's investigations into the human being's capacity to know confirmed the skeptic position and resulted in his calling for reliance on Scripture as it passed the test of common reasonableness. Hume likewise cast doubt on both the fundamental method of philosophy and theology and thus called for reliance on custom as the only faithful bulwark of the common life.

Enlightenment thinkers, especially those such as Voltaire who tended to be highly animated by their anti-clerical and anti-religious impulses, fell into the habit of being self-congratulatory concerning their skepticism. This self-consciousness, and this new openness, regarding skepticism tended to mark the Enlightenment period to such an extent that we are apt to believe that these were indeed new thoughts suddenly brought to light. Of course, they were not; and they always played a part in the dialectic of a Christian culture. It certainly is not the case, as Toulmin's *Cosmopolis* seems to imply, that an early outbreak of broadly tolerant skepticism in Europe was followed by attempts to discover foundations upon which everything could be nailed down into a tight certainty with fixed foundations. Skepticism, and the reactions to it, are not that easy to plot out. The skeptic strain in Western thought was always there and remained, and the efforts to counter it with more certain means of thought or investigation were always there, and never ceased.

Something was different, however, in the modern period. Writing on Anglican theology in the seventeenth century, S. L. Bethell spoke of the "almost violent contrast between the first and second halves of the period."[21] It should not be surprising that in every period human beings tend to rely on their strengths, especially when they meet with a crisis. The modern period, especially as it began in the midst of religious wars and political upheavals, is no exception. The change in our view of the world that occurs remarkably during this period gives a clue as to how and why we respond in the way we do. It also tells us why the skeptic disposition might lie easily and at peace in a whole panoply of intellectual touchstones, and then seem subversive and revolutionalry at a later time, at the time of the Enlightenment.

The key component in all of this was a change in the view of the world that takes place, to a large degree, although not entirely, in the seventeenth century. Looking back on that time, the tendency now is to reduce it to a caricature. We know now, and we assume they did not know, that the universe is no Ptolemaic sphere with the earth at the center and ascending spheres rising like layers of an onion to the moon and beyond. We know that the lower reaches are not dominated by Fire, Air, Water, and Earth, while the upper reaches are filled with ether that extends to the heaven of heavens that is not subject to change. But then, also, we can be sure that the average educated European took these fanciful pictures no more literally than we do.

What we do know, however, about the sentiment which these pictures represent, is that it *did* operate on one level. That is, they easily believed in a universe of graduated value, a hierarchy of being, from the most common of things to the most rare and noblest. That language, the language expressed in what Pope refered to as "the vast chain of being" (in the *Essay on Man*), was a language that people of the sixteenth century understood and felt and that they had begun to lose in the latter part of the seventeenth.

This was a very different view of the universe than what replaced it. What replaced the earlier hierarchical vision was a universe reduced to "bodies" and motion, one that could be measured, weighed, and calculated with mathematical precision. This new vision of the world, so reliable in the uses it could be put to because so predictable, was nevertheless a seriously reduced world. If the world is only "atoms in a whirl" then it can to a certain extent be understood. But it will not be understood in the same way as a world that also has moral weight, and value, and nobility or its opposite, and that has *purpose*. This earlier world, the pre-Enlightenment world, calls upon faculties other than those capable of counting, measuring, and calculating. It is a richer world, a world given to be understood by reason in a fuller sense, but also by intuition, and feeling. Pascal, for instance, saw how calculations could so overwhelm us with their power that we might *forget* what else was meant when we thought that we knew things, and—the genius that he was—he never lost touch with the non-calculating human sentiment. There are two excesses, he said, "to exclude reason, to admit nothing but reason."[22] Though he was among the greatest of mathematicians—and perhaps because he was among the greatest—he did not concede the whole field to the mathematician: "One must know when it is right to doubt, to affirm, to submit. Anyone who does otherwise does not understand the force of reason. Some men run counter to these three principles, either affirming that everything can be proved, because they know nothing about proof, or doubting everything, because they do not know when to submit, or always submitting, because they do not know when judgment is called for. . . . Skeptic, mathematician, Christian; doubt, affirmation, submission."[23]

This different "texture"—this capacity to reason in a fuller and richer sense—that has been radically weakened in the modern world is never fully lost. We do not cease to think and behave as human beings. And we do not cease to relate to a world of things that are true simply because we do not understand them. As Pascal, once more, pointed out, "Everything that is incomprehensible does not cease to exist."[24] We still make judgments about right and wrong, about the nobility of things and actions. Matters strike us as beautiful, heroic, courageous, perverse, ignoble, barbaric, and so on. But there is now the tendency to quarantine these judgments from the scientifically reliable calculations about the world and call them value-judgments. The world in which (even if by stealth) human beings attempt to live has depth and height as well as length and breadth. In the world in which we privately move about, one can do more than *count* people the way the daily and ubiquitous political polls do, as if everyone's political response counted for the same thing. The secret world of both modern and ancient human beings is a world of weight as well as numbers: it is a world in which people count for something even if we have lost the language to say what that something is.

Shakespeare's advantage —and we still listen to Shakespeare, don't we?—was that he had at his disposal a sense of the world that still included not only the object available to the immediate senses but also its *intention*, its purpose, its *telos*, and therefore its *value* in a sense more significant than personal preference. Such a view of the world— or more properly, the sentiment attendant to that world—included more than bodies affected by material and efficient causes, but things and persons occupying a place within an articulated hierarchy and within providential anticipations. That hierarchy was given its meaning by virtue of the way everything is related to God, through the orders of creation and redemption.

Sir Walter Raleigh, an Elizabethan contemporary of Shakespeare, describes such an articulated universe in his *History of the World*:

> Man thus compounded and formed by God, was an Abstract, or Model, or brief Story in the Universal: in whom God concluded the Creation and work of the World, and whom he made the last and most excellent of his Creatures, being internally endued with a Divine Understanding, by which he might contemplate and serve his Creator, after whose Image he was formed, and endued with the Powers and Faculties of Reason and other abilities, that thereby also he might govern and rule the World, and all other God's Creatures therein. And whereas God created three sorts of living Natures, (to wit) Angelical, Rational, and Brutal; giving to Angels an Intellectual, and to Beasts a sensual Nature, he vouchsafed unto Man both the intellectual of Angels, the sensitive of Beasts, and the proper rational belonging unto Man: and therefore (saith Gregory Nazianzen) *homo est utriusque Naturae*

vinculum, Man is the bond and chain which tieth together both Natures: And because in the little frame of Man's body there is a representation of the Universal, and (by allusion) a kind of participation of all the parts there; therefore was Man called *Microcosmos*, or the little World.[25]

From this, one can understand how a type of reasoning becomes possible that varies considerably from the empirical notion of cause and effect. Here there is not simply cause and effect but *correspondence*. It becomes natural to understand the nature and function of things or events in terms of analogy, a rearticulation of something. If the human being is a "microcosmos," then it becomes reasonable to think that anthropology will help to inform cosmology, and likewise that cosmology helps to inform anthropology. There is an insight here that moves beyond cause and effect and proposes to illuminate areas of thought, feeling, and imagination that the empirical approach cannot. The point is not that the insight that analogy yields is infallible. But only the most unreflective Baconian would think that empirical logic did not also yield false results as well as reliable ones, depending on the premises. The point *is*, however, that here is a different operation of the mind that evidently medieval and ancient people appreciated more than those, especially, who came along after the seventeenth century.

A species of this sort of thinking is found in the Apostle Paul's teachings on the *anakephaliasis* of Christ, the recapitulation of Christ, in Ephesians 1:9 and 10. St. Irenaeus made this concept in Paul's thinking the basis for a major component of his theology. The passage reads: "He made known to us the mystery of his will, according to his kind intention which he purposed in him with a view to an administration suitable to the fullness of the times, that is, the summing up of all things in Christ, things in the heavens and things upon the earth."[26] We come to understand by analogy the true nature of the human being and the nature and destiny of the world through what has been revealed concerning Jesus Christ. Since Christ is the summing up of creation, we can understand the order of things, and their ultimate purpose, and their relative value. Calculation of efficient causes, on the other hand, will never in a thousand years yield this kind of judgment.

The world left behind by modernity, therefore, was a world in which comparisons could be made in a sense that claimed to be more than the statement of an opinion. Analogies illuminate both nature and that which is beyond nature. Since there must be a correspondence between the Creator and that which he creates, one must be able to learn *by analogy* through the realities disclosed in nature some things that are true concerning God. At the same time, those things which God reveals through his unique actions in history, and through the singular disclosure to prophets, must say something about the purposes to which nature is put. The sorts of reasoning—this analogical reasoning—presupposes a universe existing in community with the God who creates, sustains, and redeems it, so that what is true on one level speaks indirectly about what is true at a different level. In a created world, a world under providence, a world of personal intention, there are correspondences. This allows for a dimension of reason that will not be allowed by the bare-bones world of Newtonian cosmology and Baconian science.

For all of the images that ancient people have used to illustrate this world, and which distract unreflective modern minds, the difference in this world is one of *telos*. The ancient world accepted that human beings seem not to be able to conceive of a world and a life without purpose. Modern people have struggled with this by saying that, although no purpose can be calculated, we must act as if there is one. There, simply, is the choice that must be made. Either we understand life as one in which there is meaning (even if we admit we only "see as through a glass darkly") or we understand life as one in which we must determine our own meaning. Life is a gift— the ancient intuition—or life is virtual reality, an artifice of will and imagination.

From Will to Power

What happens, then, in a world in which the intellect is foreshortened, such as I have argued might have happened for modern people? If we cannot live without purpose (and it seems that we cannot) and if we are not likely to dissolve into collective despair, then by default we turn to the will. If I come to a fork in the road and have no way of *knowing* which way to go, then rather than stand still forever, I— by an act of the will—choose one and proceed. In my more reflective moments I know the truth of what the Cheshire Cat said to Alice at her own fork in the road: "If you don't know where you want to go, then it doesn't matter which road you take."

How does the loss of confidence in moral responsibility translate into the rise of power, especially political power? The transition is not a complicated one. We have already detected the direction we must take when we see that the loss of an intelligible order, with intelligible and believable goals for the individual and society, ends in resorting to the will. But now we can go a step further.

Associations such as families and religious groups bind us together with ties that are not always consciously detected. In societies where the family is strong, for instance, members understand their obligations rarely as choices: they treat the obligation with a sense of acceptance. It is an authority the strength of which coincides with that sense of unquestioning inevitability. My occasional encounter with Chinese families outside of mainland China gives me the impression that the sense of family obligation is still quite strong there, especially in comparison with families in the modern West, where individual choices of vocation, religion, and political party bind more tightly than family ties.

The strength of these informal and natural associations has diminished over time, especially in the West. That is among the most remarkable and obvious features of modern life. And the strength of the formal, organized, national ruling authority has increased. This situation is in no way assuaged by the fact that Western nations are largely representative democracies; in fact, this form of government in many ways makes the authority of the central power all the more secure. When this increase is measured over four centuries, the trend is unmistakable. We must consider together, first, the society in which authority resides in diverse centers, and at various levels, some transcending national boundaries (such as the church), some unrelated to the state, having existed from before historical memory (such as the family), and second, that this society loses its strength, vis-à-vis a society focused upon organized, formal authorities residing in more or less remote political centers and ruling by the formal agencies of laws and bureaucratic regulations.

At issue in this transition is the rather thick slice of moral philosophy that we have scrutinized all along: if the *telos* or the multiple goals that govern our actions are fundamentally artifacts of our imagination and will, rather than disclosures to us of what is authoritative, then the natural, timeless, and informal associations have no *necessary* authority in human lives. The artifice of human "values" is well matched by the artifice of the national state. As the inevitability of these other associations—treated with such seriousness by Thomas Aquinas, Johannes Althusius, Edmund Burke, John Calhoun, and a number of the West's most luminous political theorists—is diminished in people's consciousness, then the state proves to be the benefactor. And we can think of the state as the benefactor without the least conspiratorial implications as long as we keep in mind Bertrand de Jouvenel's insight that power necessarily and inevitably seeks to increase itself.

In a world where power inevitably finds its place and seeks to expand its authority, the state eventually proves to be the only legitimate authority to which the increasingly isolated individual can resort. More than ever, the individual finds himself bereft of the resources of society in the normal, traditional sense.

The individual casts his lot with whatever agency takes on the office formerly belonging to the family, the guild, the church, collegial friends, and the like. Differences once arbitrated on a personal level, calling upon obligations of kinship and collegiality, are now arbitrated through the more or less indifferent machinery (indifferent, ironically, when it functions properly; personal only to the extent it has become corrupt) of the courts or the public agencies. Loyalties of individuals once distributed to a variety of informal and largely organic associations, are later absorbed into the reified state.

Bertrand de Jouvenel presented an arresting picture of how this absorption of authority in the state bore tragic fruit in the twentieth century. He began by remarking on the surpassing viciousness and barbarity of the Second World War, which "surpassed in savagery and destructive force any yet seen by the Western World."[27] It was a war that effectively drew upon the resources of the entire populations of several large nations, especially Germany, France, Great Britain, the Netherlands, Japan, and the United States. Even women were recruited and, in the case of Great Britain, subject to conscription. Farm products, industrial capital, raw products of the mine—all were at least subject to the "emergency" needs of warfare. Hitler successfully focused the "total" resources of Germany upon the war; and so he was indirectly responsible for a similar "total war" response by the Allies.

Jouvenel points this out in order to remark that this was not always so, that "if we arrange in chronological order the various wars which have for nearly a thousand years ravaged our Western World, one thing must strike us forcibly: that with each one there has been a steady rise in the coefficient of society's participation in it, and that the total war of today is only the logical end of an uninterrupted advance towards it, of the increasing growth of war."[28] Society has been increasingly "sucked into" a project of primary interest to the survival and prosperity of the state. He cites, in a footnote, a line from the *Frankfurter Zeitung* on December 29, 1942: "the needs of the civilian population must receive sufficient satisfaction *to ensure that its work on war production will not suffer.*"[29]

Surely earlier regimes could have used this level of resource from the civilian population and economy at times of national crisis. One thinks of the English against Napoleon or the Austrians against the Turks. Why did they not call upon these resources? Why did they not mobilize their entire populations and a large part of the materials available in the land?

They did not because they *could not*! The secret of the comprehensive wars of the twentieth century is the extent to which authority once distributed and multicentric became, over time, concentrated in national governments.

Tolerance as Universal Solvent

The role played by the modern doctrine of toleration is important at this point. In order to understand this, we need to clearly have in view what individuals and groups are asked, in terms of this doctrine, to tolerate.

Each group consists of persons held together out of loyalty to a common *telos*. It is of course an "end" that they generally agree upon, which they may or may not articulate in precisely the same way and which undoubtedly changes with time. However it might change, or however varied it might be presented among the group's constituents, the end holds for them a certain authority. Without that end, the group might persist out of habit for a time but would eventually die or become something entirely different. To the extent the end is an arbitrary thing in their minds it has less of a grip on their loyalty than if it is seen as obligatory and necessary—and hence out of their hands.

Groups claim an authority, moreover, altogether apart from that permitted or expressly authorized by government. The artistic collegium, for instance, imposes standards or encourages experiment among its members in the informal, communicative way that all groups do. They might conceivably enforce some sort of regulation for the sake of accreditation or membership in a formally organized guild; but among artists it is generally recognized that truly superior standards of work do not occur in that way. Accreditation ensures, perhaps (if it is done well), a minimum competence, but the only effect it has on superior work is that it ensures that the group so accredited is not an indiscriminate group of would-be's but in fact a group of artists. That sort of discipline can occur unless, of course, the artistic community itself buys into the notion that "no one can really say" what is art and what is not.

What happens when this informal association's sense of "good work" or "artistically credible work" is considered to be entirely arbitrary and might better be made subject to the greater aims of society? That sort of thing did happen, in a very dramatic way, under the influence of some of the twentieth century's ideologically based totalitarian regimes. The Nazis saw art as useful for *their own* sense of values and felt no compunction about usurping the artist for political rather than artistic ends. "So long as there remains in Germany any non-political art," said Goebbels, "our task is not finished." What makes the totalitarian regime *total* in its effect is that it denies the ends that make the artist an artist instead of the citizen of the state. It denies that which is constitutive of the artistic community.

The same can be true of any group, any association, that exists by virtue of its own sense of *vocation*, its own sense of why it exists. It is probably important, however, to realize that this sort of thing is not simply done by the regime to innocent healthy groups with a strong sense of their teleological vocation. First comes the profoundly enervating realization that there is really nothing *necessary*, or vital, or significant in any transcendent sense, about what they formerly took to be their calling. Thus, families, with the given roles and obligations of mothers and fathers, are taken to be arbitrary arrangements, accidentally passed on in a given culture, bespeaking more the dearth of imagination in former generations than a divine and irrevocable call to duty. The church is taken to be one socializing agent alongside a number of others, some of which are not burdened with a sense of transcendent origin nor the bigotry of thinking that the world somehow depends upon their doing well.

Under such conditions, the political aim of the state can easily encroach upon the aims of the family, the collegium (such as the artistic community), the profession, the church, the local village, the province. Yet, first the *telos* of these entities must be called into question. That is where tolerance comes in—not the practice of tolerance which is entirely productive of lively community life but the kind of tolerance that essentially demeans the status of groups along with their provincial, familial, or ecclesiastical sense of authority.

In chapter one I mentioned the 1995 UNESCO "Declaration of Principles on Tolerance." This statement might be taken as a fairly standard notion of toleration in the closing years of the twentieth century. In many ways the language is reassuring in that it expresses respect for groups rather than immediately exposing attitudes that might diminish the strength of group identity. Beginning on an ambiguous note, it says that the meaning of tolerance is "respect, acceptance and appreciation of the rich diversity of our world's cultures," and adds (significantly) "our forms of expression and ways of being human." More reassurances are given at the end of the section on the "meaning of tolerance": "Consistent with respect for human rights, the practice of tolerance does not mean toleration of social injustice or the abandonment or weakening of one's convictions." Yet even these reassurances are stated in terms of the *individual*, not the group. Rather, tolerance "involves the rejection of dogmatism and absolutism and affirms the standards set out in international human rights instruments."

The most striking feature of this document is the easy and almost absent-minded transitions from tolerance, spoken of in individualistic terms, to a clearly political agenda in terms of the modern notion of the state. "Tolerance is harmony in difference" is immediately followed by "It is not only a moral duty, it is also a political and legal requirement." Further, tolerance is evidently not, by this document, inclusive of just any political arrangement but a very specific kind: "Tolerance is the responsibility that upholds human rights, pluralism (including cultural pluralism), democracy and the rule of law." Individual freedom, in terms of the free choice of cultural and moral commitments, is linked to the state that adheres to the agenda of liberal democracies. Between the lines is the advice that the bonds that maintain loyalty to groups be slackened, and the loyalty to a particular kind of state (or at least one that espouses a certain political ideology) be strengthened.

The state that we have learned to expect is a fairly faithful representation of what we might have learned from Hobbes. Yet this Leviathan was always preceded by a shadow. It was preceded by a kind of society in which this state has a chance of coming into being, a society of individuals and dispirited, jejune groups, void of the kind of conviction for which men and women sacrifice and even die. It is the Shadow Leviathan, that loss of power that invites the excess of power. It is tolerant not in the sense that it expects to learn from others but in the sense that its expects there is nothing really to learn of any consequence. It makes impossible, almost, the kind of reflection that occurred to Dean Inge in the midst of the Second World War, the battle of Titan States: "In the first place, there is no reason why the state should be chosen as the sole object of loyalty. We all belong to several different groups, some narrower, some broader than the state. Such are the family, the locality, the trade or profession, the church, the whole comity of civilised nations, humanity itself. Each of these has a limited but definite claim upon our loyalty. St. Peter's words, 'Honour all men; love the brotherhood; fear God; honour the king,' embody a much truer philosophy than state absolutism."[30]

9

Nihilism and the
Catholic Vision

It was on the truth of the sentence that God is
One that the "Third Reich" of Adolf Hitler
made shipwreck. Let this sentence be uttered
in such a way that it is heard and grasped, and
at once 450 prophets of Baal are always in fear
of their lives. There is no more room now for
what the recent past called toleration. Beside
God there are only His creatures or false gods.

—Karl Barth

THE STUNNING ACCOUNT of Lance Edward Armstrong and his victory in the 1999 Tour de France, which he repeated in the 2000 Tour, dominated sports news for days. In the *New York Times* he is pictured, the very image of health, posing with his beautiful wife and his beautiful mother, a strong arm around each, as they stand on either side.

Three years earlier he was diagnosed with advanced testicular cancer; the disease had spread to his lungs, his abdomen, and his brain, and doctors gave him no more than a 50 percent chance of survival. Enduring surgery and chemotherapy first, he then tried to return to cycling and failed. He dropped out half way through a race in France in early 1998. He returned to Texas partly convinced that he should try no more.

Then a change occurred. The stricken and discouraged cyclist went riding for ten days with a friend in the beautiful North Carolina mountains. Armstrong merely says that he learned during that time that "its not just the convalescence of the body, but it's the convalescence of the spirit as well." What the convalescence of the spirit means in concrete and personal terms is a story he has yet to tell. What it clearly means in more general terms is this: At the end of that time, he knew what he *had* to do. He came to a point that, though the means were uncertain, the end or the goal became clear. And against great odds, he has twice won the world's greatest cycling championship.

By Armstong's and many like stories we know the power of a goal. But what happens when power *becomes* the goal, or when it is taken to be the goal? That, as I will hope to show, is a partial description of what has happened in modern times, for the very good reason that power has become so very much available to us, so impressive that it overawes us, and in every way tempts us to worship it. The question for modern people is not whether it has become a goal. The question is rather if it has any legitimate place in a discussion of human aims.

Community and the Catholic Vision

Nietzsche detected that the sense of a purpose is so much with us that we will even make its negation our purpose. It is well to remember Nietzsche's oft-repeated words in *The Geneology of Morals* that "man would sooner have the void for his purpose than be void of purpose."[1] There are two things to keep in mind here, and both tend to confirm Nietzsche's characteristically keen insight: we *will* have an end, and the void is, properly speaking, an end. Each of these is important in understanding the dynamics of the present state of our culture in the West in particular, and to the extent that the world has become caught up in aspects of Western culture, even in its decadent phase, it is true of the world at large.

First, we *will* have an end. As long as human beings, or at least those whom Nietzsche thought of as among the more enlightened, believe in God, then God defines the purpose of life. But Nietzsche thought it now prudent and in fact necessary to say that God no longer stands as the "purpose" for modern men and women. In *Thus Spake Zarathustra*, Nietzsche's awakened prophet of the new world encounters a desert saint and says, "Could it be possible! This old saint in the forest has not yet heard anything of this, that *God is dead!*"[2] The time for believing in God is past and irrecoverable for those who understand the state of the world in modern times. Yet something in this, for Nietzsche, has not died. We must yet give ourselves to that which stands as a purpose for living. For Nietszche that something, in these modern and enlightened days, is absorbed into the human being himself: "But let me reveal my heart to you entirely, my friends: if there were gods, how could I endure not to be a god!" That which the human being cannot part with is the purpose that keeps him alive. So, "God is conjecture; but who could drain all the agony of this conjecture without dying? Shall his faith be taken away from the creator, and from the eagle, his soaring to eagle heights?"[3]

Therefore, the second part of Nietzsche's insight is equally important: the void is, properly speaking, an end. He thinks indeed we can live without God, but not without that which God stands for in us. If the void means life without God, it stands at the opposite extreme of the spectrum, but it is nevertheless what will authentically serve the purpose of an end. If, indeed, there is no God to which to give life, in the sense that Saint Paul meant when he said, "present your bodies a living and holy sacrifice" (Rom. 12:1), then the honest alternative is to say there is none. It is a despairing end unless we are prepared as "creators" and as the "overman" to seize the obligation to make it our end. The spectrum of honest choices looks like this: at one end "life" lived with some great object in mind, some object worthy of life and therefore greater than life; and at the other end "nothing." In between are strategies to avoid the stark contrast of these choices.

The intriguing feature of the alternative moral philosophies that we have briefly examined in the foregoing chapters is that they are presented to us as real choices. Yet, upon close reading each proves to be a way of negating—shall I say bargaining with?—the one real choice. They are, as it were, some variation on a third choice. While Hobbes, Bayle, Locke, Nietzsche, Dewey, and Foucault all are rather certain about the need to live on the basis of a *telos*—none attempts even to imagine that human life is conceivable otherwise—and they all to varying degrees see some significance to that fact, each nevertheless calculates in various ways how the question of *telos* might be settled in a way less ultimate than the gravity of the choice implies. For Hobbes it is settled vicariously by the magistrate. For Bayle and Locke the matter is relegated more or less to the private sphere. For Nietzsche and Foucault the *telos* is illusory but necessary and must be settled in the realm of myth and the inventive imagination. And for Dewey, the end is a pragmatic concept that responds to the situation at hand (the end-in-view) that only reads and feels as if ultimate. These are bargaining positions. They never deny the apparent irrevocable need for the human being to respond on the basis of some idea of an end, a purpose. Yet their reasoning remains dependent upon some choice other than what is given, a "possible reality."

Fortunately, we are not bound by Nietzsche's dismal second choice. Such being the case, we can perhaps think in a different way about how life's goals are not the lonely choice of those who dare but the truth about human purpose that draw us together.

The *telos* of a group, that which makes it a group, can seem, on the scale of things, quite trivial and mundane. It can even seem, and often is, self-serving and morally deplorable. Yet any goal which draws individuals together—whether trivial or grand, whether ignoble or noble—counteracts the self-centered impulse, draws individuals out of themselves, and causes them to open themselves toward the larger whole. We would not always applaud this as a good thing. I am not forgetting that mob action and the persecution of a scapegoat create a community of sorts, as René Girard tirelessly reminds his readers.[4] Nevertheless, the bare fact that a goal creates community means that an anti-egoistic impulse is both possible and is a very attractive and satisfying impulse in the human experience. It is an impulse whose full implication is universal in nature. That the individual merges for a time in self-forgetfulness, and that the group with narrow, limited, even ignoble purposes can do the same, implies that—at the farthest reaches of hope—the ultimate horizon embraces all of existence. It is an impulse not fully satisfied short of the inclusion of all that God has created. This is not necessarily universalism in the sense of anticipating the salvation of all people. But the awareness of this universalizing impulse is so strong in the Christian message that it is yet no wonder that some of the most prominent early teachers of the church, such as Origen and Gregory of Nyssa, considered such a prospect inevitable. This universalizing tendency, this consciousness of a "catholic vision" came to be seen as a "mark" of the authentic church. Along with the marks of unity, holiness, and apostolicity, the church's catholicity signified the true nature of the church.

Heresy in the early church was seen as an offense against catholicity. It is not simply that it introduced schism, which would be serious enough. And the term heresy did, in fact, originate in the idea of a party spirit, in that it "signified a choice, membership in a special group."[5] But the idea of "heresy" came to be this: that the teachings were judged by the church as *incapable* of producing wholeness. Instead of speaking a truth that transcended special considerations and limited experience, a heresy embodied one-sided ideas that failed in its relevance to every person, everywhere, and through all time. Heresy was incapable of building toward a universal community. Although it may well express *a* truth, it is not the full truth. It is limited, provincial in its outlook, with the necessary result of party spiritedness. One thinks today of the various forms of liberation theology that intend to express theology for, and out of, a particular group or "context." It seems to me that these deliberately abandon the catholic vision of the church and introduce the notion (actually a very old notion) that truth can only mean what is in the *interest* of given groups or segments of the world's population.

Of course, early in the life of the church, the idea of some universal principle that would overcome barriers of culture, religion, and nationality was also of importance to the Roman empire. Various attempts to bring a unifying principle to the empire were made. None of them was as successful as the Constantinian adoption of Christianity as the official religion. Thinkers from Eusebius to the present time have struggled with the question of whether this marriage of empire and church was a net gain or a net loss for the church. One thing, however, is quite certain: the empire with its ecumenical mission did not last, while the church did last.

A question perhaps more important than whether the Christian mission suffered or gained by its alliance with worldly powers, is why one ecumenical intention lasted and the other did not. Might it have to do with the fact that the aim of the Roman adoption of the church was in fact motivated by the desire for power? And might it be that the church's catholic vision, while it was often tainted and distorted by those lusting after power, was not *in principle* based upon worldly ambitions for power? The reach of the gospel was and is intrinsically universal, for its true goal lies outside this world and includes the world.

The question of power as an aim comes down to our time, however, in a different form. We have seen, I think, that the spirit of the modern age can only be understood in view of a terrible fascination with the prospects of power. And we have seen that modernity proven to be a time of terrible alienation, with devastating results in providing for life together. Where modern thought has been the strongest, there we also find the strongest sense of the loss of community and the isolation of the individual. People today are both lonely and afraid, and tend to act (or react) out of fear precisely where the modern project (which at bottom is an organized quest for power) has been most successful.

When Power Becomes the Goal

Nietzsche knew very well what Christian theologians of every age had taught, that to say the end or *telos* of human nature and to say God is very nearly the same thing, at least from an anthropological point of view. The Shorter Catechism says, "Man's chief end is to glorify God and to enjoy him forever." A strange thing happened about four hundred years ago to Christian thought about God. The way was opened to make power itself the goal or aim of the human life. How did that come about?

It happened right along with the realization that what later came to be known as modern science or positive science carries with it impressive achievements in the realm of technology. And when Bacon said, "Knowledge is power," it was clear he meant a certain kind of knowledge and that he could point to important achievements in the areas of technology and commerce to back up what he said. What happened in theology was that God came to be defined as *potentia absoluta*, absolute power. This redefining of God began to lose sight of the orthodox doctrine of the Holy Trinity in which God's oneness was joined with the mutually indwelling relationship, yet distinct Persons of the Father, the Son, and the Holy Spirit. Emphasis gradually but definitely migrated to an idea of God as principally defined by his absolute power. This change marked an important transformation in the Christian sentiment regarding God. Earlier the attributes of God would include not only the so-called "natural" attributes of spirituality, personality, life, and infinity (which includes the idea of power), but also the "moral" attributes of holiness, justice, truthfulness, faithfulness, and love.

The first category refers to God in himself, and the second category is always considering God in terms of a relationship. The classical formulation of the Trinity includes the idea that God is One and that he is Three Persons, each Person equal in that they are each God, and distinct in that the Father is not the Son, the Son not the Spirit, and the Spirit not the Father. The formulation of the Trinity, therefore, includes both the uniqueness of God and the community of the Godhead: he is One *and* Three. It includes what he is in himself, but also who he is in relationship. By this we can see that the power of God is hardly the sole or the chief attribute of God. Yet when the modern sentiment accorded, by degrees, divine power *alone* the status of divine attribute, it is clear that it was not so much informed by Christian theology in any normative sense but by the new achievements that people of the West came to look upon in almost an idolatrous fashion. They were tempted by the conviction that, if the chief object of life is to gain power, then God must be the One who has more power than anyone.

This development in theology means that there was a consequent leaning toward the oneness of God, in the modern West, as opposed to keeping clearly in view the Three Persons. The image of the Three Persons naturally suggests community and a harmony of wills, even the centrality of love. But the idea of One God, taken alone, suggests something else.

If I live alongside someone else, we might have quite different ideas about how things in our neighborhood ought to be done. And if I consequently seek to use whatever means available to see that my will is enforced and my neighbor's is negated, then I am not seeking a harmony or community of wills; I am seeking to establish my will as the only one that counts. So, if our image of God neglects community of persons and focuses solely upon the unity of will, then we have a very different picture of God.

That, of course, is always the temptation in monotheistic religions: the temptation to reduce God to mere dominant will. And it is the temptation, moreover, to which modern people have succumbed. They were not quite aware when it happened, but eventually, looking back, it dawned on some of them that they had stopped worshipping the Christian God and begun to worship power. It became apparent that Augustine's idea of knowledge at the beginning of the middle ages was very different from that of Francis Bacon's at the beginning of modernity. "We know the extent to which we love" is Augustine's reflection upon the idea that we participate in a community of people and things and to know them is to participate with them in love. But for Bacon, who said "knowledge is power," knowing is a way of asserting the will. The first emphasizes community as the end of knowledge, while the second emphasizes power and domination as the goal of knowledge.

God, therefore, whose reality ultimately expresses the end of all existence, is identified with power. The idea that a feature of modern life is the worship of power should not be an entirely surprising point to make. Walt Whitman saw this as essentially modern in his poem, "To a Locomotive in Winter": "Type of the modern—emblem of motion and power—pulse of the continent." And when asked why he wanted to become president, John F. Kennedy was not ashamed to reply "Because that is where the power is." The modern orientation to the world is not one of responding to powers, or a Power, that is already a given reality, but it is in *gaining* power. It is not in understanding and thus cooperating with a First Cause, but it is in coming as close to being a primary cause of things as possible. Several years ago, the Southern Baptist Theological Seminary had as its motto, "We're Out to Change the World," words that one could not imagine on the lips of Saint Paul. Paul's ambition could hardly be construed to be "like God" in the sense of sharing his power, but that of being a "bond servant" of God and thus "like God" in the sense of his moral attributes.

The Modern Theology of Power

No theologian in recent times has done quite as much as Jürgen Moltmann to illuminate the role that power, or the idea of power, has played in modern theology and modern thought generally. He sees that in modern times a great displacement has taken place that, in Christian theology, has made it more difficult to understand what a Trinitarian view of God was actually seeking to articulate, and furthermore what sort of errors a healthy Trinitarian theology might prevent. The displacement that takes place comes as a result of a basic, though very subtle, redefinition of God's relationship to creation.

Interestingly enough, Moltmann makes his case over against those who accuse the Jewish and Christian ideas of creation and the human being's dominion over creation for being the harbinger of exploitative practices that have ruined or badly compromised the natural environment. It was not, in fact, the Old Testament idea of the nurturing, cultivating human being that is responsible for ecological sins, claims Moltmann, but a much more recent change in our understanding of the central place of power in modern times. In a remarkable paragraph in his Gifford Lectures of 1984-85, *God in Creation*, he summarizes his case:

> The Jewish-Christian tradition is often made responsible for man's usurpation of power over nature and for his unbridled will to power. It was this tradition, we are told, which decreed that human beings should rule the earth. In return that same tradition has stripped the world of nature of its demons and its gods, and has made it the profane world of human beings. Yet this allegedly "anthropocentric" view of the world found in the Bible is more than three thousand years old, whereas modern scientific

and technological civilization only began to develop in Europe four hundred years ago at the earliest. So there must have been other, more important factors in its development. Whatever the economic, social and political changes that may require mention, another factor was more important still in determining the way people four hundred years ago saw themselves. This was the new picture of God offered by the Renaissance and by nominalism: God is almighty, and *potentia absoluta* is the pre-eminent attribute of his divinity. Consequently God's image on earth, the human being (which in actural practice meant the man) had to strive for power and domination so that he might acquire *his* divinity.[6]

In an essay from approximately this same time, he writes of how the Chinese culture has been affected by the introduction of Western ideas, especially through Marxism. In Chinese culture, he sees a clear delineation between two different possibilities in the way a society views itself. The older culture, influenced by Taoist and Confucian teachings and practices, valued balance and harmony as the central objects of social life. With the introduction of *modern* Western ideas of history and progress, there was a shift to the social emphasis upon *power* as the aim of social life. In the West it is understandable that people should experience such an orientation as inevitable. The sudden and dramatic changes that have taken place in the East remind us that not all cultures have preferred to place such enormous emphasis upon the acquisition and use of power. Moltmann raises the question, with his Chinese readers, if the alternatives are not worth considering at a deeper level. He paints a dark picture of what has happened to Chinese life under the new quest for power:

> Industrial production is directed towards maximizing work productivity and profit. More must be produced and more must be consumed. It is therefore programmed for growth and expansion, for innovation and accumulation of power. Because it is in principle unlimited, it is also universal in tendency. . . . The

fight for a position in the market and for workplaces dominates the scene. As a worker, each person is left to themselves. The family doesn't play a role anymore. In place of the traditional, natural community of generations, the free associations of single individuals appear. What has appeared in the highly industrialized West after 200 years, must be introduced into the industrial cities of China through the intervention of the state: control of human reproduction. The modern Chinese one-child marriage is enforced through tax legislation.... The one-child family and the indiscriminate cremation of the dead breaks up the old Chinese family culture just as the family as the primary institution for social help and for giving people their home has been broken up in the West. It would be good if the Chinese people and their government would recognize the human costs of Western "modernization," which consists of the separation, isolation and alienation of people from one another. Does the street committee replace the village community? Does the Party replace the solidarity of the family? ... Are the benefits really worth the costs?[7]

Moltmann's analysis of the dangers inherent in the accumulation and abuse of power is more than a theological refinement or an ethical afterthought. It has proven to be central to many of the emphases he has brought to theological issues ever since he burst on the scene prominently in the 1960s with his book *Theology of Hope*. In his concern for oppressed people, his criticism of war, and in his writing about ecological issues, he goes back to the touchstone issue for him, which is the modern idolatry of power, its almost unselfconscious acceptance of power and whatever serves power—in politics, economics, and the sciences—as the epitome of value. That this suspicion of power is strongly rooted in his thinking doubtlessly is a product of experiences from the time he was a child.

He grew up in the midst of Germany's being swept along in the tide of an ideological movement that finally brought the nation's destruction and their leader's humiliation. In 1943, at sixteen years of age, Moltmann and his entire class were drafted to man the antiair-craft guns in Hamburg. He witnessed the fiery destruction of his city, and the death of those around him, including a classmate who had been his lifelong companion and friend. He was rushed off to the front lines, where he was soon captured by Allied troops and sent to prison camps for three long years. He was touched early by the effects of those who wanted power more than anything else and those who responded with the total war that was not only the Nazi propaganda but the Allied resolution as well.

When he studied theology later at the University of Göttingen, he had ample time to reflect upon what had befallen his country and his times in the mad acquisition of power over the previous decades. He realized at the same time, however, that Christian theology had not so much prevented this madness as, in its own way at times, promoted it. In 1934 theologians signed a statement in Württemburg that in effect affirmed Hitler as the instrument of God's power in bringing judgment against the enemies of Germany. "We are full of thanks to God," they wrote, "that He, as Lord of history, has given us Adolf Hitler, our leader and savior from our difficult lot. We acknowledge that we, with body and soul, are bound and dedicated to the German state and to its Führer."[8] By the 1980s, in his forward to my book on his theology of history, he still recalls that experiences in his own life-time helped to inoculate him against the temptation to identify God too easily with power itself. In the book, *God, Hope, and History*, I had questioned whether his critique of monarchistic monotheism necessarily obliged him to take up the case against any form of hier-archy. His response to me was revealing of his own theological de-velopment: "Dr. Conyers's problem with me obviously concerns my attitude toward authority and power, toward theocracy and hierarchy. With this he, first of all, touches upon a personal problem: I grew up during the German dictatorship and as a young man spent five years in barracks and prison camps (1943-1948). I therefore have person-ally experienced authority and power as not especially healing—in fact, the reverse. Quite early, I believe it was in 1947, a sentence from *Abraham Lincoln* fascinated me: 'I do not want to be any lord's slave nor any slave's lord.'"[9]

His response was to be somewhat distrustful of the dominant theological movements of his day, and even though he was more influenced by Karl Barth than any other contemporary theologian, he said, "I could not march well in step with others, and so I became a divergent thinker, a nonconformist in that theological school to which I owe the most: the Barth school." The school of thought that gave him some sense of a different direction, a direction perhaps out of the modern intricate web of power and its apologists, was a seventeenth- and eighteenth-century movement within Reformed theology known as federalist, or covenant, theology. Theologians such as Heinrich Bullinger and Caspar Olevian, and later Johannes Coccejus, saw that personal relationships are built upon the mutual give and take of peoples on many different levels and are described biblically in terms of the covenant. This presented a picture of God's work among people that did not so much resemble the political arrangements of empires and bureaucracies as the subtle work of mutual affection and piety that operates in healthy families and in the collegium. In connection with this insight into the federalist structure of relationships, Moltmann was also drawn to the political insights of Johannes Althusius, whose influence upon early modern thought we have already had some time to explore. Moltmann speaks of him this way: "[Federalist theology] found a political complement in the thought of Johannes Althusius who, following the model of the 'league' of Swiss farmers, declared the covenant to be the essence of the political life of the people. Humans are symbiotic creatures and organize their common life on various levels in tacit or explicit covenants. The covenant is the form of political power in which justice can be accomplished best. These federalist ideas . . . became the foundation for the development of modern democracy in the struggle against absolutism during those centuries."[10]

Yet, certainly from an outside view of things, the federalist idea of political association has given way during most of modern times to one form or another of absolutism, even if that absolutism has rejected every semblance of the *imperium* and the monarchy and speaks the language of democracy as a native. There is a reason for this that resides at the root of things in our own culture, Moltmann maintains. It is because, in Christian theology which lies about as close to the root of things as possible in Western culture, there has been for a long time a subtle weakness, a sort of *plague bacillus*, that affects attitudes toward power in a way not necessarily harmonious with the fundamental direction of Christian thought. Its virulence is especially noteworthy in the culture of modern life with its ready access to an amazing array of powers—powers that arise and magnify themselves on the basis of political arrangements that have discovered the strength of bureaucracy, economic arrangements that are fortified by ease of exchange and transport, and technological advances that have dazzled even those most resistant to the allures of power. That subtle weakness is on the side of Christian monotheism. It is the monotheism that early Christianity both cultivated in a certain way and resisted in a certain way, as it encountered and eventually made its place in the Roman empire.

So accustomed are we to the language of monotheism that it seems to be a very gross heresy indeed, casting us back into some kind of Druidic paganism, to even call it into question. It is well to remember that monotheism does not specifically distinguish Christianity, and to the extent that Christians identify themselves as monotheists it may have more the result of linking them to the Greek monotheism of antiquity and the Islamic monotheism of the early middle ages. Even Karl Barth warned that a certain abstract loyalty to monotheism may be only a disguise for a subtler polytheism. Rather than worship of the God of the Bible, it may prove to be only a "glorification of the 'number one'." "Necessarily, then, we must say that God is the absolutely One, but we cannot say that the absolutely one is God." To say merely "God is One" and mean by that that God stands alone at the apex of cosmic power tells us absolutely nothing about the character of that one power. Thus, the "cosmic forces in whose objectivity it is believed that the unique has been found are varied," Barth writes. And then, "It is only by an act of violence that one of them can be given pre-eminence over the others, so that to-day it is nature, and to-morrow spirit, or to-day fate and to-morrow reason, or to-day desire and to-morrow duty.... For all his heavenly divinity each Zeus must constantly be very anxious in face of the existence and arrival of very powerful rivals.... Monotheism is all very well so long as this conflict does not break out. But it will inevitably break out again and again."[11]

Moltmann's point is strengthened by these observations and warnings about abstract monotheism. But he also makes a more particular and historical case. It is that the early Christian emphasis upon God as the theoretical *One*, the abstract One, which came at times to overshadow his threeness and his incarnation in the particularity of flesh, arose along with the need to identify with the idea of *monarchia*, one rule. They were following the example of Josephus who had made the case that the Jewish belief in one God corresponded to the Aristotelian formulation of one God, one rule for the cosmos. He sees evidence of political accomodation in the expression *monarchia* itself, which is a "curious hellenistic word-formation, deriving from *monos* and *mia arché*." In Alexandria the term was used to emphasize the economy of one rule both from heaven and on earth, and then was employed by Philo in his reformulation of Jewish theology. As Erik Peterson has shown, "The God of the Jews was fused with the monarchical concept of Greek philosophy." The unified rule of God became an appropriate theological backdrop for the notion of empire and the absolutist ambitions of the emperor.

These political implications of the theological principle, Moltmann says, are inevitable: "Strict monotheism has to be theocratically conceived and implemented, as Islam proves."[12] Again, "let me point out at once here that this monotheistic monarchianism was, and is, an uncommonly seductive religious-political ideology. It is the fundamental notion behind the universal and uniform religion: One God—one Logos—one humanity; and in the Roman empire it was bound to seem a persuasive solution for many problems of a multinational and multireligious society. The universal ruler in Rome had only to be the image and correspondence of the universal ruler in heaven."[13]

Thus, "religiously motivated political monotheism has always been used in order to legitimate domination, from the emperor cults of the ancient world, Byzantium and the absolute ideologies of the seventeenth century, down to the dictatorships of the twentieth."[14] By contrast, the doctrine of the Trinity has acted to prevent and expose the excesses of monotheism. For, by virtue of the Trinitarian nature of God, the significance of God's unity is shared with his diversity. In answer to the question "What is real, the unity of things or the diversity of things?" the Trinity answers *both*. In political terms this might be asked by questioning whether it is the larger, centralized nation that makes up a people, or is it the local, the informal, the organic associations. Tutored by a strong, principled monotheism (such as Islam, for instance) we might be persuaded to answer in favor of the more comprehensive political body. Taught, however, in the school of Trinitarian thought, we might be persuaded that both the local and the national, both the particular and the comprehensive, have their distinct and significant roles to play. In a word, Trinitarian thought prepares us for thinking of society in terms of distributed roles, separation of powers, and a federalist view of social associations.

For Moltmann, the "correspondence between the community's religious ideas and its political constitution counted as being one of life's self-evident premises."[15] Therefore, he sees the doctrine of the Trinity being developed among Christians as an effective resistance against the centralization of power; it is a "theological doctrine of freedom" and points toward a "community of men and women without supremacy and without subjection."[16]

Hierarchy and Power

At this point I feel the need to call attention to a sense in which I believe Professor Moltmann has overstated the case in a way that I have thought was hardly necessary. I dealt with this point at some length in *God, Hope, and History.* But here I will state the matter more briefly in order to distinguish between what I think might be an extremely valuable insight in Moltmann's thinking on monotheism and power, on the one hand, and what he enters under that heading with regard to hierarchy. He writes, for instance, "as father of the universe he is the universe's highest authority. All other authorities take their powers from him, so that patriarchal hierarchies grow up on this pattern: God the Father—the father of the church—the father of his country— the father of the family. This partiarchal religion is quite obviously not Trinitarian; it is purely monotheistic."[17] And in the foreward to my book dealing with this subject, he wrote: "There are radical ways to deal theologically with power: sanctification and damnation. If power is theologically justified and sanctified, the 'sacred power' is produced—that is, *hierarchy.* If power is theologically deprived of rights and cursed, then the opposite arises—that is, *anarchy.* The expression of hierarchy is, for example, the acknowledgement: 'For God and my country.' The expression of anarchy is: 'Ni Dieu—ni maitre' ('neither God nor state')."[18]

The problem I found in his inclusion of hierarchy in his critique of monarchical monotheism, along with the coercive sorts of power arrangements, is that hierarchy does not always imply power and oppression. We are ruled in different ways. Besides being ruled more or less against our wills by some alien power, we are also ruled by our desires and by our expectations. Love itself constructs for us a hierarchy of values: we love, or should love, those things most valuable more than those things that are of less value. We make judgments on the basis of that hierarchy of values. We anticipate or hope for things that are of proximate and immediate importance, or of ultimate importance. Hope also arranges our world in a type of hierarchy. Our thoughts and our actions are always to some degree ruled by those things that we love and that we hope for. If our hopes and loves are directed toward that which is less worthy, then the disorder shows up in our lives. By contrast, the ordered and peaceful life is ruled by properly ordered love and hope. If monarchical monotheism, in Moltmann's analysis, implies a kind of coercive oppression, then it still does not implicate hierarchy in this broader sense.

My point is that society naturally articulates its sense of values in a hierarchy that reaches into and affects every area of life. In rank, in manners, in speech, in the courtesy afforded age and prestige, or the protection afforded the young and the infirm, in all these and a thousand other ways we express and make incarnate a hierarchy of values. It is certain that they do not reflect infallible or even fair judgment, certainly not in every case. But a society that lacks these becomes, as Shakespeare pointed out long ago, one fit only for the ravenous wolf, in which power alone counts for anything. It seems to me that the better part of Moltmann's argument is directed against that possibility and not against the mere fact of hierarchy.[19]

Monotheism and Centralized Power

Moltmann is not alone, of course, in seeing the connection between monotheism and power, especially political power expressed in the growth of empire. There is little doubt that the emperor Constantine viewed Christian "monotheism" as opportunistically aligned with the need for unifying principles of a theological sort in the empire. Eusebius, the church historian and panegyrist of Constantine does not fail to draw the connection between Constantine's power and the power implied by a sovereign god: "[The Emperor Constantine] openly declared and confessed himself the servant and minister of the supreme King. And God forthwith rewarded him, by making him ruler and sovereign, and victorious to such a degree that he alone of all rulers pursued a continuous course of conquest, unsubdued and invincible, and through his trophies a greater ruler than tradition records ever to have been before. So dear was he to God, and so blessed; so pious and so fortunate in all he undertook, that with the greatest facility he obtained authority over more nations than any who had preceded him, and yet retained his power, undisturbed, to the very close of his life."[20]

To this passage by Eusebius, Garth Fowden, a modern scholar, responds: "Constantine does not just Christianize the Roman Empire; he unifies it too. And he expounds a worldview to which, though it was not absolutely original, he gave new force: one god, one empire, one emperor."[21] Giuseppe Ruggieri summarizes Eusebius's main argument as beginning with the idea that the end of separate nations and "their incorporation into the one Roman Empire was due to divine providence." Consequently, the gospel was aided by the disappearance of national frontiers and the unification of administration in the Empire. Second, the end of national existence and the forging of a unified empire brought about peace, which was promised by the prophets. Third, the one absolute authority on earth corresponds to the one ruler in heaven. And, fourth, a "pluralist world produces a polytheist metaphysic." Therefore, the ending of nation-states means that "polytheism itself lost the right to exist."[22]

Both Moltmann and Ruggieri refer back to the famous essay by Erik Peterson entitled *Der Monotheismus als politisches Problem* in which Peterson denounces the European Enlightenment for its reduction of the fullness of Christian belief in God to mere monotheism." Peterson saw this essentially political heresy as addressed, especially, by the Cappadocian fathers with their elaboration upon the doctrine of the Trinity. This became, in a sense, the verdict of early Christianity upon the Augustan tradition of the divine monarchy. And it was because of the development of a Trinitarian doctrine of God that Christians were prevented from a wholesale adoption of classical philosophical monotheism, which, as Arthur O. Lovejoy has said, "had almost nothing in common with the God of the Sermon on the Mount."[23] Nevertheless, monotheism remains a kind of permanent temptation to dissolve the Christian vision into a justification for unitary rule: if it is true in heaven, then it ought also to be true on earth. It becomes, in a way, a theological Manifest Destiny.

Yet the complaint against monotheism which we find in Moltmann and others leaves us naturally somewhat unsettled. Moltmann does not deny the "oneness" of God, yet for him it must be understood as an inviting and attracting oneness of community: it is a oneness that includes the world because it is the destiny of the world, not a oneness that compels and forces its pattern upon things. That does make a difference in that it is not an abandonment of unity and catholicity which we might have thought were practically the same as monotheism. But is it enough to satisfy what one finds as a tour de force throughout the prophetic writings of the Bible and influences all else? Does it satisfy that strong emphasis upon the exclusiveness of One God, whose rule in Israel is to be shared by no other and whose claims upon the earth deny (eventually) even the reality of other gods? As Bernard Lang points out, "The monotheistic profession of faith became the yardstick for the formation of the biblical canon. It could adopt only what was compatible with the Yahweh-alone idea or its advanced form, monotheism. Everything else was transformed in the process of revision, or thrown out."[24] Furthermore, after Deutero-Isaiah and the Deuteronomic literature of the sixth and fifth centuries, "Judaism possessed its monotheistic creed, which it bore unaltered through the ages, to be handed on to Christianity and Islam." Thus, Lang draws the conclusion that "Monotheism is the gift to mankind of the religion of the Bible."[25]

Must we choose between these two alternatives? Is monotheism either the baneful influence that Erik Peterson, Jürgen Moltmann, and others have seen it to be, promoting the notion of unitary coercive power in the political realm and justifying violence on every level?[26] Or is it instead the great "gift to mankind" that Bernard Lang, Pinchas Lapide, and others would argue?

Could it be argued, that neither view is entirely without merit? Might it be that the danger lies in either extreme? In the Christian understanding of the triunity of God, there is both the unity of God and the differentiation of his three persons. In principle we find theological justification for a view of the world that is Catholic or universal: something that tells us that indeed we are all related to each other and taken up along with the whole of creation in one great destiny. At the same time, the idea of real distinction within the godhead also helps us to know that distinctions are not swallowed up in the unity of things, as some illusion—the *maya* of Hinduism—but they are real and significant. As persons, we are part of the world, and we stand over against the world. Both are true. There is theological justification for our communal existence, even for viewing ourselves as sharing our humanity with all other human beings. And there is also theological justification for thinking of ourselves as individuals. This balance is made real for us in the Incarnation. The danger which Moltmann rightly warns against is, to my mind, not monotheism itself so much as it is monotheism alone—monotheism taken as a replacement for Trinitarian doctrine.

Power and the Secular Illusion

The problem is seen in yet another dimension when we consider *what* we purport to worship or to recognize as the end of human existence, once God has been reduced in the modern mind to mere abstract power. For power, properly speaking, is no end or goal. It is, instead, a means. We have the power—or we do not have the power—to do something. A man has the power to lift a three-hundred-pound rock and heave it into the Brazos River (to take one that's nearby). In this case, power is antecedent to lifting and heaving the rock. Power is the means. Tossing the giant stone in the river is the end. Power itself will always be a means to accomplish something else. Hobbes recognized this when, in *Leviathan*, he said, "The power of a man is his present means to obtain some future apparent good."[27]

We should look at this in terms of some rather common speech about the nature of our times. Our era is often described as "secular." What is meant by this term is usually nothing more complicated than that it is not a "religious" age, that it is not remarkably shaped by religious beliefs but by other, non-religious categories. Yet anything that takes seriously the question of the destiny of things is called religious. Plato's philosophy has a "religious" quality about it because it delves into what is "good" in an ultimate sense. And if that is the character of religious talk, then secular talk must be primarily that which involves something other than ends. Or one might say more accurately that it is talk that *avoids* discussion of the ultimate purpose of life and action.

What we find here is that a secular "culture" is one that either neglects or resists dealing with the problem of the *telos*. And it might do so stubbornly even though some more reflective inhabitants of that culture—even its defenders, like John Stuart Mill and John Dewey—know and readily confess that you really cannot avoid formulating something that serves for ends. They talk naturally about means instead of ends, or as if they were ends. The most abstract and concise way of talking about means, of course, is by talking about *power*.

Allen Tate described secularism in a way that precisely fits what we have been discussing. "Secularism," he said, "is when the ends are replaced by the means." It is when much discussion centers around how to do something and not what to do. A secular culture is one in which the ends are largely assumed—and are therefore unexamined. It is why Bertrand de Jouvenel could say of our technically rich times,

"Every day we can do more and more, until now we can do more than ever before in history . . . but what on earth shall we do?"

We have become experts in the former consideration, but amateurs, in fact barbarians, in the latter. Experience—as well as those we have summoned to speak on that topic—tells us that, though we might well postpone thinking about the goal of life or the goal of our existence, we cannot do so forever. Snatching at straws in our drowning condition, we will attempt to make means our ends, as Allen Tate says, but the reality cannot be forever hidden: means cannot be ends, they are *for* ends. The hammer is for hitting nails, the fish hook is for catching fish, money is for buying food and shelter, food and shelter nourish and protect life . . . and living is for. . . . That is the question. We will always come to it, sooner or later.

The Illusion of Power

When power becomes in some sense the object of pursuit, as it has increasingly in modern times, we are therefore engaging in an illusion. It is rather like the proverbial dog chasing its tail. Much effort is being expended, and a chase of sorts is taking place, but the pursuit is taking the dog nowhere. The illusion of a grand pursuit allows us to imagine we are in control of life and of our destiny. And control is very much the issue, when at a deep level we suspect that things are not under control, at least not under *our* control. This anxiety for control is a form of despair: having found nothing to "rest" our hopes in, we grasp for the lesser things of the created order, just as a drowning man grasps for straws, or a dying man grasps for the most unlikely occult cure.

In its outward expression this despair might take many forms, forms we will recognize in contemporary social problems. It may take the conventional form of depression, resignation, and lethargy. Many astute observers, surveying the creative product of this age, say that we are simply not producing and not displaying the energy that we once did. Our culture has stopped building, ceased the kind of creative production that comes from deep in the human psyche. We have become repetitive, superficial—in a word, lethargic. Paul Tournier once wrote of the immense fatigue that seems so prevalent in modern life. "Our fatigue" he says, "is above all the sign of an estrangement from God and the great fatigue of the modern world expresses its immense need of rediscovering God."[28]

It was a triumph of modernist culture that it was able to suggest that high culture of medieval civilization was static, while its own was full of activity, dynamic in the highest degree. We see that "redefinition of the time" suggested in the early modern juxtaposition of the earlier emphasis upon "rest" as the aim of life and the later modern emphasis upon "motion." Augustine's "our hearts are restless until they find rest in thee" is then seen in the most superficial light, as the aim for a lethargic life. Thomas Merton refused the modern propagandists' version of the idea of "rest," saying "Man was made for the highest activity, which is, in fact, his rest."[29] Such an idea of a high state of vigor is clearly the impression one could gain from the church fathers as a whole. It is also quite clear, as Henri Bergson suggested, that whenever there has been an irruption of mystic awareness, there has been a concurrent high state of activity, resulting in social renewal, charitable institutions, and the like. We have only to think of the enormous and widespread works of charity, in our own day, that occurred because of a small, frail Mother Theresa of Calcutta, to know that there are actions that take place of a higher order than the ordinary push and pull of the uninspired life. St. Francis of Assisi perhaps can claim to have changed Europe more than any single person in history, yet he was not a modern, but a medieval, man.

When we see that the modern self-congratulatory talk about "taking action" can be illusory and may not compare as favorably with other cultures as we think, then we can also imagine that in our culture despair may often take the form of this pretense of action. It can take the form of rage, violence, and attempts to dominate. The air traveler flies into a rage because the aircraft is not exiting the gate on time and he will miss his appointment in another city. He cannot effectively change his situation so he takes it out on the cabin crew and his fellow passengers. The irate driver, angry from a dispute at home, is pushed over the edge by a slowpoke automobile ahead of him, so he pulls a gun and fires two rounds through the rear window. Of course, we know that many worse things have happened because of uncontrolled and inexplicable rage. One reacts to the large things in life by raging against the small things. The boss chews you out at work, and you kick the dog at home (suspecting perhaps that he chases his tale out of a mocking imitation of his master).

Another way of reacting when things appear out of control is to call upon some larger power in order to solve the more immediate issues. It is much as when biblical Judah found itself hard pressed by its small neighbors, Israel and Syria. To relieve its oppression, it called upon the help of the new superpower in the region, Assyria. Assyria did, in fact, lift the oppression of the Syro-Ephraimite aggressors, but they themselves brought a much more serious oppression. It was a move that Judah was soon to regret, as Isaiah prophesied: "Because this people has refused the waters of Shiloah that flow gently, and melt in fear before Rezin and the son of Remaliah; therefore the Lord is bringing up against it the mighty flood waters of the River, the king of Assyria and all his glory; it will rise above all its channels and overflow all its banks; and it will sweep on into Judah as a flood, and, pouring over, it will reach up to the neck."[30] We find something similar when seventeenth-century thinkers such as Pierre Bayle are so concerned with the oppression of local Catholic authorities that they see the solution in greater authority exerted by the state. Hobbes and Locke, likewise exercised by the influence of the clerics, call for an authoritative state, even if—as in Locke's case—the state takes on the form of a bourgeois republic more than an absolute monarchy.

These measures only delay and partially disguise the full experience of despair. They are disguised by their own *activist* form. Rage exhausts, leaving us feeling even more helpless than before. Dreams that some comprehensive power arrangement—a more powerful government, a more powerful ally—eventually disappoint the ones it intended to help as they find themselves freed of their former oppressors only to be more powerfully bound even than before:

> As when a man flees from a lion,
> And a bear meets him,
> Or goes home, leans his hand against the wall
> And a snake bites him.[31]

It eventually disappoints because one finds that the problems that created oppression on the local level exist at the more comprehensive level as well. But because power has become both greater and more remote, the oppression it brings with it inevitably becomes more difficult to remove. At the local level people whose character is more likely to be known to us oppress us. As the centers of power become further removed from us, they act upon us in a more impersonal way, but also—because the machinery that makes it all possible is bureaucratic in nature—in a more inflexible way. We are saved from the personal animosity of the malicious neighbor only to be delivered into the hands of the indifferent, faceless, nameless, unknown functionary—or else the celebrity ruler who we only think we know. The anonymity and abstractness of the whole process fixes us all the more firmly in its grip.

At the conceptual level, what makes this process possible is the steady conversion of society, over a long period of time, but at an accelerated rate in the twentieth century to the notion that social life is framed by a national government at one end and the autonomous individual at the other—the bipolar vision of society. It is a vision that serves the interests of centralized power. This vision contrasts, as we have seen, with Johannes Althusius's understanding of society as a symbiotic relationship of many groups, some more comprehensive than others, from the family, to the collegium, to the community, to the region, to the state, to the church, to the human family as a whole. Each association or group has about it its own goals and its own internal discipline, each linking by degrees and in its own way the individual with the whole of the world, including the state. By this idea, and by the similar Catholic social doctrine of subsidiarity, the state is by no means the only significant social association that an individual belongs to, nor does it constitute what it means for a person to belong to a society. The individual is not first and foremost, let alone exclusively, a citizen of a state.

What we have seen is that the modern doctrine of toleration plays a key role in this process of the bipolarization of society. It has done so, and continues in this role, for the following reason. Each association and group develops out of a sense of its purpose. The purpose might be quite practical and limited, such as one might find as the *raison d'etre* of the collegium or association of workers and professional people. Or it might exist out of a sense that is highly refined, transcendent, and even theological in nature, such as one finds in the case of the church or a religious body. The more the group exists on the basis of a *telos* or purpose that transcends in significance the practical purposes of the state (or the ideological vision of the state), it becomes thereby an indigestible, alien, and resistant object that frustrates the simple bipolar power arrangement.

The society that exists easily between the poles of state and individual is a society that has become featureless. It is a society in which "voluntary" organizations decline, as many sociologists have lately observed in the United States. It has become a "mass" society. Its mode of existence is a secular one. And the individual in such a society stands more or less defenseless against the demands of a powerful state. Commenting on the results of the French Revolution, Benjamin Constant saw this operation clearly: "The interests and memories which spring from local customs contain a germ of resistance which is so distasteful to authority that it hastens to uproot it. Authority finds private individuals easier game; its enormous weight can flatten them out effortlessly as if they were so much sand."[32] The idea of toleration, in the modern sense, calls into question the validity and even the ethical appropriateness of attaching oneself too strongly to the kinds of loyalties and the kinds of transcendent convictions that are the very *soul* of the association. It targets the intractable loyalties, along with the intrinsic disciplines and moral commitments, of the family and the church or the synagogue. It does so not out of a commitment to a certain conspiracy to undo these institutions but out of the tacit and almost intuitive recognition that here are the most formidable barriers to the spreading efficiency of central administration and the centralization of authority. The passions must be harnessed to the larger agenda and not be distributed and made disorderly in the untidy natural associations that spring up so freely in a society not well organized, nor rational, nor subservient to the goals of commerce and power.

It is again the old struggle between Baal and Yahweh, the god of fertility and wealth over against the God of sociability, peace, and righteousness. The modern tale of an ideology of toleration has, as we have seen, increasingly served the priests of Baal. But when we look carefully at the practice of toleration that has its legitimate place in the temple of Yahweh, the whole notion of toleration has not thereby proved to be a selling of the soul.

10

High Tolerance

TOLERANCE, AS IT HAS COME TO BE UNDERSTOOD, is given re-markable form with the experiments in "multiculturalism" that have taken shape in American universities. Stanford, considered by many the best of American universities, was one of the first to engage in a virtual orgy of multicultural experiments, reshaping its curriculum, hiring faculty, and policing student life and speech according to the new standards of multicultural thought. In spite of the fact that the Stanford experiment was a colossal failure, other universities have continued to follow the example of the abortive project. What became apparent at Stanford was the degree to which multiculturalism issued in gross *intolerance*, even though it ostentatiously marched under the banner of tolerance.

In an account by two Stanford graduates, *The Diversity Myth,* we can see where the experiment went badly awry. David Sacks and Peter Thiel write of "liberal Mexican-American students who were 'encircled' and threatened for not uniting with the radicals; a liberal male student hounded out of an all-female feminist studies class; and black students who were 'blacklisted' and persecuted for befriending white students." Sacks and Thiel conclude that the "problem on America's campuses has more to do with intolerance than with ideology."

Obviously, the modern idea of toleration has turned upon itself, producing in many cases greater bigotry than anything it sought to eradicate. The question then becomes how we achieve authentic toleration without merely shifting to another political perspective from which a new kind of intolerance becomes acceptable?

The Difficulties of a Secular Virtue

As we have seen, the very character of modernity has accorded tolerance the status of a secular virtue. It is a virtue inasmuch as it strengthens a certain predisposition toward life together. It is secular in that the predisposition it strengthens is one of postponing or diverting the quest for meaning that is an essential component of social cohesion and the forming of groups or associations. Religion, of course, is what we call that quest, along with the practices and habits of the heart that it engenders. The religious impulse is strong enough to bind people together, and also strong enough to set them at deadly odds with one another.

Toleration, as we modern people have defined it, is the decision to replace that quest with another one both practical and material in nature. Thus, it actually lessens the binding authority of community life, an authority that makes subtle appeal to manners, traditions, group sanctions, and respect for elders. At the same time, the ersatz virtue increases the need for organization, authority exerted from outside the group, formal laws, as well as emphasizing the protection of abstract "rights" that are divorced from what the living community calls the "good." In recent American culture, one need only take note of the lessening authority of the family and the increasing role of government policy to get a sense of what this means at the street level. Recently, Texas, along with a few other states, passed laws over stiff opposition to ensure that parents are informed if their minor child, shepherded usually by school counselors and Planned Parenthood operatives, plans to have an abortion. Never mind permission, this was only to assure that the parents *know* what is happening to their teenage daughters. Authority in such a case was once, not so long ago, assumed to belong to the family and only by default to a public agency.

The natural tension between the authority of government and religious authority was once treated much more forthrightly than it is today, when we listen uncritically to claims that the government is guarantor of freedoms on every front. In the 1880s there was reported in the press a conversation concerning a new religious group in France. Someone with republican sentiments raised serious doubts:

> "It's dangerous, this machine of M. Desjardins."
> "Why?"
> "A religion could come out of it, and not an old tired religion but a new just-born religion, that is an adult religion, for religions have the special quality that they are never more adult than when they are just born . . . ."
> "Well?"
> "Well, this will embarrass government."
> "Why?"
> "I'll bet you, it will embarrass government. Anything with a strong moral life has a will of its own. Anything with a will of its own embarrasses government."[1]

But since the working out of what is "good" is difficult at best in any context, it becomes increasingly difficult as the opportunities for power and wealth expand the horizons of possible social organization. The organized community (the state) outstrips the natural community which is organic in its growth and development, growing out of forces and needs that are internal to the life of the group. The organized community's size and the fact that it is actually constituted by external authority makes commitment to an ecumenical concept or what is indeed the *summum bonum,* the highest good, all the more difficult to maintain. For while an idea of the good is clearly essential to the organic community, it is not strictly necessary to the *orga-*

nized community; for the organic community grows out of its purpose, but an organized community reflects its alien authority or its formal principle. At the same time, economic and political opportunities thrive on efficiency, while the philosophical and religious questions take time. Conflicts are expensive, not often productive of wealth, and are probably unresolvable in the short run. Modern people have elected efficiency and the superficial accord of common pragmatic goals rather than the protracted struggles for ideals, which have all too often, historically, erupted into violent conflict. It is easy to see why toleration is often the virtue of the middle class, the class that values above all comfort and safety. It is also the virtue that the elite most wish for the middle class to have, making the business of ruling all the more efficient and profitable.

At the beginning of this book, I questioned whether toleration or tolerance could be considered a virtue at all. And I concluded that, in the traditional sense, which is to say a religious or even a Christian sense, it is not. But it is a secular virtue, if by secular we mean that the quest for power (or means) has replaced the quest for ends.

Reclaiming the Practice of Toleration

There is, however, as I suggested in chapter one, another side to this issue of toleration. There is a practice of toleration that comes naturally to the religious disposition and is often admirably displayed in the best expressions of religion. I will not say that this is an exclusively Christian predisposition, for the practice of toleration is often touchingly and effectively expressed in such religious philosophies as one finds associated with Hinduism, Taoism, Confucianism, and among the Sufi mystics of Islam. But there is something about Christian faith that promotes this practice, and that sets forth the possibility of authentic toleration so reliably that it is remarkable. And it is, by the way, out of Western (that is to say Christian) culture that tolerance has found such a natural homeplace and that we find it exercising unusual influence over public policy and the expression of a public ethic. The very fact of its modern expression (even if somewhat perverse at times) is witness to an underlying predisposition that could only have come to us out of the centuries, old tutelage of Christian practice. Therefore, it is worth considering what it is about toleration that in our times is well worth an effort to recover. Once the predisposition toward tolerance is disentangled from its questionable alliance with power and the will to power, there is still the memory of a certain practice that makes abundant sense to those who seek peace in a world (whether of the seventeenth or the twentieth century) too thoroughly practiced in war. How might this recovery proceed? How can one, in a word, disentangle the authentic practice of toleration from the modern doctrine of toleration?

We begin with the problems that toleration seeks to address. What are they? First, it is a commonplace to say that the world has grown smaller. It is quite true, however, that technology, communication, and travel, have brought each of us into closer proximity to people all over the globe. That much is no surprise, nor is the sense of urgency with which we might feel that this situation calls for measures, both personal and political, that relieve the clash of cultures.

In addition, however, there are deep cultural divides in modern life that arise, not from the clash of traditional cultures, but from the Enlightenment agenda itself, the results of which are carried forward to our own time. These divides occur because of the attempt to neutralize or even abort the normal processes of culture within groups or associations. For instance, in the United States, it becomes ever more difficult for religious groups to express their core convictions in the public arena—in schools or at public assemblies—because the public space is more and more understood as the province of the state. We need only notice how severely curtailed are the protests of pro-life activists against abortion or how limited now the legal opportunity for a community that might wish to have prayer in its public functions to do so.

But even the discussion of these matters is coming to be more difficult. It is difficult because a large portion of society takes discourse about human meaning and purpose to hinge on personal preference. It does not hinge, that is, on a common acknowledgment of the problem under discussion but on the very thing that makes common agreements impossible. John Gray, the Oxford political philosopher, admits the difficulty, especially, this late in the modern era. "Consider," he says, "the traditional Christian and the person for whom religion has no importance": "The difference between these two may be far greater than that between the traditional Christian and the traditional atheist, such as Bradlaugh, say. For the latter pair had a conception of deity in common and differed only as to its existence, whereas the genuine post-Christian unbeliever (such as myself) may find the very idea of deity repellent, incoherent or flatly unintelligible."[2] Gray calls this the "radical tolerance of indifference." It has its application in the realm of the moral life as well, and perhaps touches us most often at this point. For there is an incommensurable difference between one who thinks this or that course of action to be more just or right, and one who believes it all depends on personal preference and private choice. Whereas two who differ on a course of action but believe there *is* a course of action that is right (or more or less in the right direction) have profoundly more in common.

The differences described by the former more accurately depict our modern divide. Two people who differ as to whether homosexual behavior is right or wrong can still have a basis for conversation. Imagine, however, one who believes it is wrong, placed at the table with one who believes it merely a "lifestyle," something given its place by virtue of personal preference alone. These two have little to talk about and will probably not understand one another. This is at least part of the intractability of the modern question of toleration.

But if it is an acutely modern problem, it is still not an exclusively modern problem. It is a perennially human problem, and it has always reached a certain level of acute distress on the borders between nations and cultures, and in the growth of urban life, and in the expansion of trade, and in the spread of religion. The difference today has to do with the worldwide impact of cultural conflicts along with their swift and perhaps cataclysmic consequences.

Yet the problem itself, the problem to which toleration is addressed, remains the same. The problem—as the last two chapters have attempted to make clear—is that the most deep-seated cultural conflicts have to do with what we conceive (or tacitly sense) as the *telos* of life. *These ends are both necessary for living and incapable of any final resolution.* They are ends because we live *for* them; they are beyond the value of any particular life, and therefore we are often persuaded to give up all else for the sake of them, even to die for them. As people of the seventeenth century were painfully aware, religious conflicts sometimes create wars. They were also well aware that they frequently spoil commerce: so the modern dilemma was in part a conflict between doing good and doing well, and the dilemma drove men mad—mad with bigotry, on the one hand, and mad with greed, on the other. But the radical nature of the problem was expressed in the extremities to which societies went in response to their religious convictions; it was a conflict about the nature of the ends and goals of human life.

The modern response, as we have seen, was an attempt to forestall or bargain with the ultimate questions of human existence, and to do so while profiting from the newly available opportunities for prosperity and power. It was an attempt to achieve a kind of ecumenicity on the material level instead of an ecumenicity of the spirit. It was an attempt to satisfy the human longing essentially without God.

The question we want to ask at this point, therefore, is this: "Is there a basis for tolerant practice that is neither evasive of the deepest quests of the human spirit nor materialistic and secular in its aim?" The answer, I think, is found in one of the central mysteries that has animated Christian culture and that, in fact, has made some

of the greatest intellectual and artistic achievements of the West possible. It is a certain conviction about the incarnation of God in the
particularity of human flesh: the enfleshment of God in Jesus Christ.
I am beginning, therefore, not with speculation or abstract moral
principles. Instead, I am calling attention to the simple historical fact
that here is a pervasive belief that has had enormous impact upon the
traditions of the West, is at the same time not confined to the West,
and offers a basis for practice. And the practice it engenders is, by
the force of its own internal logic, one of tolerance and openness
toward other human beings.

The Incarnation as a Basis for Tolerance

First, I would like to say why I think the theological idea of the Incarnation has a place in this discussion, a discussion that traditionally attempts to give wide birth to theological issues. To begin with,
it highlights the effective nature of an earlier *practice* of toleration, a
practice which we have all along distinguished from the modern doctrine of toleration. The Incarnation, in the first place, is not strictly
speaking, a doctrine. There is, indeed, a doctrine of the Incarnation,
developed and passed on in Christianity; but I say it is not strictly
speaking a *doctrine* because it speaks of what is believed to be a reality. And if it *is* in fact a reality, then the doctrine might be off the
mark by several degrees, or even by a mile, and the essential thing is
not affected in the least. It is either real, or it is not. And if it is real,
it means that the highest spiritual aspirations of the human being and
the most particular elements of existence are bound together eternally
in a community of meaning and purpose. If such a thing is true, then
the implications are for all men and women everywhere and for all
time. No one is excluded. If it is true, it is not just a good idea; it is
a powerful fact. Toleration in this case does not mean that we all
grasp this reality, or even that any of us do so adequately. It means
simply that the reality grasps us, comprehending what it means for

any of us to be human beings. While we cannot comprehend that which comprehends us, we nonetheless owe a certain loyalty to it. That loyalty includes the humility to listen to others, even those whose honest seeking after truth takes a different shape than our own. To do so—to listen in expectation of hearing truth from others whose doctrine differs from our own—is the highest form of loyalty to the insight that we all rely upon a common reality, created by the One God who makes himself known in human flesh.

In the first part of Saint Thomas Aquinas's *Summa Theologica*, question XVI, "On Truth," the greatest of the medieval theologians proceeds to explore the meaning of "truth" by showing various *valid* definitions of truth. He draws first from Augustine, who wrote that "Truth is that whereby is made manifest that which is." Then he turns to Hilary, who wrote, "Truth makes being clear and evident." Then Anselm: "Truth is rightness perceptible by the mind alone." Next Avicenna, a Muslim teacher (tenth and eleventh century) is quoted: "The truth of each thing is a property of the being which has been given to it." And finally Aristotle, the pagan philosopher, who says that a statement is true "from the fact that a thing is, not from the fact that a thing is true."[3]

What are we to make of this unpretentious move by Saint Thomas, in a work of Christian theology, from the church fathers, to medieval Christians, to a Muslim, to a pagan? There is no self-conscious celebration of diversity here, not even the thought of it. Nor is there the resigned air of "everyone is entitled to one's own opinion, since no one can gainsay opinion." Just the opposite is the case, in fact, because there is the resolute pressing forward to an idea of truth that is common to everyone simply because it is *real* for everyone. It is inclusive not in the easy modern way that makes its claim before any effort has been expended to find common ground but in the more arduous medieval way. It promotes not a unity that is assumed and goes unquestioned at the beginning but one that is found at some cost to those who search. Furthermore, it is a response to issues that divide us, settled on the level of the intellect and the affections, whereas the modern response to ultimate issues only leaves the way open to resolving them by the use of power and a contest of the wills. Here, then, we find a practice that recognizes the very complicated way God has of making himself known to us in the partiality of human experience, yet always with the aim of leading us to wholeness.

To enter into such a practice is to enter into the mystery of the Incarnation. It is to acknowledge the God-ordained *end* of human existence—an end not imagined or willed, an end that serves no evasion of the human vocation, but a true end: an end in which we might *rest*. Which is to say, it is an end that embodies our highest activity and our deepest motivation as human beings.

Now I want to say, in as few words as possible, why such conditions for tolerant practice might exist in a society convinced of the Incarnation, and why it is that the church founded by Jesus Christ might be the natural culture for the authentic recovery of toleration.

The Incarnation promises to resolve the problem of finding a modus vivendi in the midst of cultural ambiguity and human uncertainty. It does so in three ways: by asserting that there is meaning in existence without reducing that meaning to given propositions; by revealing the paradoxical relationship of authority and humility; and by opening the way toward trust rather than fear as the key to relationships among human beings and between human beings and the world.

The Restoration of Purpose

Thomas Merton said, "we have a way of seeking the good things of this life as if they were our last end."[4] My seeking for a purpose is a search that includes myself *and the world*. It embraces all that is, all that has been, all that is yet to be. It asks the question "Why am I here?" And by *here* we are including all of reality. Our sense of place is certainly local and particular, but it is inevitably universal. Primitive cultures quite strictly bound to their own locale, and seeing the world through the eyes of a limited group of people, often locate in their terrain a site they refer to as the center, or the "navel," of the world. The human spirit might be said to be imperialistic in the sense that it must understand its place in the midst of everything.

From the standpoint of theistic reflection, the picture becomes quite clear. The world does constitute a whole, and we are included in that whole because of the unity of God who created all and redeems all. So, he is the proper object of our seeking. And when the end and goal of our seeking is something other than God, it is necessarily partial. It is inevitable that the search for genuine destiny will be frustrated. Mircea Eliade wrote of this as the essential thing in all religions. It is what religion attempts to articulate: "That the dialectic of hierophanies, of the manifestation of the sacred in material things, should be an object for even such complex theology as that of the Middle Ages serves to prove that it remains *the* cardinal problem of any religion. One might even say that all hierophanies are simply prefigurations of the miracle of the Incarnation, that every hierophany is an abortive attempt to reveal the mystery of the coming together of God and man."[5]

To state such a thing is easy enough. Something within us responds to the notion that somehow we are related (we know not how) to all things, and all things are somehow related to each other. But what we experience is not whole but partial. Furthermore, it is *daily*: it is presented to us in little slices of time. It is like riding through the Smokey Mountains, seeing bits of the landscape hedged in by mountains, forced to follow winding roads down ravines and canyons, limited in our sight by banks of fog in the early morning or profound darkness at night. It is hardly the same thing as holding a roadmap in one's hand and comprehending the entire region in a glance. In that case, we can place a finger on our destiny, and with a bit of calculation we make sense of where we are and where we are going. Life, of course, is not that simple. Nevertheless, we have what might be called an experience of the *telos* even in the most ordinary processes in life, from learning to traveling to creating.

Let me attempt to describe that experience in a way that helps to make sense of the problem we are dealing with, the problem of how we might respond to the fundamental differences among people in a community or in a world. Let me say further, for which we have the urgent impression that it ought to be whole, that it ought to bear within it what we call "peace"—a dynamic harmony of all its disparate parts—or "rest," a settled direction in all its disparate movements.

An experience that everyone has in life is what I would call the dialectic of order and disorder. We move, each of us, from the clarity of a few things whose relationship to each other and to us is clear, to the inclusion of a greater number and variety of things that in turn create confusion until some principle or intuition unites them in a greater whole. We find this in matters as basic as learning mathematics to something as rare as the spiritual journey of a mystic. It is captured in the civilizing effort to extend a culture essentially local and tribal to a framework which accommodates strange people, strange lands, and strange customs in a framework more cosmopolitan and catholic. Both the climb to more or less ecumenical civilizations and the decline from them are occasioned by periods of brilliant but always incomplete clarity. Mystics tell of experiences of simple faith, followed by doubt, followed by intense awakening, followed by a dark night of the soul, sometimes followed by a more complete illumination. Life is a process of composition and decomposition, of simple clarity in which the gain of greater clarity only follows the disorder of expansion to include more of the whole.

Almost always the experience of greater inclusion appears as something that comes to us from the outside. It was not "with us" as a part of our logical calculation, but it came to us as an intuition. The rarer and higher of those experiences we call revelation. Insight on this level is not available to everyone but to a very few, even though it is *for* the many. Lockean clarity, you will recall, required the even availability of common sense—and "Christianity that will be comprehensible for laboring and illiterate men."[6] Before modern times it would have been considered eccentric to require such a broad source. For ancient peoples, without exception, the source of civilizing wisdom was narrow and its benefits broad, for its truest expression is in the common life of the people. For modern people, the process is turned on its head: the sources of wisdom are broad and its truest expression is narrow. They are broad in that they are especially validated when almost anyone can understand them and approve them, and they are narrow in that their truest expression is the ideology of an intellectual elite. Hence, as Leo Strauss once insisted, philosophy for the ancients was esoteric and for moderns it is exoteric.[7]

What I have described from one point of view is the seeking of that *telos* which we find in God. What I have described from the other point of view is the grace by which that seeking becomes effectual. One involves faith and the looking in anticipatory longing toward that which is the fulfilling of faith. The other involves grace through God's self-disclosure in revelation, which comes to us through the esoteric channels of tradition. Man finds his *telos* in God; God finds his *telos* in man. The twin sense of disparity and unity in the world is found satisfied in community: in the incarnation of God in man. It responds to the question coming so naturally to the Psalmist's lips, "What is man that You take thought of him, And the son of man that You care for him?" It is the articulation of a mutual *telos*—man in God and God in man.

The Paradox of Power and Humility

The Incarnation, therefore, means not only that man finds his chief end in God but God finds his chief end in man. Revelation tells us not only who God is, but who we are. At one and the same time it

reveals true God *and* true man, *vere Deus, vere homo.* The humiliation of God in man is at the same time the exaltation of man in God.
The idea of power flowing from God on high, distributed among men
and women, and exercised over nature—this notion of a one-way
sacred rule—does not adequately articulate what the Christian believes to be true. It is only one side of the picture, and taken alone it
is false, just as every heresy embodies a truth, but a truth taken alone
and without other truths. The other side of the picture is expressed
in the teachings of the apostles that emphasize the authority with
which the human being is endowed by God.

At Caesarea-Philippi, Jesus' famous prophesy concerning the
church is not one of subordination so much as one of exaltation. To
Peter he says, "I will give you the keys of the kingdom of heaven; and
whatever you bind on earth shall have been bound in heaven, and
whatever you loose on earth shall have been loosed in heaven." This
lifting up of the human authority is confirmed in Mark's use of the
word *exousia* (power or authority) to describe Jesus' authority over
demons, over death, over nature, regarding the Sabbath and so on; and
then using the same word as Jesus authorizes his disciples in the same
way: "And He summoned the twelve and began to send them out in
pairs, and gave them authority (*exousia*) over the unclean spirits"
(Mark. 6:7). Paul's letter to the Ephesians describes the Christians
there as belonging to those "heavenly places" from which Christ himself now rules "far above all rule and authority and power and dominion, and every name that is named, not only in this age but also
in the one to come" (Eph. 1:21). The picture is clearly not simply one
of power distributed from on high but power exercised as a cosmic
exchange. It is not the love of power but the power of love: God has
become man, and that man, the representative of the race of men, is
indeed God, so that human beings can participate in all that God is.

Therefore, power is never understood unambiguously and directly as some kind of achievement or possession but always para-

doxically: "whoever wishes to be great among you shall be your servant, and whoever wishes to be first among you shall be your slave" (Matt. 20:26). Power is truly exercised as it is given up. Humiliation and exaltation go together. The picture here is not one of power flowing downward from some centralized authority but more one of the condescension of God in Christ on the cross in which his power to save is made perfect and by whose example believers come to be exalted along with him. The picture is painted beautifully in Philippians, where Paul enjoins disciples to "have this attitude in yourselves which was also in Christ Jesus: Who, although He existed in the form of God, did not regard equality with God a thing to be grasped, but emptied Himself, taking the form of a bond-servant, and being made in the likeness of men. Being found in appearance as a man, He humbled Himself by becoming obedient to the point of death, even death on a cross. For this reason also, God highly exalted Him, and bestowed on Him the name which is above every name, so that at the name of Jesus every knee will bow, of those who are in heaven and on earth and under the earth, and that every tongue will confess that Jesus Christ is Lord, to the glory of God the Father" (Phil. 2:5-9).

But when power is taken unambiguously, as the mere exercise of one will over another, or the exercise of "mind over matter," it becomes the worst sort of idolatry and heresy. That is why Marion Montgomery said that "the opposite of love is not hate, but power."[8] And by that he meant not the power that attends to the attraction of love but power that is seized directly, coercive power, the power to execute one's will upon other people and things.

Yet we cannot miss the fact that this very heresy is the legacy of modernity. It is confidence in power as the mere exercise of will. It is what Francis Bacon had in mind when he said "Knowledge is power" and Descartes when he hoped science would make us the "masters and possessors of nature."

The Recovery of Trust

When one considers, with any sense of detachment and distance, thinkers of the early modern period such as Hobbes—not the dissenting thinkers, but the ones whose ideas and attitudes tended to prevail—then is it not natural to sense a certain pervasive pessimism? Descartes is driven by doubts that our minds naturally yield to us anything about the world that we can know with any certainty. The world does not so much lie before us to be discovered and known (and, according to Augustine, known in order to be loved) as it is clouded over by the very real possibility of doubting anything and everything, except one's own doubting mind. Hobbes believed the world populated by men and women who were fundamentally in a state of war, "each one against each one." The life of human beings without the intervention of some self-serving artifice in the form of governmental powers is destined to be "solitary, poor, nasty, brutish and short." Montaigne, Bacon, Bayle, and Kant were especially impressed with the notion that tradition and authorities were not to be trusted; one must, as Kant put it, "trust one's own intelligence."

The modern world has been profoundly affected by doubt, fear, and distrust. Knowledge of the world has been cast in the role of that which assures safety, control, and relative certainty. Knowledge is, as Bacon said, power. It is that which makes us, according to Descartes, the masters and possessors of nature. For the real world is not so much to be known and loved as it is to be conquered, subdued, possessed, and made safe. Along this same line the modern doctrine of toleration played a part in this program of making the world safe and subduing its unruly nature. The seventeenth century supplied much fertilizer for the growth of this dangerous jungle of a world; but nevertheless, the world modern men and women visualized was a dangerous one, with much to be feared and little to be trusted.

The Incarnation, however, inserts into this picture a new reason to hope and to trust. It asserts that though the world is full of suffering, and often warrants the fear and mistrust, it is nevertheless not destined to remain that way, and it is therefore not essentially a reality to be feared and distrusted. It is destined to be fully in harmony with the will of a good God who created men and women for good things.

To a large extent, therefore, modern people were impressed by the disharmony between the Judeo-Christian understanding of God and the world as they found it. They reacted to that picture not with the openness of soul and mind that characterized the earlier practice of tolerance that we find in figures such as Thomas Aquinas and Clement of Alexandria but with an effort to call off any further discussion of those matters that gave rise to the dangerous disputes of the modern world. While the older practice of toleration brought men and women to the table to discuss those things that most concerned them—their purpose here in this life, the goal that motivates them and makes them truly human—the newer doctrine closed the discussion so that one might get on with the practical agenda. The modern world has attended to means but not ends: the very essence of secularity.

The Incarnation announces the accomplishment of reconciliation between God and man. It therefore announces the essential goodness of that creation. It is not something to be feared. One's efforts to know the world are in the end fruitful, even if not in the present. And human beings are not intended to live in deadly conflict, but in the bonds of love and friendship. One can therefore have hope. And if one can have hope, then one can live with trust instead of fear, confidence instead of doubt, openness to the world and its men and women rather than locked into an endless cycle of fear and conflict.

The Recovery of Authentic Toleration

I do not apologize for, or regret in any way, my turn to theology in these latter pages, though I began the book in the realm clearly of

political theory. In truth, the argument has been a theological one
from the beginning. For however we define toleration, the idea is
necessarily a theological one. It concerns whether and how men and
women shall proceed to deal with the ultimate questions of the meaning and purpose of human existence when these issues so strongly
divide us. The modern strategy, called toleration, is to postpone or
divert those questions and to attend instead to other questions—to
think about means rather than ends. But that also is a decision that
has strong implications with regard to theology: in a word, it says
something about God, and about what we think in reference to God.
So our return to theology is not only appropriate, it is necessary. It
is taking up the question that, at the dawn of the Enlightenment, was
set aside. And it is asking whether it was right to set it aside, or
whether the modus vivendi provided in a life shaped by theology has
not a *better* chance of achieving the practice of tolerance than otherwise. And it is asking whether a return to those questions, motivated
by nobler ends, might not really provide more tolerance than the
secular evasion of questions that, after all, can never be entirely set
aside, just as they can never be entirely settled.

The important thing is to make appropriate distinctions. There
is a tolerance that serves the interest of power, economic and political power. That has been the burden of much of this study, because
I thought it important to see a connection that is often overlooked,
one which sheds light on what modern people mean by toleration.
And there is also a tolerance that serves the interest of knowledge—
not knowledge in the Baconian sense of knowledge-as-power but in
the Augustinian sense of knowledge in order to love. It serves the
interest of knowledge because our knowledge is partial, it is imperfect and plagued by our imperfections. It is an expression of the virtue of humility.

What I am distinguishing as the *practice* of toleration, over against
the *doctrine* that emerges from development of democratic liberalism,
is the logical result of a recognition that our imperfections oblige us

to listen to the insights of others. We are utterly dependent upon the gifts of society and tradition—even traditions other than our own. It is a toleration that recognizes not the implied self-sufficiency of the individual or of various idiosyncratic groups in a supposed pluralistic world but the insufficiency of these limits and the ultimate need for a catholic vision. Even as the doctrine of toleration promotes isolation, the practice of toleration gently nudges us into community. Therefore, authentic toleration serves, and does not hinder, the forming and the functional life of groups within society. It does not hinder in that it does not discourage the quest for ultimate meaning that is the inner light and life of any social group of any lasting importance.

By contrast, the latter day doctrine of toleration serves the agenda of *organization*, the attempt to use groups for purposes not strictly demanded by the nature of the group itself. It uses the group more than serves the group. Its purposes are detached from the life of the group, unlike that of the natural group whose *geist* is its purpose. Just as the organized social entity relies upon sanction and force from outside the group, this pseudo-toleration is intended to interfere with the honest seeking of every normal social group or association which is to *find its vocation* and to give it concrete expression in morals, manners, art, language, and in every way that gives full scope to its own prejudices.

The idea can now be given up that the kind of toleration that has become so important a part of the ideological arsenal of liberal democracies has served to preserve individual liberties. Too often, in our times, the observation of Bertrand de Jouvenel has been proven true that democracy, "in the centralizing, pattern-making, absolutist shape which we have given to it is, it is clear, the time of tyranny's incubation."[9] And we do well to listen to D. W. Brogan's warning from a few years ago that "some modern deifiers of the state, democratic as well as totalitarian, preach and practise a doctrine of Divine Right far more uncritical than Filmer's. For their rulers, the führer or the duce, the party or the sovereign people cannot do wrong, morally or intellectually. We are, most of us in the West, immunized against the doctrine of political infallibility and impeccability when it comes to us in the discredited forms it took in Berlin and Rome or even in the more sophisticated form it takes in Moscow. But we are not immune from 'democratic' arguments which state or imply that a majority can do no wrong, if it is *our* majority; that, if we are part of it, it cannot do anything disastrously silly. It can and does."[10]

Because authentic toleration is a reflection of humility, it militates against the egoistic tendencies of the individual and makes the formation of groups possible and meaningful. It draws naturally from the spirit of self-sacrifice. It endures assaults upon its most long lasting dogmas for the sake of making dialogue possible, because the process of dialogue even about, or perhaps especially about, the most cherished convictions, is the heart and soul of the group, whether a family, a church, or a community of professionals, or a region that shares distinct practices and manners and patterns of language. By contrast, pseudo-toleration wants to make dialogue possible only so long as it conforms to certain "rules" that preordain its result. Thus do universities impose strictures on the speech of both faculty and students that does not conform to ever changing notions about gender, "sexual-orientation," minorities, and an anti-Western bias. The role of the "Anglo-American academic class" in promoting such an agenda has been held up to ridicule by John Gray. They are the self-appointed "voice of an alienated counter-culture, hostile to its own society and enamored of various exotic regimes—of which it knows, in fact, nothing." As such, it "has acquired a Monty Pythonish character, as the peoples and even the rulers of these regimes have exposed their failings to a pitiless scrutiny in which the pretensions of their ruling ideologies have been devastatingly deflated."[11] Just as pseudo-toleration answers power with power, it answers bigotry with bigotry. The hallmark of authentic tolerant practice should be the listening heart for which the wise king prayed[12] and not the management of language and appointing itself the arbiter of all public discussions.

Finally, authentic toleration's anti-hubristic character takes us in an altogether different direction from the modern doctrine with its individualist preoccupation. Not only does it open the individual toward the larger group but the group toward even larger connections. Its impetus is inevitably catholic, and its ultimate horizon, the world itself. For the wound of broken fellowship which Christian belief posits as lying at the foundation of our human pathos is satisfied by nothing short of total restoration. It is as Grace Westerduin has envisioned it, and as we all sense it deep within us:

> Time's running out,
> (as life-blood seeps
> out of a mortal wound).
> Nothing now,
> Short of eternity,
> Shall ever serve to staunch it![13]

Such toleration reaches outward toward an ecumenical goal, with eternity as its ultimate horizon, because its practice is essentially the practice of the open soul. It springs not from the fear and self-protection that Thomas Hobbes was so sure animated all things in human society where life is naturally "solitary, poor, nasty, brutish and short," but it springs from a propensity toward magnanimity and a predisposition toward faith. The recovery of this *practice of toleration* would mark the reversal of a very old prejudice in the modern mind. It would reverse the deep-seated suspicion that undergirds much of modern thought, the suspicion that the world cannot be known, much less loved, and that it must be conquered in order to be made safe. The recovery of toleration would now have to be a recovery of faith itself and a rediscovery of the freedom afforded men and women to think and act in a world designed for human beings to inhabit in peace.

Notes

Preface

1 Hannah Arendt, *On Violence* (New York: Harcourt Brace and Company, 1970), 82."

1   *The Cunning of History*

1 Johannes Althusius, *Politica: An Abridged translation of Politics Methodically Set Forth and Illustrated with Sacred and Profane Examples*, ed. and trans. Frederick S. Carney (Indianapolis: Liberty Fund, 1995), 77. Althusius wrote, for instance, "Moderation should be observed . . . . For no mode of thought has ever come forth as so perfect that the judgment of all learned men would subscribe to it. Aretius concludes that if the principle articles of faith are preserved, nothing should stand in the way of disagreement on opinions in other Christian matters." It should be remembered that European references to religious toleration, or in this case "moderation," almost always, in the sixteenth and seventeenth centuries, considered it within the context of a Christian polity.
2 Michael Walzer, *On Toleration* (New Haven: Yale University Press, 1997), 25.
3 Ibid.
4 Dietrich Bonhoeffer, *Ethics* (New York: Touchstone Books, 1995), 147.
5 Frederick S. Carney, "Introduction" to *Politica* by Johannes Althusius, (Indinapolis: Liberty Fund, 1995), ix.

6   Althusius, *Politica*, 17.
7   Ibid.
8   Ibid.
9   Daniel J. Elazar, foreward to *Politica* by Johannes Althusius, xxxviii.

2   *The Ecumenical Impulse*

1   The fact that arguments for "human rights" are compelling does not mean that they are adequate. The "rights" tradition suffers from the same one-sided emphasis on the individual that we find in much modern thought. But it is there because of a sense, fostered by Christianity, that each human being shares in a dignity that belongs to all human beings. It is, in fact, an ecumenical claim.
2   William H. McNeill, *The Pursuit of Power: Technology, Armed Force, and Society since A.D. 1000* (Chicago: University of Chicago Press, 1982), 133.
3   Robert A. Nisbet, *The Quest for Community* (New York: Oxford University Press, 1953), 164.
4   A. J. Conyers, "Communism's Collapse: The Receding Shadow of Transcendence," *Christian Century* (May 2, 1990): 466. This article deals with the fact that communism's collapse is not strictly speaking a corresponding victory for a Christian view of the world since its failure in part stems from the same forces of secularism and the loss of transcendence that undermine a Christian sense of reality.
5   *Troilus and Cressida* 1.3.116-124.
6   Carl J. Friedrich and Charles Blitzer, *The Age of Power* (Ithaca: Cornell University Press, 1957).
7   Simon P. Wood, *Clement of Alexanria: Christ the Educator*, viii. He writes, "The famous Neo-Platonic Alexandrian, Philo the Jew, a century and a half before, had left a deep Hellenistic imprint upon the culture of that city. . . . It was only natural, then, that the Christian community in Alexandria should turn to a deeper study of the faith than prevailed in earlier missionary regions. Such was the origin of the catechetical school which Clement found under the leadership of Pantaenus." And on page x, we read, "Clement also shared Philo's Hellenism, his humanism. More than any previous Christian writer, Clement recognized the integral relationship between all that was worth while in pagan literature and the new Christian faith. Like Philo, he calls on Homer and Plato, the dramatists and the Stoics and all the best writers of Greece to substantiate his arguments."
8   St. Thomas Aquinas, *On the Eternity of the World* (Milwaukee, Wisc.: Marquette University Press, 1964). A clear comment on this text is found

in Ralph McInerny, *A First Glance at St. Thomas Aquinas* (Notre Dame: University of Notre Dame Press, 1990), 103-08.

9 Clark Pinnock, *A Wideness in God's Mercy: the Finality of Jesus Christ in a World of Religions* (Grand Rapids, Michigan: Zondervan, 1992). Pinnock perhaps goes too far in accommodating the tastes of pluralistic and overly-sensitive culture, but he draws upon a solid tradition of what might be termed toleration for other cultures and other religious traditions in the Bible.

10 Henry Chadwick, *The Early Church* (London: Penguin books, 1993), 74, 75.

11 Colin Brown, *Christianity and Western Thought* (Downers Grove, Ill.: InterVarsity Press, 1990), 88, 89.

12 Chadwick, *The Early Church*, 76, 77.

13 F. L. Cross and E. A. Livingstone, eds., *The Oxford Dictionary of the Christain Church*, Third Edition (Oxford: Oxford University Press, 1997), 364.

14 Chadwick, *The Early Church*, 99.

15 *Stromata* 1:94.

16 David Burrell, *Knowing the Unknowable God: Ibn-Sina, Maimonides, Aquinas* (Notre Dame: University of Notre Dame Press, 1986), ix.

17 Ibid., 109.

18 Burrell notes that "one suspects that not even Aquinas, who executed the major act of synthesis, would have seen it as an intercultural acheivement. He seemed rather to have been imbued with an intrinsic respect for human understanding, inherited from the Greeks through the Arab *falasifa*, which counseled him to acknowledge truth wherever it may be found" (*Knowing the Unknowable God*, 109).

19 *Oxford English Dictionary*, 2nd ed., s.v. "tolerance."

20 Article I, Meaning of Tolerance, Declaration of Principles on Tolerance (UNESCO: Nov. 16, 1995).

21 Arendt, *On Violence*, 83, 84.

3   A Feeling of Uncertainty

1   John Dewey, *The Quest for Certainty* (New York: Minton, Balch, & Company, 1929), 6, 27, 33.

2   Stephen Toulmin, *Cosmopolis, The Hidden Agenda of Modernity* (Chicago: University of Chicago Press, 1990), 77.

3   Ibid., 79.

4   Samuel Taylor Coleridge, *The Statesman's Manual, or the Bible the Best Guide to Political Skill and Foresight: A Lay Sermon Addressed to the*

Higher Classes of Society, in *Coleridge on the Seventeenth Century,* ed. Roberta Florence Brinkley (Durham, N.C.: Duke University Press, 1955), 408.

5 A. Lloyd Moote, *The Seventeenth Century: Europe in Ferment* (Lexington: D.C. Heath, 1970), 17.

6 Bertolt Brecht, *Mother Courage and Her Children,* trans. Eric Bentley (New York: Grove Press, 1966), 23-24.

7 Henry Kissinger, *Diplomacy* (New York: Simon & Schuster, 1994), 59.

8 *Lettre secrète à Louis XVI* (1694 or 1695).

9 William H. McNeill, *The Pursuit of Power,* 117.

10 William H, McNeill wrote: "A well-drilled army, responding to a clear chain of command that reached down to every corporal and squad from a monarch claiming to rule by divine right, constituted a more obedient and efficient instrument of policy than had ever been seen on earth before. Such armies could and did establish a superior level of public peace within all the principal European states. This allowed agriculture, commerce, and industry to flourish, and, in return enhanced the taxable wealth that kept the armed forces in being. A self-sustaining feed-back loop thus arose that raised Europe's power and wealth above levels other civilizations had attained. Relatively easy expansion at the expense of less well organized and disciplined armed establishments became assured, with the result that Europe's world-girdling imperial career extended rapidly to new areas of the globe" (*The Pursuit of Power,* 117).

11 Thomas Hobbes, *Human Nature* and *De Corpore Politico* (New York, Oxford: Oxford University Press, 1994), 141, 155, 162.

12 Thomas Hobbes, *Leviathan* (New York: Touchstone, 1997), 317, 299, 132.

13 Bertrand de Jouvenel, *On Power: the natural history of its growth* (Indianapolis: Liberty Press, 1993), 417. He continues: "Tocqueville, Comte, Taine, and many another redoubled their warnings in vain. . . . Useless Cassandras! And why so useless? Perhaps societies are governed in their onward march by laws of which we are ignorant. Do we know whether it is their destiny to avoid the mortal errors which beset them? Or whether they are not led into them by the same dynamism which carried them to their prime? Whether their seasons of blossom and fruitfulness are not achieved at the cost of a destruction of the forms in which their strength was stored? After the firework display, the darkness of a formless mass, destined to despotism or anarchy."

4 Thomas Hobbes and the Fears of Modernity

1 "Authority, not truth, makes law" (*Leviathan,* chapter XXVI).

2 Noel Malcolm, "A Summary Biography of Hobbes," in *The Cambridge*

Companion to Hobbes, ed. Tom Sorrell (Cambridge: Cambridge University Press, 1996), 15.

3   A. E. Taylor, *Thomas Hobbes* (London: Kennikat Press, 1970), 5.

4   Thomas Traherne. Also there is the remarkable piece by Augustine on the "weight of love": "A body tends by its weight towards the place proper to it—weight does not necessarily tend towards the lowest place but towards its proper place. Fire tends upwards, stone downwards. By their weight they are moved and seek their proper place. Oil poured over water is borne on the surface of the water, water poured over oil sinks below the oil: it is by their weight that they are moved and seek their proper place. Things out of their place are in motion: they come to their place and are at rest. My love is my weight: wherever I go my love is what brings me there."

5   Malcolm, "A Summary Biography of Hobbes," 12.

6   Leo Strauss, *The Political Philosophy of Hobbes* (Chicago: University of Chicago Press, 1952), ix.

7   Michael Oakeshott, introduction to *Leviathan* by Thomas Hobbes (New York: Touchstone, 1962).

8   At the other extreme we find Pelagianism, which relies on the goodness of creation and fails to take seriously the extraordinary intervention of God in redemption. So the extremes that normative Christianity has always struggled against is that of "all creation and no redemption" (Pelagianism) and "all redemption and no creation" (gnosticism). Puritanism tended toward the latter; and some, such as Eric Voegelin, would classify it as a modern gnostic ideology along with other Calvinistic movements. For the record, I would not. However, I can see his point, and it illuminates something important about the Protestant-Calvinist-Puritan trend in theology.

9   The close association of Hobbes with the charge of being an atheist (a quite serious charge in those days) is perhaps indicated by a case in which Daniel Scargill, Fellow of Corpus Christi College, Cambridge, was subject to expulsion until he delivered a recantation which included: "Whereas I . . . being through the instigation of the Devil possessed with a foolish proud conceit of my own wit and not having the fear of God before my eyes: Have lately vented and publickly asserted in the said University divers wicked, blasphemous, and Atheistical positions (particularly, that all right of Dominion is founded only in Power: That all moral Righteousness is founded only in the positive Law of the Civil Magistrate), professing that I gloried to be an *Hobbist* and an *Atheist*; and vaunting, that Hobbs should be maintained by *Daniel* that is by me." Samuel I. Mintz, *The Hunting of Leviathan* (Cambridge: Cambridge University Press, 1962), 50-51.

10 Hobbes, *Leviathan*, 100.

11 Ibid., 132.

12 Ibid., 35.

13 Thomas Hobbes, *The Elements of Law*, ed. J. C. A. Gaskin (Oxford, New York: Oxford University Press, 1994), 36.

14 Hobbes, *Leviathan*, 45.

15 Ibid., 47.

16 Cited in Marion Montgomery, *Why Hawthorne was Melancholy?* (LaSalle, Ill.: Sherwood Sugden & Co., 1984), 70.

17 Dr. Joy Brown, radio broadcast of September 27, 1999.

18 Hobbes, *Leviathan*, 131-32.

19 Ibid., 118.

20 Ibid., 123.

21 Ibid., 113.

22 Hobbes, *Elements of the Law*, 104-05.

23 A classic study of the true goals of large states, over against the offered rhetoric, is Edmond Wilson's *Patriotic Gore*, concerning the literature and speech during and after the American sectional war of the mid-nineteenth century.

24 Note that Hobbes's *Leviathan* was published in 1651, and Althusius's *Politica* was published only a few years earlier, in 1643.

25 Donald W. Livingston, "The Very Idea of Secession," *Society* 35:5 (July/August 1998): 39.

26 Hobbes, *Elements of the Law*, 113.

27 Ibid., 112.

28 Hobbes, *Leviathan*, 157.

29 Ibid.

30 Ibid., 142ff.

31 Hobbes, *Elements of Law*, 115ff. (esp. xx.15).

5 *Pierre Bayle and the Modern Sanctity of the Individual*

1 Elisabeth Labrousse, *Bayle* (Oxford: Oxford University Press, 1983), 15.

2 Labrousse, *Bayle*, 34.

3 Amie Godman Tannenbaum, "The Impact of Bayle's Life on the Philosophical Commentary," in *Pierre Bayle's Philosophical Commentary: A Modern Translation and Critical Interpretation* (New York: Peter Lang, 1987), 307.

4 Labrousse, *Bayle*, 35-36.

5 Thomas Aquinas, *Summa Theologiae*, 1.19.13 and 1-11.19.5-6.

6 Labrousse, *Bayle*, 60.

7 Pierre Bayle, *Historical and Critical Dictionary: Selections*, trans. Richard H. Popkin (Indianapolis/Cambridge: Hackett, 1991), 194.

8 Bayle, *Dictionary*, 195.

9 Bayle, *Dictionary*, 195-96.

10 Craig Brush, in *Montaigne and Bayle: Variations on the Theme of Skepticism* (The Hague: Martinus Nijhoff, 1966), 383, writes "What does Bayle mean when he says that one must make Pyrrhonists feel the infirmity of reason? That is certainly carrying philosophical coals to Newcastle. As has been shown, there are two facets of Pyrrhonism, one that Bayle admires, one that he rejects. As long as skepticism is the critique of natural reason, he agrees heartily. If, however, it results in complete paralysis of judgment, he finds it pernicious. This is borne out by the hundreds of times that he accuses a doctrine of resulting in disastrous Pyrrhonism."

11 Tannenbaum, *Pierre Bayle's Philosophical Commentary*, 154.

12 Ibid., 155-56.

13 Ibid., 156.

14 I am referring here to the excellent book on twentieth-century music, driven by the popular market rather than by true aesthetic concerns, entitled *The Triumph of Vulgarity: Rock Music in the Mirror of Romanticism* by Robert Pattison (New York: Oxford University Press, 1987).

15 Pattison, *The Triumph of Vulgarity*, 8-9.

16 Christopher Lasch, *The True and Only Heaven* (New York: W. W. Norton, 1991), 17.

17 Harry Blamires, *The Christian Mind* (Ann Arbor: Servant Books, 1978), 13-14. He had in mind writers such as George Orwell, Albert Camus, and George Andrzeyevski.

18 Tannenbaum, *Pierre Bayle's Philosophical Commentary*, 149.

19 Donald W. Livingston, *Philosophical Melancholy and Delirium: Hume's Pathology of Philosophy* (Chicago: University of Chicago Press, 1998), 147.

20 Immanuel Kant, "What is Enlightenment?" [1784], in *The Philosophy of Kant*, ed. Carl J. Friedrich (New York: The Modern Library, 1993), 145. On the issue of individualism and its effects, the entire paragraph is worth reciting: "Enlightenment is man's leaving his self-caused immaturity. Immaturity is the incapacity to use one's intelligence without the guidance of another. Such immaturity is self-caused if it is not caused by lack of intelligence, but by lack of determination and courage to use one's intelligence without being guided by another. *Sapere Aude!* Have the courage to use your own intelligence! Is therefore the motto of the enlightenment."

21 Mrs. Clinton's book, *It Takes a Village*, is a perfect example of the illusion that many people indulge that the centralized state, in this case one that

takes in most of a continent, is the same as a "village." The difference
between the highly organized state and the natural associations developing on a local basis is not one of mere degree; it is a difference of kind.

22 Pierre Bayle, *Selections from Bayle's Dictionary*, ed. E.A. Beller and M. duP.
Lee, Jr. (Princeton: Princeton University Press, 1953), 135.

23 Ibid., 121.

24 Ibid.

25 Labrousse, *Bayle*, 76.

26 Ibid., 78.

27 In Scotland, for instance, it was well into the nineteenth century before
the judiciary powers of clan chiefs were brought under the supervision
of the state; and in France at the early part of the twentieth century, it
was common for people to identify themselves as citizens of a province
rather than as French. In Germany and Italy, notoriously, the development of a comprehensive nation-state was quite late, so that institutions
independent of the government continued in the nineteenth century to
exercise considerable influence of their own. In parts of Africa and Asia,
natural social groups still exist almost without reference to any state
whatever, even though the pressures are great to establish the "sovereignty"
of a given territory, under the auspices of an organized government.

28 F. H. Hinsley, *Sovereignty* (Cambridge: Cambridge University Press, 1986),
315.

29 Dietrich Bonhoeffer, *Ethics* (New York: Simon & Schuster, 1995), 197.
Specifically in reference to the state, and suggesting the results of the
state's incursion into areas normally falling under the influence of these
"natural" social groups, Bonhoeffer suggests, "Whenever the state becomes
the executor of all the vital and cultural activities of man, it forfeits its
own proper dignity, its specific authority as government" (239).

6 *John Locke and the Politics of Toleration*

1 John Jenkins, *Understanding Locke* (Edinburgh: Edinburgh University
Press, 1983), ix.

2 H. R. Fox Bourne, *The Life of John Locke*, vol. 1 (London: 1876), 15.

3 Kraynak's argument is found in "John Locke: From Absolutism to Toleration," *American Political Science Review* 74 (1980): 53–69.

4 John Locke, *Essay on Toleration*.

5 Robert Kraynak, "John Locke: From Absolutism to Toleration," 62.

6 John Locke, *A Letter Concerning Toleration* (Buffalo, NY: Prometheus
Books, 1990), 18–19.

7 Ibid., 22.

8 Ibid., 20.

9 Eric Voegelin, *The Collected Works of Eric Voegelin*, vol. 24, ed. Barry Cooper (Columbia: University of Missouri Press, 1998), 171.

10 Ibid.

11 Ibid., 173.

12 Francis Fukuyama, *The End of History and the Last Man* (New York: Avon Books, 1992), 153.

13 Ralph Waldo Emerson, *Self-Reliance* (Mount Vernon, NY: The Peter Pauper Press, 1967), 13.

14 Charles H. Monson Jr., "Locke's Political Theory and Its Interpreters" in *Locke and Berkeley: A Collection of Critical Essays* (Notre Dame: University of Notre Dame Press, 1968), 195-96.

15 Voegelin, *Collected Works*, vol. 24, 172.

16 Ibid., 176.

17 Ibid., 177.

18 Ibid., 178.

19 Ibid., 179-80.

20 John Locke, *The Second Treatise of Civil Government*, ed. J. W. Gough (Oxford: Basil Blackwell, 1946), 55, 56.

21 Ibid., 48.

22 Ibid., 103.

23 Ibid., 73.

24 In Chapter xv, "Of Paternal, Political, and Despotical Power Considered Together," Locke wrote that "Parental power is nothing but that which parents have over their children, to govern them for their children's good, till they come to the use of reason or a state of knowledge wherein they may be supposed capable to understand that rule, whether it be the law of nature or the municipal law of their country, they are to govern themselves by—capable, I say, to know it as well as several others who live as freemen under the law" (Locke, *Second Treatise*, 84, 85).

25 I will use the capitalized form for autonomous Reason as understood by Locke, and lower case for reason in its ordinary sense.

26 Leo Strauss, *Philosophy and Law* (Albany, NY: SUNY Press, 1995), 103 (emphasis mine).

7 The Triumph of Toleration

1 Henry Kamen, *The Rise of Toleration* (London: World University Library, 1967), 217.

2 Eric Voegelin, *History of Political Ideas*, vol. VIII (Columbia and London: University of Missouri Press, 1999), 252.

3 Melvin J. Lasky, *Utopia and Revolution* (Chicago: University of Chicago Press, 1976), 151.

4 Since historians are not completely agreed upon Locke's influence on the writing of the Carolina constitution, I would like here to quote a fairly balanced statement on the issue: "The extent of Locke's contribution to the authorship is a vexed matter. Several scholars have mistakenly claimed that the 1669 manuscript is wholly in Locke's hand. Others have held Locke could not have articulated the Constitution's 'antiquated feudalism', but that is not an accurate description of its regime. The Constitution is very unlikely to have originated with Locke: he was acting as secretary to the lords proprietors of Carolina. Some suggest he was no more than a copyist. What probably happened was that Locke was handed a draft and asked to comment and amend. However, for the rest of his life he closely associated himself with Carolina and its Constitution. He was made a landgrave (nobleman) of Carolina, and Locke Island (today Edisto Island) was named after him. Important evidence is a remark in 1673 by Sir Peter Colleton, one of the lords proprietors: 'that excellent form of government in the composure of which you had so great a hand' (Letter 279)." John Locke, *Political Essays*, ed. Mark Goldie (Cambridge: Cambridge University Press, 1997), 160-61.

5 A late medieval forerunner of Unitarianism.

6 Locke, *A Letter Concerning Toleration*, 52.

7 Hans Aarsleff, "Locke's Influence," in *The Cambridge Companion to Locke*, ed. by Vere Chappell (Cambridge: Cambridge University Press, 1994), 252.

8 Locke, *A Letter Concerning Toleration*, 3.

9 The argument against both of these views, one put forward by Robert Filmer and the other by Hobbes, is found in Locke's *Two Treatises of Civil Government*.

10 See David A. J. Richards, *Toleration and the Constitution* (New York: Oxford, 1986), 88-95.

11 Locke, *A Letter Concerning Toleration*, 3.

12 Ibid., 15.

13 See also John Locke, *The Reasonableness of Christianity*, ed. I.T. Ramsey (Stanford: Stanford Univ. Press, 1958), 70-71.

14 Richards, *Toleration and the Constitution*, 62-100.

15 John Locke, *Two Treatises on Government*, ed. Peter Laslett (Cambridge, 1967), 418.

16 Locke, *A Letter Concerning Toleration*, 64.

17 Ruth Borchard, *John Stuart Mill: The Man* (London: Watts, 1957), 117-18.

18 Gertrude Himmelfarb, *On Liberty and Liberalism: The Case of John Stuart Mill* (San Francisco: ICS Press, 1990), 12.

19 This appears in his autobiography and is cited in Himmelfarb, *On Liberty and Liberalism*, 3.

20 Himmelfarb, *On Liberty and Liberalism*, 15.

21 Locke, *A Letter Concerning Toleration*, published as *A Letter Concerning Toleration: In Focus*, ed. John Horton and Susan Mendus (London/New York: Routledge, 1991), 23.

22 Joseph Hamburger, "Religion and *On Liberty*," in *A Cultivated Mind*, ed. Michael Laine (Toronto: University of Toronto Press, 1992), 139.

23 J. S. Mill, *On Liberty, The Collected Works of John Stuart Mill*, vol. xviii (Toronto: University of Toronto Press, 1977), 228n.

24 Ibid., 262.

25 Ibid., 265.

26 Martin Buber, *I and Thou*, trans. Ronald Gregor Smith (New York: Macmillan, 1987), 11.

27 Mill, *On Liberty*, 215. The superscription is from Humboldt's, *Sphere and Duties of Government*, trans. Joseph Coulthand (London: Chapman, 1854), 65.

28 Ibid., 265.

29 Ibid., 266.

30 Ibid., 266-67.

31 Herbert Marcuse, "Repressive Tolerance," in Robert Paul Wolff, Barrington Moore, Jr., and Herbert Marcuse, *A Critique of Pure Tolerance* (Boston: Beacon Press, 1965), 90.

32 See David Edwards, "Toleration and Mill's Liberty of Thought and Discussion," in *Justifying Toleration*, ed. Susan Mendus (Cambridge: Cambridge Univ. Press, 1988), 87ff.

33 Lasch, *The True and Only Heaven* (New York: W.W. Norton, 1991), 87. He cites Mill's essay "The Spirit of the Age," (1831).

34 Mill, *On Liberty*, 224.

35 Ibid., 262.

36 Ibid., 257.

37 Ibid., 263.

38 The expression used in the text of the Old Testament Book of Judges to express the profound disorder of pre-monarchical Israel. See Judges 17:6 and 21:25.

39 Quoted in "Philosophical Schools and Doctrines," *Encyclopedia Britannica*, 15th ed., vol. 25, 647.

40 John Herman Randall Jr. "Dualism in Metaphysics," in *Essays in Honor of John Dewey* (New York: Octagon Books, 1970), 315.

41 See the excellent study of this reverence for progress in Christopher Lasch's *The True and Only Heaven*.

8   *The Shadow Leviathan*

1   Modern thinkers such as John Dewey want to express this as a "fixed" point of reference, as if the adequacy of the idea is totally dependent on the adequacy of a certain metaphor. To say that the "good" is fixed and stable is only an attempt to say that it does not depend upon us but is something that stands over against us—it is *given* and perhaps discoverable but not invented and the product of artifice.

2   Thomas A. Spragens Jr., *The Politics of Motion: The World of Thomas Hobbes* (Lexington, KY: University Press of Kentucky, 1973), 205.

3   Kant, "What is Enlightenment?", 145.

4   From the notebook of Marx and under the title *ad Feuerbach*. The eleven theses on Feuerbach are published in *Gesamtausgabe*, 5:533-535.

5   Gerhart Niemeyer, *Between Nothingness and Paradise* (Baton Rouge: LSU Press, 1971), 98.

6   John Stuart Mill, *Utilitarianism* (Amherst, N.Y.: Promotheus Books, 1987), 9.

7   Ibid., 16-17.

8   Ibid., 17.

9   Ibid., 18.

10 Ibid., 43.

11 Friedrich Nietzsche, *The Genealogy of Morals*, in *The Birth of Tragedy and the Genealogy of Morals*, trans. Francis Golffing (Garden City, N.Y.: Doubleday, 1956), 298.

12 Ibid., 299.

13 Ibid., 231. Translated here: " . . . a basic trait of the human will, its fear of the void. Our will requires an aim . . . ."

14 John Dewey, *Experience and Nature* (New York: Dover Publications, 1958), 84.

15 Ibid..

16 Ibid., 84-85.

17 Ibid., 85.

18 Michel Foucault, *Truth and Power* (New York: Pantheon Books, 1980), 133.

19 John Dewey, *A Common Faith* (New Haven: Yale University Press, 1934), 24.

20 Ibid.

21 S. L Bethell, *The Cultural Revolution of the Seventeenth Century* (London: Dennis Dobson, Ltd., 1951), 13.

22 Pascal, *Pensées* (New York: Penguin Books, 1983), 85.

23 Ibid., 83.

24 Ibid., 101.

25 Bethell, *The Cultural Revolution of the Seventeenth Century*, 46.

26 New American Standard Bible (LaHabra, California: The Lockman Foundation).

27 Jouvenel, *On Power*, 1.

28 Ibid., 3.

29 Ibid., 383.

30 William Ralph Inge, *The End of an Age, and Other Essays* (New York: The Macmillan Company, 1949), 196. At this point in an essay entitled "The Philosophy of the Wolf State," he also writes, "The state is neither a person nor an organism; it is only an organisation. The General Will is a figment, a stick for the backs of minorities; there is no will apart from the wills of individual citizens." A similar insight was revealed by Dietrich Bonhoeffer in his *Ethics*, when he distinguished between organized and organic social groups.

9 Nihilism and the Catholic Vision

1 Nietzsche, *The Geneology of Morals*, 299.

2 Friedrich Nietzsche, *Thus Spake Zarathustra*, trans. Thomas Common (New York: Russell & Russell, 1964), 6.

3 Ibid., 99. Nietzsche here, of course, speaks of the human being, not God, as the creator.

4 See René Girard, *The Scapegoat* (Chicago: University of Chicago Press, 1990).

5 G.C. Berkouwer, *Studies in Dogmatics: The Church* (Grand Rapids, Michigan: Eerdmans, 1976), 116.

6 Jürgen Moltmann, *God in Creation: A New Theology of Creation and the Spirit of God* (San Francisco: Harper & Row, 1985), 26.

7 Jürgen Moltmann, "In Search for an Equilibrium of 'Equilibrium' and 'Progress'," *Ching Feng* 30:1-2 (May 1987): 1.

8 G. C. Berkouwer, *The Providence of God*, trans. Lewis B. Smedes (Grand Rapids: Eerdmans, 1952), 162.

9 Jürgen Moltmann, foreword to A. J. Conyers, *God, Hope, and History: Jürgen Moltmann's Christian Concept of History* (Macon, GA: Mercer University Press, 1988), vii.

10 Ibid., viii.

11 Karl Barth, *The Doctrine of Reconciliation: Church Dogmatics*, vol. 2, pt. 1, ed. G. W. Bromiley and T. F. Torrence (Edinburgh: T. & T. Clark, 1956), 448-49.

12 Jürgen Moltmann, *The Trinity and the Kingdom: The Doctrine of God* (San Francisco: Harper & Row, 1981), 131.

13 Ibid.

14 Ibid., 192.

15 Ibid.

16 Ibid.

17 Ibid., 163.

18 Conyers, *God, Hope, and History*, viii.

19 For the fuller treatment of this aspect of the question of monotheism see especially Chapters One, Seven, and Eight of *God, Hope, and History*.

20 Eusebius, *Vita Constantini*, 1.6.

21 Garth Fowden, *Empire to Commonwealth* (Princeton, N.J. : Princeton University Press, 1993), 88.

22 Giuseppe Ruggieri, "God and Power: A Political Function of Monotheism?" in *Monotheism*, eds. Claude Geffré and Jean-Pierre Jossua (Edinburgh: T. & T. Clark Ltd, 1985), 17.

23 Cited in H. Richard Niebuhr, *Radical Monotheism and Western Culture* (Louisville, KY: Westminster/John Knox Press, 1993), 12n.

24 Bernard Lang, "No God but Yahweh! The Origin and Character of Biblical Monotheism," in *Monotheism*, 45.

25 Ibid.

26 See, for the argument of violence, Regina M. Schwartz, *The Curse of Cain: The Violent Legacy of Monotheism* (Chicago: Chicago University Press, 1997).

27 Hobbes, *Leviathan*, x.

28 Paul Tournier, *Fatigue in Modern Society* (Atlanta: John Knox Press, 1965), 34.

29 Thomas Merton, *The Ascent to Truth* (New York: Harcourt, Brace, & Company, 1951), 24

30 Isaiah 8:6-8 New Revised Standard Version (New York: Oxford University Press, 1991).

31 Amos 5:19 NRSV.

32 Livingston, "The Very Idea of Secession," 39.

10 *High Tolerance*

1   Owen Chadwick, *The Secularization of the European Mind in the Nineteenth Century* (Cambridge: Cambridge University Press, 1975), 117. Here Chadwick cites E. Faguet, *Le Libéralisme* (Paris, 1903), 114. (This volume was the published version of the Gifford Lectures of 1973-74.) Chadwick also makes this interesting observation (in light of our present thesis) : "Revolution in the nineteenth century knew of the state and the individual but not much of the organisms in between. It exhorted sons to throw off the yoke of their fathers and of custom. . . . Religion [on the

other hand] was part of the continuity in the family. . . . Religion was at its most powerful when men stood by the open graves of their father or their mother in a churchyard" (113-14).

2   John Gray, *Enlightenment's Wake: Politics and Culture at the Close of the Modern Age* (London and New York: Routledge, 1995), 28.

3   Anton Pegis, ed., *Introduction to Thomas Aquinas* (New York: The Modern Library, 1948), 170-71.

4   Thomas Merton, *The Assent to Truth*, 277.

5   Mircea Eliade, *Patterns of Comparative Religion* (New York: Meridian Books, 1963), 29.

6   Eric Voegelin, *Collected Works*, vol. 24, 176.

7   Leo Strauss, *Philosophy and Law*, trans. Eve Adler (New York: State University of New York Press, 1995), 102-03.

8   In an interview distributed by *Mars Hill Tapes*, 39 (July/August, 1999).

9   Jouvenel, *On Power*, 11.

10 Ibid., xvii.

11 Gray, *Enlightenment's Wake*, 3.

12 Solomon prayed for "wisdom" as it is usually translated: the Hebrew metaphor is "listening heart" (I Kings 3:9).

13 Grace Westerduin, "Last Aid," in *Poetry for the Soul*, comp. Mary Batchelor (Nashville: Moorings, 1995), 451.

Index

A Note on the Author

A. J. Conyers is a professor of theology at Baylor University's George W. Truett Theological Seminary, in Waco, Texas. Among his previous books are *How to Read the Bible*, *The Eclipse of Heaven*, and *The End: What the Gospels Say About the Last Things*.

This book was designed and set into type
by Mitchell S. Muncy
and printed and bound
by Thomson-Shore, Inc.,
Dexter, Michigan.

The text face is Minion Multiple Master,
designed by Robert Slimbach
and issued in digital form by Adobe Systems,
Mountain View, California, in 1991.

The cover illustration is *St. Bartholomew's Day Massacre*
by JN Robert-Fleury,
Musée du Louvre, Paris,
reproduced by agreement with SuperStock,
on a jacket by Lee Whitmarsh.

The paper is acid-free and is of archival quality.

29